Education,
Class and
Nation

Education, Class and Nation

THE EXPERIENCES OF CHILE AND VENEZUELA

Kalman H. Silvert/Leonard Reissman

ELSEVIER

New York/Oxford/Amsterdam

ELSEVIER SCIENTIFIC PUBLISHING COMPANY, INC.
52 Vanderbilt Avenue, New York, N.Y. 10017

ELSEVIER SCIENTIFIC PUBLISHING COMPANY
335 Jan Van Galenstraat, P.O. Box 211
Amsterdam, The Netherlands

Library of Congress Cataloging in Publication Data

Silvert, Kalman H
  Education, class, and nation.

  Includes bibliographical references and index.
  1. Education—Chile. 2. Education—Venezuela.
3. Educational sociology—Chile. 4. Educational
sociology—Venezuela. I. Reissman, Leonard, joint
author. II. Title.
LA561.S54   370'.983   75-40653
ISBN 0-444-99018-6

Manufactured in the United States of America

Designed by Loretta Li

TO

Lennie

A BROTHER

Contents

Preface

"We began this study on a beautiful summer day in New Hampshire." Those were the last professional words Leonard Reissman wrote before his death early in 1975. They were his proposed beginning to this preface, the opening of his second draft in reaction to a first draft of mine which did not please him. The thought of that joyous sentence always makes my sorrow spring forth afresh, for Dr. Reissman died just as he had reached the top of a mountain. The more than nine years we worked together on this book helped us both to put things in order for ourselves. Professor Reissman felt that he had brought the passions and ideals of his young manhood into coherence with the discipline and rigor of his scholarly life. Few of us are so privileged. When the youth become man forms a harmonious fusion, one is ready for the joy of being a spontaneous creature empowered by experience and techniques.

I am not guessing about Professor Reissman's feelings, nor exaggerating them. We talked lengthily about our sense of this work and its meaning for us after completing the polishing of the final draft in December 1974. Everything herein was finished before his death except for this preface, the acknowledgments, the dedication, and the publisher's suggested copy-editing changes. We started with the ambition of enriching the theoretical literature on social change, and of contributing to the methodological sophistication of comparative political sociology. Later we added a third aspiration: to say something of ethical political worth in our increasingly harassed and self-punishing world. Although both of us shared a large dose of skepticism about the willingness or ability of most in our respective fields to accord us the time and intellectual effort to find out what we have been about, we followed the old-fashioned course of at least pleasing ourselves and vaguely hoping for some understanding from "them." This bemusement with our putative publics has to do with our rejection of much mainstream theory, method, and ideology. But our convictions and our data did not permit us to be otherwise.

Neither of us found any contradictions, in the end, within the mix of our theories, methods, commitments to social science inquiry, and general ethical beliefs. On the contrary, those elements reinforced themselves; for us, good science and "good" politics became at root the same.

Bias, passion, and cultural limitations do not negate the possibility of doing science. Instead, appropriate sets of utopian visions, commitments, and ethical stances are what make science possible in the first place. They tie the individual social scientist to his scholarly community, without which there can be no "knowing" in a scientific way. Only the workings of a community of social scientists, engaging in free interaction, produces the cumulative effort whose results can transcend gossip and partisanship and become reliably useful in interpretation, problem-definition, and, more particularly, the creation of new ideas. A prime intellectual duty of such a community is to explore the full limits of the cultures within which social scientists work. Otherwise, we will be hampered in checking the ethnocentrism which affects us all, unable to carry out our responsibility for comprehending total situations and their alternatives. The comparative study of societies, then, is not merely a technically desirable "control"; it is the only way to understand the categorical bounds of historical situations. Without such knowledge, we can have no idea of the absolute state of the political and scientific arts, no way of knowing when the possibilities of a social structure for producing desired results are becoming exhausted, and other social arrangements must be found for the pursuit of valued ends. In a world of wornout ideas and crumbling polities, no task is more socially useful than seeking an understanding of the limits of utility of given social orders.

When we started this research we knew that scholarly thinking about development was in disarray. We also knew that political life in many "modern" countries was becoming disoriented, but we did not foresee the extent to which violence would become the norm and democratic participation increasingly rare. Our original, tacit assumption was that any immediate impact of this study would be on the debate which was brewing in academic circles. But because both academy and society are in fact faced with the same critical questions, this work has become political as well as scholarly.

When democratic hopes and practices falter, any undertaking entirely dependent on a free commerce in ideas must find itself shot through with political tensions. The stress becomes especially acute when many social scientists themselves turn on the preconditions for their own work by espousing the inevitability or, worse, even the desirability of various forms of authoritarianism. But that reason is not the only one which imparts a political cast to this book, despite our original intentions. More important is that, willy-nilly, the present confluence of economic, social, and political crises imbues all acts with political meaning by destroying the routine acceptance of variety, thereby endangering the systematic confrontation of differing ideas. Science is, after all, a convention based on the belief that informed intellectual playfulness without fear of social sanction is "good" for society because it enlarges social understandings, broadens available alternatives, and enriches societies by making them more flexible, responsive, and able to take advantage of individual difference. A certain apartness from public policymaking is necessary if scientists are to escape all pressures except those which punish them for being poor practitioners of their trade. The ubiquity of crisis, however, destroys that protection, even for the ostensibly apolitical. When everything is in disorder, social habit disappears, and with it the accustomed respect for situational and institutional differentiations. Under such conditions, merely laying claim to scientific aspirations is to adopt an overtly political position.

Undoubtedly we will be accused of favoring social empathy over bigotry, open-mindedness over intolerance, and relativism over dogmatism. A narrower and nastier accusation will be that we are prejudiced in favor of "Western liberalism," that we believe "political development" equals the establishment of a polity in the style of the United States. The first evaluation of our bias is correct. Aside from what we think as citizens, a social scientist who values his profession can do no less than favor those social conditions which permit him to exercise it. The second accusation is false. The forms of social organization do not deliver up the same substance in differing historical settings. In this book we seek to examine the concrete cases of Chile and Venezuela, with special respect to certain relations binding class to nation and education. Obviously, we come to the research with a melange of ideas out of Western European and North American as well as Latin American understandings of the world. But then, the cultures of Chileans and Venezuelans are compounded of the same materials. If we employ broadly derived theories and universally applicable techniques to study these two countries, it is not for the purpose of blurring them, squeezing them into diluted generalizations, or making them the pawns of our ethnocentrism. Quite to the contrary, a major part of our purpose is to understand the ways in which they are unique. It is not paradoxical that a disciplined understanding of the unique helps us determine which aspects of a case are transferable to other situations, and which are not. We have no wish to impose the structures of our own political system on

Latin Americans or anyone else. We do, however, have the wish to assess the costs and benefits of what we as citizens favor (political freedom, equality, dignity, and so forth) and the costs and benefits of what we abhor (authoritarianism, status-based privilege, slavery, indignity, and so forth). We regret that in this book we have been able to work in only one small corner of this immense mansion.

To suggest the shape of the larger possibilities, however, we have chosen to center this research on education. The reason is plain: schools are the major public socializing agency. To that institutional setting we put only one basic question: what does formal education have to do with affecting the attitudes and abilities of students in civic life? The issue is classical, part of our inheritance from the Enlightenment. But it is also a forgotten issue, swept away in the prevailing wisdom which views schools as producing training and not culture, and labor as commodity and not productive humanity.

From the outset we did not expect that attitudinal and cognitive changes worked through formal education would have any single or even necessary correlative impact on the polities of Chile and Venezuela. In other words, we had and have no expectation that to help persons develop the capacity for participant citizenship is to produce participatory democracy. Our overt, conscious, and theoretically explained and tested rejection of automatic diffusions, lineal determinism, or the "naturalness" of social consistency is at the heart of the concepts we have tested in this study. However, because we do not think what happens to students necessarily fructifies in society at large, the reader should not jump to the conclusion that we think formal education unimportant. As we make entirely clear in this book, we have found that the "formation of people," as the phrase goes in Spanish, creates that reservoir of social understanding, relativism, and receptivity to change which can reasonably be counted as fundamental to free, secular society. Those attitudes and skills are necessary for what we deem a decent public life but they are not enough. With Jefferson, we believe that, "If a nation expects to be ignorant and free, in a state of civilization, it expects what never was and never will be." But also like the American and French revolutionaries, we believe that positive attitudes can be made effective only through appropriate social arrangements. Otherwise, the attitudes remain just that—latent, social onanism.

The practical effect of our predisposition to see an educational success only in its own terms, and not necessarily as a general social success, was to predispose us to theories concerning conflict and disjunction, to methods that would not trap us in lineal analysis, and to the mingling of attitudinal and institutional information. Certainly our purposes would have been betrayed by a standard neopositivistic use of quantitative data. Such techniques are specifically designed to find coherence and essentially lineal causality, and they presume that one goes "out there" to find "reality." Not sharing either in the theoretical or ideological implications of such techniques, we have taken another tack. The first step was to be entirely deductive: at no point did we say, "Let's ask, and see what they answer." A major benefit of this uncompromisingly deductive approach is that we avoided the usual lack of fit between our quantitative and qualitative data. Both for us are evidence in proof or disproof of theoretical views we blended out of our prior knowledge of the two countries being studied, the relevant literature on education and politics, and our past academic experience. In other words, we used induction to set up the deductive process, just like the introductory texts in methods say that one should proceed. The consequence of starting that way, however, is to discard the remainder of those methods books, with their ideology that society is a self-adjusting "system" inhabited by psychologically motored self-adjusting people.

The deductive process also leaves room for the epistemological premise that the observer himself constitutes reality, creating the relationships which give symbolic wholeness to the analytical pieces he deems significant. Therefore, we believe, with Cassirer, "that the 'understanding' of the world is no mere receiving, no repetition of a given structure of reality, but comprises a free activity of the spirit." The reader will have to judge for himself whether our attempt is successful. But he will not be able to do so unless he first enters into the spirit of our inquiry. Given the weak associations and strained interpretations of every other cross-national survey of which we know, the bald correlational strength of our analysis gives us cheer and courage. Much more important, however, is whether the strength of the patterns we see can suggest how the piece we have studied can form part of a synthetic understanding of the entire situation.

Toward this goal of synthesis, in our writing we have attempted to meld theory, quantitative and historical evidence and interpretation. These elements are interwoven throughout the first four chapters. In Chapters V and VI, however, we leave quantification and employ only documentary information. The first is a study of the historical moments in which humanistic nationalists and positivists fought for Chile's soul during the 19th century, and the second a look at the mechanistic, technocratic rationalizations of the Venezuelans during this century. The principal purpose of these chapters is to explain the source of our concepts and techniques by recreating for the reader part of the apperceptive sea from which we took the specific questions we asked in the social survey and the particular concepts we chose to test. Indeed, the careful reader will see that the Latin American *pensadores* and politicians seem to be answering our questionnaire in their speeches and writings.

I am writing this preface on a beautiful summer day in Vermont, putting on the last touches almost ten years to the day of our having begun. It's a shame that the sunniness is largely climatic. There has been a lot of bad weather in this decade, both for us and the societies for which we care. But if there is any solace that I carry away from this study, it is that our *formación* has made most of us—by no means all of us—people who do not deserve the governments we have. They make of us less than we could be, less than our educations and values and hopes might allow us to become. In the fullness of his life, Rousseau wrote in his *Confessions*, "I had attained the insight that everything is at bottom dependent on political arrangements, and that no matter what position one takes, a people will never be otherwise than what its form of government makes it."

KALMAN H. SILVERT

Norwich, Vermont
July 31, 1975

Acknowledgments

At least ten thousand Latin Americans gave of their time and good will to make this study possible. Only very few will ever know that we have tried to give them more than verbal thanks. We hope this book shows not only our appreciation, but also our respect for them.

Many prominent Chileans and Venezuelans, in and out of public life, testified to our good faith and opened many doors for us. The list would be a roster of distinguished persons, from presidents and cardinals to ministers and university professors. We do not wish to exploit them further by naming them, so that they inadvertently lend their dignity and prestige to the status of this work. But they will know who they are, and should also know that we profoundly appreciate their faith in us, and the possible risks they ran in supporting us during tense times in their countries.

Miss Roxana Balay was in charge of the field research. Through content analysis and survey, threats and gratification, disappointment and achievement, she was staunch, expert, and faithful. Without her, the work would be conceptually poorer and much less rigorous. Mr. Joel M. Jutkowitz assisted Miss Balay, and was also responsible for the major effort in gathering historical documentation. He, too, knows the great value we put on his contribution.

Small brigades of coders, interviewers, coffee-makers, and delivery boys also lent of their efforts with dedication and professional concern. We cannot give all their names, but collectively they have our *agradecimiento*.

The Carnegie Corporation provided funds and moral support. William W. Marvel was the foundation official whose interest and faith made this long trek possible. Special thanks go to him. And, for their patience with us, gratitude goes, too, to Bill's successors.

Office space and other material assistance was given us by governmental agencies in both Chile and Venezuela. We thank the responsible officials of the Center for Educational Planning in Chile, and EDUPLAN and CENDES in Venezuela for their many courtesies. In neither case were we shown anything other than consummate good will and consideration for the difficulties of the undertaking.

There are other persons and institutions whose discouragement we should also like to acknowledge. Some attacked us politically. Others hampered us administratively, even while profiting from our efforts. We shall be gracious, however, and refrain from mentioning them.

We used computing facilities at Tulane University, Cornell University, New York University, and Dartmouth College. Those, our respective host institutions, sometimes charged us and sometimes did not. So, we sometimes thank them.

The Ford Foundation graciously gave K.H. Silvert time enough away from his desk to work on this manuscript. Thanks go to Silvert's colleagues there for their unwavering and concretely expressed encouragement.

Our wives have asked to be left out of this litany.

Education, Class and Nation

one / *Intentions and Purposes*

Politics in national societies integrates the institutional order. Formal education in national societies is the institution fundamental to preparing persons for autonomous participation in secular and relativistic politics. This effect of education makes possible individual democratic activity in national societies. In *incompletely* national societies discord develops around the ability of some individuals and groups to live democratically, and the inability of others to act in effectively democratic ways. In such societies formal education is a crucial element in creating both the grounds of the conflict and the ability to perceive it. In developing capitalistic societies, the principal brake to continued development has been a stress between the opposing pulls of class and nation. The intellectuality promoted by prolonged participation in formal education, however, tends to lead educated persons to value universal national over particular class interests. Therefore, while education as an institution makes possible partially democratic as well as dictatorial national integration, through time it is inherently in contradiction with class-supportive authoritarianism.

These stark statements are our major conclusions from a study of politics and education in Chile and Venezuela. We believe they are valid for those two countries, and that inferences from those conclusions will help us to understand the situations of some other societies both more and less economically elaborated than Chile and Venezuela. In the course of telling how we arrived at those conclusions, many complexities both of data and of ideas will become apparent. Before we begin the tasks of describing and reasoning, however, we should bare some of the predispositions that led us to give politics and education two different kinds of primacy—the first in potentially shaping total social orders, and the second in preparing persons for effective personal participation in what we shall temporarily call "open" political systems.

We started our thinking with a rejection and several affirmations. The rejection was of any part of the notion that societies "progress" point by point along a single historical line stretching into an inevitable future, and of the accompanying idea that social change always occurs in un-

1

broken continua. Our view is quite different. We see social change, first, as occurring within a tapestry of varied strands and changing patterns. The inference is that at times tapestries become rudely torn, and at other times they may be woven into new patterns—but they are never made understandable by tugging on a single thread. Secondly, we see national politics as a synthesizing institution, as the creator of patterns. To continue the analogy, politics is the weaver—probably in all societies, but certainly in those stratified by class, by extended occupational specialization, by sharply contrasting patterns of institutional behavior, and by conflicting systems of explanations. Politics may enforce synthesis on such diversity despite inequalities, striving for a common basis upon which less disintegrative orders of inequality may be built. Or, conversely, politics may act directly as a function of existing inequalities and strive to maintain them through changes that reinforce the existing system of privilege. But whatever the nature of the synthesis, however loathsome or desirable it may be, synthesis there will be, and in developed and developing societies it will be enforced by a government acting within the legal frame we call the nation-state. This synthesis is not the sum of society's individual, structural, and institutional parts. Rather, it differs from other parts of the social order in that it adds sufficiency to the understanding of necessities with which we imbue society's other components.

Our predispositions concerning education were at once more prosaic and more ingenuous. We decided to look only at the *formal* educational structures, not merely because the inclusion of general socialization and informal ways of learning would have pulled us into a morass, but more positively because we are primarily concerned with social institutions and their interrelations. The ingenuousness was a true innocence: we were agnostic about what we thought we would find to be education's part in the political process. Buffeted between studies which say that education molds the whole individual, and others which say that education has little effect, we had suspicions but no firm beliefs. The suspicions were that the educational process affected basic attitudes very little, but that it had much to do with practices, habits, and overtly expressed preferences. We also thought the class factor would become entangled in the matter: that is, the ability to remain in school is related to social class, and so we presumed that the interlocked processes of going to school, growing up, and becoming identified with a given class position would reveal itself in patterns of attitudes expressed and behavior averred. Naturally, we also hoped to see some evidence of the persistence of basic values, and the changefulness of more lightly held

2

ones as occurring with some independence of social mobility, class, and other structural facets of an individual's life. As will be seen, we turned up much more than we bargained for.

So much for the baggage we brought with us. We will speak about our formal hypotheses as we deal with each major set of findings. Before we turn to those discussions, however, we need to explain why we chose to work where and with whom we did. In the appendixes the reader will find descriptions of the sample design, tables providing broadly descriptive materials on the persons whom we interviewed, and summaries of straightforward technical matters which the specialist will need in order to see how we proceeded from start to finish. In the text, however, we have decided to eschew heavy doses of data presentation, descriptions of our techniques, and justifications for our choices. We began with words, and we should like to end with them, despite the temptation to display the results of more than nine thousand interviews, some of them gathered under extremely difficult conditions. Our Chilean work was punctuated by an outcry there against Project Camelot, a piece of research supported by the U.S. Department of Defense which caused a revulsion against survey research in general and suspicion of American social scientists in particular.[1] That event, coming when it did, almost ended our survey then and there, although we did manage to complete most of our interviews and to proceed on to Venezuela after losing out only on some university students and professors we had planned to interview in Santiago, Chile's capital city. In Venezuela we ran into the tag ends of the urban terrorism that was plaguing that country in the early and mid-1960s, and an echoing protest against American social scientists. One of the nastier incidents we encountered was a threat of death against the field director of our research. Again, we managed to complete all planned interviews except those with university students and professors. Although we deeply regret the losses, and could have easily done without the added emotional and scholarly difficulties we suffered, we still were left with some basis for drawing a few broad inferences about the provincial university students whom we were able to interview. The failure to complete the entire sample design was lamentable, but not fatal.

CHOICE AND DESIGN OF THE STUDY

The choice of Chile and Venezuela, and within those countries of certain places and types and levels of schooling, requires justification. The historical chapters (V and VI) provide the best and richest explana-

3

tions. At this point, however, we shall emphasize those reasons that flowed from our theoretical orientations, for they are the underpinning of the quantitative as well as the historical analyses.

This book attempts to study social change in general and political change in particular. Although our theoretical predispositions are wide-ranging and draw on varied currents of the immense available literature, the data refer only to limited sets of relations. Because our attention has been focused upon the formal educational structure, the persons we interviewed were chosen because of their place in those structures. Our data have been generated from two sources, interview surveys and historical materials. But we should explain the following choices underlying the selection of techniques:

- Why we chose formal education as a way of getting at the general theme of social and political change.
- How we expected information about individual attitudes to tell us something about institutions.
- Why we emphasized historically specific institutional analysis rather than functional analysis.
- Why we chose to work in Latin America.
- Why we chose two countries rather than one, or even to extend ourselves to three or more.
- Why we chose Chile and Venezuela in particular.
- Why we chose particular sectors of the educational structure for study.
- Why we emphasized legal and ideological materials rather than curricula and the like in our analysis of the historical development of the educational systems of Chile and Venezuela.

The most complex of the explanations we must consider is our choice of the educational institution as the study's focus. This choice, in its turn, rests upon our view of social causality, which we must explain first. Obviously, *some* idea of cause pervades any study of change. If the research purpose is deliberately passive, if one dismisses any intention to manipulate or to judge changes, then the view held of causality is either likely to be left in the intellectual shadows or to result in the mute acceptance of a descriptive chronology of changes. Although our view of the causes of social change must stop short of questioning ultimate origins, this research was designed to inquire into the nature of social development and social action, a goal demanding an explicit statement of causal relations. As we see it, change is the result of the interaction between what is possible in any given social setting and the actual *effective* decisions that are made. Of course, the possibilities inherent in given situations cover the full range from the "ideally possible" to the more limited "realistic" alternatives comprehensible to those persons involved within each situation. The ability to perceive the ranges of possibilities clearly must vary, depending as it does on individual talent and learning, on those socially induced differences which prepare some groups and individuals more than others, on fashion and fad and the temper of the times, and on the cultural predispositions of a society.

If possibilities and their varied perceptions are necessary parts of causality, so, too, is the actual taking of a decision. Needless to say, decisions must be backed by effectiveness or power, for otherwise they are mere hopes and not decisions. Here, again, social factors enter into the causal process as they did in the selective ability to perceive possibilities. The making of empowered decisions, thus causing change, may move between two modes which are seldom found pure and unalloyed in actual behavior. Decisions may be taken in as consciously rational a way as the person or persons involved can manage. Or, conversely, decisions may be ritualistic, habitual, or modish. The mixture of rationalism and ritualism employed in making choices is a useful indicator of the degree of traditionalism or modernism (two weighted words we shall explain later) that can be used to characterize the behavior under study.

Doubtless there are those who would object to our simplification of the choice process and social change. After all, we will be told, choices are never simple. They involve complex psychological and personality variables, to say nothing of how the relative power of individuals to implement their choices in itself affects what they choose. From the structural side, too, we will be told that social changes are the complex results of "blind" forces like "technology" or "industrialization." Convenient as these two sets of ideas about change may be for the social analyst, they often turn out to be reifications—a conversion of convenient definitions into ostensibly real things, so that "personality" or "technology" become hard realities with life and force of their own. In the same manner, "traditionalism" and "modernism" have come to stand for seemingly real personality attributes or seemingly real societal characteristics. Yet, to test these definitions, and to reify them further by basing research upon the assumption that the definitions are real to begin with, is to compound the initial error. The proof of this mistake is evident in many studies that purport to uncover the "real" indicators of social modernization (kilowatt hour use per capita, newspaper circulation, and so on) or the "real" components of the so-called modern person (the ability to empathize, the use of reason rather than a reliance on fate, and so on). Therefore, we have purposely laid down a view of social change that is open so that we can explore its conditions, at least within the parameters of the educational institution. What people say they perceive as alternatives and what relation these perceptions have to their social environment are the immediate foci of our inquiry. Depending on what we can learn from this interaction, we will shape our more abstract conclusions about some elements of social change.

This view of causality, of course, can be massively elaborated. For example, choice-making that obeys habit and custom may not necessarily be traditional in effect, for these customs may well be the fruit of a previously validated rational exercise. Similarly, apparently rational choices may, on closer inspection, be little more than automatic reactions covered over with a verbal patina of reason. Our interest, then, must include not merely the causal complex just outlined, but the effect of a causal action on one's ability to take future causal actions. This theme will recur in later discussions where its utility will become more apparent. For the moment, however, this statement of the case is a necessary introduction to why we chose education as the institutional focus of the study, for our interest in development is centered on the possibilities of broadening options, of maximizing the ability of people to cause changes. We are interested in education as the social institution charged with the transmission of the cultural heritage; with the training of individuals to perceive arrays of possibilities, to discriminate finely among options; and with the creation and transmission of new knowledge, thus further broadening the known array of choices. In some settings, education also is meant to serve as a channel for altering the power potential of individuals by preparing them to hold occupational and status positions higher than those of their families of origin. No other institution so clearly permits us to capture this relation between the evolution of personal evaluative and affective skills, and possible changes in power potential, through the stages of the life cycle from childhood to emergence into the adult world. Naturally, the presentation of our research findings will tell us whether our reasons for emphasizing education were well founded.

The critical role we have assigned to education as a force for broadening perceptions and options for individuals is applied in our research specifically to politics. Undoubtedly, education similarly serves as a sensitizing force in other areas of human knowledge and choice, such as

6

in interpersonal relations, or in judgments about the good life. But our interest is in grand politics—not partisan attachments, propensity to vote, or even the anticipation and practice of political participation, but rather in the ways in which perceptions concerning relations among society's major institutions are established and changed, and the place assigned to politics in that configuration. To hark back to something already mentioned, we wished to learn the effect of the educational experience on how individuals develop synthetic views of their entire society. We were seeking to learn whether the persons we studied ascribe a patterning function to the polity, reserve that function for other institutions, or perhaps even for a supernatural force, or indeed see no patterning at all but only randomness and accident. Viewing politics as the pivot of a grand ordering process forms another element of our view of the modern person: politics provides the day-to-day power that infuses rational decision-making with public effectiveness.

Attitude data by themselves cannot, of course, tell us how persons behave. All they can tell us directly is how persons *say* they behave, how they think others behave, and their avowed reasons for such behavior. Inferences drawn from attitudes to explain behavior are the task of the researcher himself. In this study, however, we do not stretch the views we have gathered to conclusions concerning what has or will happen in Venezuela and Chile. What we have sought to establish is *latency*, the possibility that persons may act in ways we have called "modern" and "traditional" within certain institutional settings and systems of interinstitutional relations. In this respect, our inferences are narrow and directly tied to the data, for our questions almost entirely concern the perceptions and beliefs of persons in specific institutional contexts. The direction, then, of our findings is to determine the kinds of persons who will be likely to resist or to accept any one of several kinds of social and political change. We do not presume, of course that these persons themselves will actually work to institute such changes, for the simple reason that we do not have the information required for such an analysis. The historical information we have amassed, however, does permit us to speculate about behavior, so that we may estimate the degree to which latent attitudes could have supported apposite behavior in the past. By extension, then, we can speculate on how the attitudes we have studied might become motives for action in the future, although we eschew any elision from motivation to action. Thus, we do not subscribe to the old Spanish maxim that every people has the government it deserves. We expect no neat fit between what large groups of persons are

7

able and willing to do with their lives, and what they are asked or forced to do.

The emphasis we place on understanding institutions is of a piece with our reasons for studying educational systems. Institutions, the relations among them, and their interacting patterns of influence are intelligible only within actual historical situations; otherwise, they are likely to be seen as following some ordained or necessary internal social dynamic. We are concerned, before everything else, with examining education and political change specifically in Chile and Venezuela, not in testing the ways in which supposedly universal institutional functions operate in Chile and Venezuela. In other words, these two countries are *not* seen by us as mere examples of how socialization, political order, or religion might function to maintain some mystical institutional stability. Neither are we interested in applying some hypothetical model to illustrate the workings of presumed self-adjusting mechanisms as the Chilean and Venezuelan polities slip in and out of equilibrium. Rather, we mean to seek out the *particular* ways in which, among other factors, educational level and a series of attitudes about social organization and change work out in the two countries with which we are concerned. Even so, we do not surrender to historical uniqueness so completely as to argue that our findings cannot be generalized beyond Chile and Venezuela. However, such generalizations must be contained within some historical context rather than mindlessly applied to other societies.

We define institutions as clusters of routinized behavior patterns carried out about the discharge of sets of functions which are socially recognized as legitimate and valued. This definition underpins the questions we asked concerning power, its creation, uses (legitimate and otherwise), and its transmission through time. These institutional patterns require support from social values tied to them. Ethos, the "spirit" of cultures, is understood by us as the value that is given to particular social designs. The kind of attitudes we sought to uncover are at this level, descriptive of primary value sets about proper social being and organization, from which we infer readiness to participate in one or another grand pattern of life.

The fourth justification we must advance concerns our choice of Latin America as a general culture area in which to pursue this work. The explanation naturally includes personal taste, experience and aptitude, the ways in which Latin American intellectuals and social scientists look at their own societies, and the social artifacts, structures, and practices which the authors think they see and to which they ascribe significance in Latin America. We understand Latin America as evidently ambivalent in structures and norms. It is not the Indian-European dichotomy that is salient to us in terms of our research subject, but rather the conflict between the world views of Northern and of Mediterranean Europe. In other terms of reference, Latin America is buffeted by the Protestant as well as the Catholic ethos.

Throughout Latin America immediately before its independence from Spain and during the entire nineteenth century, the ideas of the democratizing capitalist nations had a strong influence on Latin American thought. Liberalism, Utilitarianism, and Positivism infused constitutions and educational systems, informed the writings of *pensadores*, justified revolution, and quite literally were employed to change the fates of nations. In its international trade increasingly a part of the market system of Western Europe and the United States, Latin America also shared in the ideologies of those regions. Marxism appeared in the early twentieth century, along with neo-Kantianism, Existentialism, and finally the North American practice of the social sciences, particularly economics and sociology. But Catholicism, even though under attack as formal religion and social institution, did not disappear as the seedbed of a total cultural view. The concept of the individual as primary unit of Liberal analysis clashes with the Catholic view of the family as the irreducible element of social being. Other Liberal precepts also implanted themselves, describing marketplaces as naturally desirable for the free play of goods and ideas within a pluralist structure of contending interest groups and a politics of intrasystemic compromise. But Catholic views remained, too, and continued to emphasize the importance of the organic unity of man, society, and the sacred within a harmonious social setting in which absolute rights and duties, and the correctness of order and authority, assured comity between the sacred and the secular.

The acceptance of one or another of these world views has immediate consequences for the way in which "proper" institutional orders are constructed. Mediterranean organic ideas recognize institutional differentiation as necessary, but would deny the political institution an overriding priority in ordering relations among institutions. In addition, most organicists, and certainly most Church leaders until recent years, did not see institutions as legitimately employed to change the social pecking order, but specifically underwrote institutional orders which maintained existing class systems. The corporate social model is the organicist ideal—separate and parallel institutions, "pillars" of society, laced together by their leaders, who form a pluralist oligarchy.

9

The Liberal model is much less neat. Its pluralism is addressed to individuals, not groups. Recognizing the fact of institutional differences, autonomy, and specialization of functions, the Liberal ethos usually assumes that individual equality of access to institutional participation, and action judged by merit, will guarantee the proper functioning of the social order. Thus, personal equalitarianism, not group or class equalitarianism, is a premise of Liberal pluralism, a premise which comes up against the inhibiting facts of "class," defined as the categories of transmission of life-chances from generation to generation, the potential for access to a given array of institutional roles. This view of the good social organization is secular and assigns a mediating and watchdog role to the state, whose primary responsibility it is to maintain the desired conditions for the proper functioning of each institutional "market."

The uneasy coexistence of these two ideal visions is characteristic of Latin American thought and social life. The split is overtly apparent in the area's more developed countries, such as Argentina, where formal democracy and populist, corporate-leaning "nationalism" have been in open contention for two generations. The tension has also been clear in Chile, although in other forms. There Christian Democratic developmentalism, with its civil-libertarian and yet organic tinge, came into conflict with both traditional Liberals and quasi-Marxists, all three succumbing now to military-led dictatorship. With variations appropriate to each country, the same ideational clash can be traced clearly in all of Latin America's more industrially and urbanistically elaborated countries. No other major world area for so long has been so clearly grappling with the implications of falangist and democratic models, or has so patently generated ideology and partisan practice about this disagreement.

The reason for working in two countries is methodological: we wished to test the utility of our approach on a comparative basis. Having two sets of study groups provided us with something equivalent to an experimental control. That is, by studying two cases we were, in some measure, able to hedge against the possibility that our data were culturally idiosyncratic in some way that could not have been determined if we remained inside only one political system. We built a cultural parameter around the study by remaining within Latin America, of course, but Chile and Venezuela are sufficiently dissimilar in so many political, social, and economic respects as to submit our theoretical approach and the survey to a reasonably solid comparative test.

Chile and Venezuela were selected for many reasons. They are both small and manageable countries for research, each having populations of between eight and nine million at the time of our study. The historical literature on each is adequate, if not overwhelming or fully satisfactory for the study of educational systems. Officials in both countries were receptive to the study. Aside from these reasons of convenience, political criteria provided the basic positive motives for our selection. Chile had Latin America's longest unbroken history of a persistent development of formal democracy. At the time of our study, only during two short periods since the 1830s had Chile experienced interruptions in its constitutional order, and none between 1932 and 1973, despite extreme inflation, economic depression, political disturbances in neighboring countries, and worldwide turbulence and confusion. But since Chile's national community cannot be said to include all of its citizens, political issues—as distinct from economic and social problems—stand out. Chile also has a long history of educational development, buttressed by the writings as well as the direct action of some of Latin America's most renowned social thinkers.

Venezuela, on the contrary, has had a troubled and simplistic political history, played out by *caudillos* in the context of a divided and weak citizenry. Often called by its own people "a country without a history," Venezuela experienced its first constitutional presidential succession only within the past decade. Provincial, its educational system thin and archaically catering largely to the children of the privileged, the country some forty years ago began an economic expansion propelled by the foreign exchange earned through oil sales. With rapidly increasing momentum, Venezuela since World War II has seen its gross national product become the highest per capita in Latin America, although income distribution patterns harshly reflect privilege and power, and not the economic concomitants of a general growth in participation. Chile was Latin America's first constitutional, but incomplete, nation-state. Venezuela is as yet a national community in little more than legal name, although the striving for social definition is contentious, serious, and sustained.

Because national samples were impossible to take in either country, we chose to work only in certain places which would provide us internal comparability and again act as a surrogate control. In both countries we chose schools in the capital cities (Santiago in Chile, Caracas in Venezuela), in port cities influenced by direct foreign investment and resident foreigners (Antofagasta in Chile, a copper and nitrate port; and Maracaibo in Venezuela, an oil center), in provincial capital cities away from the seacoast (Chillán in Chile, Barquisimeto in Venezuela), and in rural areas affected by such national stimuli as land reform and political

11

party organization (Molina in Chile, Ocumare in Venezuela). This distribution also provided us with an urban-rural comparison to buttress the difference in urban and rural origins we expected to find among persons involved with the other schools we were studying.

Naturally, we also wanted to break down our data by age, sex, indicators of social class, and other such common measures, as well as by type of school—whether religious, private secular, or public—and the prestige commonly accorded the school in the community. The prestige rankings were obtained through soliciting the opinions of informed persons. In accordance with that ranking, as well as categorical listings of schools by their status as public, private, or religious, we took samples of participants in primary and secondary schools. Once having selected the schools, we sought to interview students in the last grades both of primary and secondary education. Our reasons for selecting those grades were several. By the time a student has reached the last year of his primary schooling, educators usually consider him firmly literate. He may backslide thereafter and become "functionally illiterate," but at least for the time being the student should be able to handle a comparatively simple questionnaire without difficulty. In addition, students at this class level are between twelve and thirteen years of age, still tied to childhood but poised for the difficult transit through adolescence. Students in the last year of secondary school are usually about eighteen years of age, no longer adolescents, and in Latin America considered to be young men and women, ready for the adult roles implied in university training as well as for direct entry into the job market. Our presumption was that between those two stages, a loosening of family and religious ties takes place, and the individual goes through a period of at least potential relative freedom in his participation in institutional behavior, except for education. That is, he can loosen the ties of his childhood, yet is still not fully obliged to take on economic and political tasks. We were interested in knowing whether this freedom from obligation permitted individuals to perceive other, more positive aspects of freedom of choice.

The third group of students we attempted to interview were enrolled in universities. As we have already said, we failed to gain access to the national universities in Caracas and Santiago, giving up the attempt as dangerous after several delicately planned forays. Provincial university students, however, were more hospitable. The reasons for refusing to collaborate in the study are certainly more complex than anti-Americanism or a suspicion generated only by the Camelot episode. The tendency toward refusals increases sharply as one goes up the social scale in major urban areas, without regard to political persuasion or even specific institutional affiliation. Suspicion of survey techniques appears to be a function of urbanity and information, phenomena that are clearly class-related. We also experienced some difficulties with the better-off parents of students, but skilled interviewers and home visits as well as the official support of governmental and Church authorities permitted us to complete those samples without undue difficulty.

Our desire to see the school as a total institution led us to interview teachers, professors, and parents as well as students. In each school selected for study, we tried to interview all teachers at all grade levels. As for parents, we took a subsample of students and interviewed the parent deemed to be the head of the household. Primary and secondary students were given questionnaires that they filled out during a fifty-minute class period under the supervision of an interviewer. University students, professors, teachers, and parents were interviewed individually, their replies noted by the interviewer. Our interest in parents and teachers was clearly motivated not alone because we have a special concern for them as such, but because their responses assisted us in understanding the setting in which the students find themselves, and in comparing the attitudes of parents and teachers with those of students at different educational levels.

Lastly, we should explain why the historical discussions will emphasize ideological and legal components in Chilean and Venezuelan education. By now it should be apparent that we put great store in intentions and in overarching ways of understanding. The infusion of events with meaning is what converts a mere occurrence into an event of social significance, a concept basic to our view of causality. As we have said, we assume that the fit is rarely neat among differing sets of meanings given to the same occurrences; similarly, there is seldom comfortable concurrence among institutions, between values and behavior, or between social class and social consciousness. But our concern with the ideologies of education does not stem from any perverse pleasure in pointing out the difference between what educators and legislators intend and what they work. Instead, we are interested in the degrees of congruity and incongruity between avowed goals and historical accomplishments, as well as between what institutional leaders think they are teaching and what is being learned. In this fashion, we once again reinforce our interest in institutional patterns, avoiding psychological reductionism but still not totally burying the individuals whom we have studied in the limbo of categories, typologies, and scales.

These, then, are the justifications we advanced to ourselves, and pass on to the reader, before field work began. Needless to say, our hypotheses did not emerge unblemished, a process of refinement we found exhilarating rather than dismaying. After much debate between us, and a long period of internalizing our newly gathered information, we decided that interpretation should be blended with data throughout this book, rather than following the style of encapsulating theory in one chapter and data in another. In our thinking, analysis, and exposition of the results that follow, we maintained an open and dialectical exchange between the data and our interpretations, so that each activity continually informed the other.

We have decided to organize this book around an examination of four major issues. The word "issues" is appropriate, for the four major clusters of data we have decided to emphasize are problematical in theory, method, and ideology. Let us conclude this chapter with a brief statement of these issues.

THE EMERGENCE OF THE THEMATIC ISSUES

The data with which we have worked can be easily imagined: the usual masses of books, documents, and ephemeral materials on Chile and Venezuela; notes of depth interviews, jottings and formal reports about each site studied; reports of interviewer reactions; and the interview data. A tight and restrictive organization, however, was imposed from the start, a consequence of the design of the interview schedule. It was composed of four major parts:

- •The usual identification questions, including some queries concerning aspirations and a few questions we were asked to add by Chilean and Venezuelan officials for their own use.
- •A battery of questions designed to inform us about the sense of institutional commitment held by each respondent. Half the questions were normative, asking what *should* be done; the other half inquired about what *is* done, in the attempt to contrast perceptions of propriety with perceptions of practice. These questions were asked about each major institutional sphere—the family, religion, education, the economy, and the polity. The questions were posed and analyzed in that order, in the presumption that we were generally following a chain of institutional effects on the individual as he grew into an adult. The same questions, by recombination, also served as a basis for analyzing types of motivation for behavior in each institu-

tional sphere, the anticipated range of effect of such behavior, and attitudes concerning change in each area. Both the substance of the questions and the meaning of the forced responses were deliberate and logical inventions on our part. We came to the study, in other words, with a fairly definitive image in mind of what constituted the major aspects of each institutional sphere and what constituted rational or ritualistic responses. In this sense, the forced choice of answers to these questions was a deliberate assumption on our part of what comprises modern or traditional attitudes, an assumption that was tested by the logical consistency of the responses given by those people we interviewed.

•A short series of questions designed to learn from those whom we interviewed the importance ascribed to each institution relative to the others. These questions were an important internal check on the consistency of responses in the other questions about institutions and were also an important source of information concerning nationalism in particular and, inferentially, secularism in general.

•Another short series of questions concerning cause and effect, providing a check on student attitudes as distinct from explanations given in their civics and history textbooks, and valuable in itself as an indication of intellectual subtlety.

Behind this grouping of the materials lie the principal themes. The first has to do, simply, with the sequences into which the perceptions of the institutions fall. Our interest here is in learning how the institutions are seen as alike or different, into what families of likeness and difference they are put, and the ways in which institutional differentiation is perceived.

The second theme has to do with the way the individual perceives himself with respect to his society and the universe. For example, does he see himself as swept by blind forces in all aspects of his life, or does he see certain areas as open to his voluntary, effective control? Merging these perceptions with those concerning institutional differentiation can help us see how persons synthesize the structure of the society in which they live, how they see institutions not only as separate, but also as falling into a pattern.

The third issue has to do with the depth of the attitudes described above. Are they at the level of ethos, part of the cultural air? Or are they closely subject to variations in age, sex, place of residence, or social class?

The last theme has to do with the comparability of our findings, their usefulness in describing important differences between the groups in Venezuela and in Chile.

As we proceed, we will try to amend some currently accepted notions about development and change. We will also attempt to draw a picture of many differing persons and groups, and to describe some of the experience of growing up and living in contemporary Chile and Venezuela. Throughout all the steps of this study, we have developed respect and fondness for those who answered our questions. Absurdity does not describe how the students we have studied are growing up, or the views of their teachers and parents. It may well describe their societies, however.

two / Social Institutions: Differentiation and Interrelationships

Fashion has decreed that the words "modern" and "traditional" should be weeded from our thoughts. Political and intellectual currents have combined to judge those concepts as being in bad taste, a slur against countries of the Third World, and of doubtful intellectual worth. In combination, racial and student disorders, inflation, unemployment, and international warfare characterize "modern" and industrial societies much more than they do developing countries. Politically, therefore, many persons doubt the validity of any traditional-modern dichotomy that implies a movement from "less desirable" to "more desirable."

Academically, too, the concepts are in difficulty. The standard search of social scientists for universal principles, functions, and balancing mechanisms in all societies seriously weakens the ability to distinguish clearly among societies. As a consequence, scholars have more or less been able to separate the "modern" from the "traditional" only at the cost of conceptual clarity, and even, we might add, at the cost of an enlightened understanding of social realities. It has become common, for example, to separate "modern" from "traditional" societies by measuring occupaitonal specialization, achievement motivations, urban population concentrations, literacy, and the consumption of energy resources. Yet, what can such a universalistic classification mean unless those societies are also placed in a realistic international, political, and economic setting? It is not enough, in other words, to rely entirely upon mechanical measures to make the distinctions for us, if the aim is to identify significant differences among societies.

To escape these problems, scholars have moved in several different directions. One path has been to assume the operation of evolutionary or quasi-evolutionary forces that are inherent in all social systems. In the first variant, it is assumed that there is a more or less unilineal progression of societies toward greater complexity, specialization, and differentiation forced by changes that demand functional responses. In the second variant, this explicit assumption of evolutionary processes is replaced by a more contained premise involving sets of social variables that appear as necessary clusters (urbanization and industrialization, occupational specialization and social classes, for example), making it seem that all societies must pass through "stages" of development. By this latter assumption, then, all societies can be arranged in a hierarchy meant to represent the level of "development" any particular one may have attained.

A second path, as Costa Pinto has noted, is to blend all societies into a global system in order to understand "the transition of the modern world as a whole, a world characterized above all by its asymmetries and inequalities. To approach the real problem, we need a more complex set of variables, free from any idea of hierarchism of the situations under study and clean of the thick layers of intellectual prejudices, wishful thinking, and ethnocentrism so apparent in the so-called 'theories of modernization.' "[1] A growing number of explanations fits this view of the world as total social system; among the more important of these approaches are those that see the growth of an international stratification system, as in the works of Horowitz, Frank, and the school of "dependence" thinkers.[2] Finally, yet another solution is suggested by those who view contemporary industrial society as in transition toward its full realization, and who extrapolate from the present to postulate a modernism that will be found only in the future. Left and right seers of post industrialism[3] have sought this style of solution to the definitional dilemma.

Our own preference is to maintain a distinction between modern and traditional personal and societal attributes, although retaining the complexities necessary to explain variations within the attitudes of a single individual, and especially within a national institutional structure. In arriving at this decision, we do not wish to deny utility to evolving theories of a global system of international relations, or to surrender unthinkingly to submerged prejudices concerning the "better" and the "worse." Still, we think it retrogressive, and indeed self-deluding, to deny, for example, that some persons are better able to tolerate ambiguity than others, and that some social orders are better able to contain dogmatisms and promote relativism than others. We choose to call sacralists and organicists "traditional," and to call secularists and relativists "modern." If some men living and working in industrial situations, and some industrialized societies, imbue the state with sacred authority and hunt down heretics in the name of ideological purity, then—by our terminology—they are traditionals wrapped in the trappings of modernism. In other words, at the personal level, we speak of "traditional" and "modern" as referring to the totality of attitudes and

18

acts that express an individual's orientation toward and his view of his society. However, these attitudes and acts are grounded in specific life-situations of earning a living, raising a family, and dealing with politics. We employ the same concepts with respect to society by examining the relationship among institutions and the purposes to which the entire configuraton is put.

In getting at matters affecting the traditionalism and modernism of the Chileans and Venezuelans studied, we have attempted to discover attitudes concerning the motivation for behavior, the standards for behavior, and the perceptions of behavior appropriate to given views concerning change. In order to anchor the varied responses expected from each individual, we have related each set of attitudes to the major institutions—the family, religion, education, the economy, and the polity. This approach also permits us to look at the attitudes as a whole, revealing how each person sees the entire institutional structure, and also to understand which institutions are seen as primary and which as secondary, and which in conflict situations should prevail over others. Before presenting the first set of findings, some of our reasoning should be set forth.

A modern person was defined by us, in part, as someone who accepts rationality as a reason for acting, as distinct from the traditionalist, who will tend to justify his acts on the basis of ritual. Appositely, a rationalist should also be a relativist. That is, the notion that reason should be used in decisions to act also implies that new situations will arise, and reactions to them will have to weigh better against worse action, as opposed to some absolute best against absolute worst. Rationalist and ritualist motivations for behavior, then, can be linked to expected effects—relative as opposed to total or organic—anticipated as flowing from the action. The traditional person, by this construction, will tend to see every act as immediately related to the universal, thus affecting everything at the same time. Sanctions, too will necessarily be religious as well as secular. The modern person does not assume universal consequences from his day-to-day actions, but tends to see historical time as absorbing the shocks of the effects of immediate activity. In this associated stream of attitudes, the third correlative element concerns perceptions of change. It is not that a modern individual is changeful, and a traditional one static. Rather, the former assumes the ineluctability of change and behaves (if he is entirely rational) in such a way as to anticipate it, on the assumption that the effects of change will be sufficiently partial to continue to permit him to react with some effectiveness. The traditional man, on the contrary, assumes either that change cannot be anticipated or, if so, that it cannot be affected. His reasons, of course, are that change is caused by factors beyond human control, and that any change affects total situations whose direction is also beyond human control.

As has been said, these three dimensions of attitudes toward behavior were examined in the context of activities involved in familistic, religious, educational, economic, and political endeavors. Naturally, we expected erratic responses among the three kinds of attitudes themselves, as well as with reference to the several institutions, not as an abnormality, but as an entirely natural occurrence. We assumed, with Germani, that

> . . . a person may be a legitimate participant (i.e. may be integrated) into the modern productive structure (as worker in a modern industrial plant), objectively mobilized in the sphere of politics (as a militant in a radical, nonlegitimate political movement), psychosocially mobilized with regard to modern consumption (because of his unfulfilled aspirations), and still "unreleased" and traditional in the area of family and kinship relations. Most important of all, the "modern" and the traditional are not separated within the same area of behavior, or in the same institutions. They may be "fused" in various ways.[4]

The usual description of disjunction is that social change is not a smooth and continuous process, but an asymmetrical, asynchronous, erratic, uncertain, and variable process that does not move through an unbroken continuum toward "progress." We have no quarrel with that view, but we would strip it of its negative connotations by adding explanation to description: even in conditions of very slow change, of a smooth flow of experience from generation to generation, and of great institutional stability, attitudinal sets will still vary as they apply to the full institutional gamut so long as there is a socially recognized differentiation among institutions and the behavior appropriate to each set of functions. In other words, we see the ability to differentiate among institutions as a token of nontraditionalism, and presume that the very ability to make such discriminations is tantamount to an ability to tolerate ambiguity and difference—to see different institutional roles differently along scales having to do with the motivations for, expectations from, and future effects of actions. Thus, the need to remain with the traditional-modern dichotomy is reinforced by tying attitudinal stances toward action to the ability to discriminate among institutional processes and roles. Drawing this relation also furthers our pursuit of the ability to infer institutional structure from data on attitudes.

The emphasis upon differentiation is widely accepted by social scientists today as the prime feature of social development, a concept that had its origins in nineteenth-century evolutionary theory. The earlier notion, however, has undergone severe modification:

> In the older evolutionary school . . . stages have been construed mostly in terms of "specialization" and "complexity." In recent works these concepts have been to a large extent replaced by that of "differentiation." This replacement is not merely semantic: it reflects an important theoretical advance in the study of society—an advance that greatly facilitates critical reevaluation of the evolutionary perspective in the social sciences.

> Differentiation is, like complexity or specialization, first of all a classificatory concept. It describes the ways through which the main social functions or the major institutional spheres of society become disassociated from one another, attached to specialized collectivities and roles, and organized in relatively specific and autonomous symbolic and organizational frameworks within the confines of the same institutionalized system.[5]

The writings on differentiation, however, are curiously detached, strangely remote from the facts of social systems and the heat of political argument. The developmental literature makes a clear distinction between the separation of Church and state, and the state and the economy. It does not tell us, for example, why we say "Church-state conflict" and not "state-Church conflict," or why we say "political economy," but cannot say "economic polity" without sounding grotesque or implying bookkeeping. In other words, the literature on differentiation does not tell us about *types* of institutional relations, but instead posits a drifting apart of bunches of activities in a way that creates neat clusters and permits heightened freedom of action (or subinstitutional "autonomy") within each general institutional setting. In this abstracted view, much contemporary theory is reminiscent of classical Liberal social thought. Adam Smith, for instance, described the desirable marketplace as one that, as institution, was to function only on the basis of informed and rational behavior, divorced from all other considerations. Within the market, the actors were to behave in entirely autonomous ways, each rationally pursuing his economic goals within rules which would weed out the less fit. The role of the state was to guarantee the integrity of the market's differentiation from all other institutional spheres. However, neither classical nor many contemporary theories of differentiation appear to have touched base with insistent fact.

As a vulgar generalization, it is safe to say that in all contemporary industrialized societies the areas of secular determinations have increased, and religious considerations have become separated, or at least very distinguishable from, mundane political, economic, and even educational activities. As another vulgar generalization, it is equally safe to say that in all contemporary industrialized societies the political and economic structures have become intertwined with ever increasing complexity and interdependence. Whether we examine systems that call themselves socialist or capitalist, we still find planning, government controls, bureaucratization, and other examples of governmentally and politically affected rationalization. The implication is not that "capitalisms" and "socialisms" are the same, but that "development," even loosely defined, brings with it no neat disaggregation of economic and political functions. On the contrary, it can be powerfully argued that one of the more useful ways of describing the differences between self-labeled socialisms and capitalisms is precisely on the basis of how each kind of system ties its political and economic orders together.

The same point can be made even more obviously about the educational institution. The transfer of some socialization functions from the family to the school does not mean the establishment of a self-regulating and institutionally self-contained apparatus. The history of education in Chile and Venezuela, as everywhere, is the story of strife between those who would manage instruction for religious ends, national goals, or individual purposes. It will be argued that this view of differentiation has nothing to do with what most writers on the subject have been talking about. They have been addressing themselves to functions, not purposes. Thus, it is beside the point to argue that schools may be employed to deepen religious conviction, *if* that objective is sought through creating a set of processes peculiar to the formalization of the function of socialization. By the same token, it matters not if a polity is put to the ends of the leaders of an economy, if the political function is carried out in its own specialized way. This view of differentiation strips away both purpose and form, leaving us only with abstract function, technique, or process.

We have little interest in the subject from the purely functional point of view. Our concern is not with the procedural aspects of analytical bits of the total array of social behavior, but with the ways in which those pieces are put together. The construction of the whole pattern of institutional relations can provide us with an idea concerning the purpose of social organization as well as its shape. The reason, of course, is that seeing how groups distinguish institutions within an organizing frame also tells us which institutions they consider more important than others. An examination of the patterns of institutional differentiation *and* interrela-

22

tions can then permit us to draw inferences concerning the priorities of social purposes as well as the situses, procedures, and values through which those purposes might be served.

INSTITUTIONAL SETS

At this point let us present a summary of the responses given us by the Chileans and Venezuelans we interviewed with respect to their views of the five grand institutions—the family, religion, education, the economy, and the polity. Later, we shall discuss some of the implications of these findings for general views of differentiation as well as for the specific cases of Chile and Venezuela.

All of the 30 questions upon which the present description is based are included in the appendixes, but here we should describe briefly what they are about and how they were constructed. We framed a set of 6 questions for each institution to cover the person's motivation, the standards guiding his behavior, and his reactions to change. Here is a paraphrase of selected questions about the family to illustrate these three dimensions:

•Is society basically formed for the unity of families or for individuals?
•Is the family basically the same in all societies or does it vary according to the society?
•As time passes, do you expect your relations with your family to remain more or less the same or will they change greatly?

Additionally, for each of these three issues, we asked what a person believed *should* be the case and what he thought it actually was, thus giving us insight into his perception about his beliefs and his perceptions about his behavior. The alternative answers provided for each question were meant to be either a "traditional" response (given a value of one) or a "modern" alternative (given a value of 2), but they were not always presented in this 1-2 order. Each individual's total score for every institutional area thus fell in the range of 6 for the most traditional to 12 for the most modern.

In no sense are we suggesting that the people we interviewed read our questions and answered them with the same awareness of purposes that we have just sketched, any more than a witness always understands the purpose of the questions asked him by a trial lawyer. Rather, our

23

specifications of detailed components served as a guide in formulating the questions with explicit goals in mind, much as the trial lawyer constructs an outline to guide his questioning. In this way, we felt reasonably sure that we were asking parallel sets of questions about aspects of the subject that we believed were critically important. Our questions, in short, were explicitly deduced from our theoretical conceptions.

Further, we approached the formulation of the questions with some dissatisfaction with earlier attitude studies of the subject. Specifically, there were two interrelated assumptions in those studies that we meant to avoid. One was the conception that individuals hold more or less homogeneous packages of beliefs which can be expressed as a single statistic, usually derived from factorial and other correlational analyses. We could not accept such a neat picture, implying that individuals are so utterly consistent in their belief structure. Rather we pursued our assumption that most individuals hold mixed attitudes leading them to be more traditional—or modern—in some areas than in others.* The other feature of earlier studies we deliberately sought to avoid was their assumptions about a *Weltanschauung* that would distinguish modern from traditional outlooks. In earlier studies this has usually led to the phrasing of generalized, wide-ranging questions about one's outlook on life and fate rather than about the more specific decisions that have immediate relevance for individuals.

Compare, as examples, the thrust of the questions used in two of the best-known studies. Alex Inkeles and his colleagues questioned persons in six countries and, through detailed correlational analysis, developed several different forms of what they call an "individual modernity" scale, which they believe

> shows unmistakably that there is a set of personal qualities which reliably cohere as a syndrome and which identify a type of man who may validly be described as fitting a reasonable theoretical conception of the modern man. Central to this syndrome are: (1) openness to new experience . . . (2) the assertion of increasing independence from the authority of traditional figures like parents and priests and a shift of allegiance to leaders of government, public affairs . . . and the like; (3) belief in the efficacy of science and medicine, and a general abandonment of passivity and fatalism in the face of life's difficulties; and (4) ambition for oneself and one's children to achieve high occupational and educational goals.[6]

---

*For this reason we see no purpose in summing up the responses on all 30 questions about the institutions to achieve some single "traditionalism" or "modernism" score.

Joseph Kahl, in his study of workers in Brazil and Mexico, constructed fourteen scales to measure "the core values of a modern orientation."

> Further statistical analysis showed that seven of these scales were closely tied to one another: they composed a single pattern or syndrome which we have labeled the "core" of modernism. They are Activism, Low Integration with Relatives, Preference for Urban Life, Individualism, Low Community Stratification, High Mass-Media Participation, and Low Stratification of Life Chances.[7]

The thrust of the questions formulated by Inkeles, Kahl, and others is toward a goal of establishing some unified "core" of attitudes that would allow the researcher to designate a more or less total orientation held by individuals. By contrast, our assumptions about the asymmetry of beliefs and the distinctiveness of the several institutional sectors led us away from accepting any such notion of an internally consistent set of attitudes. We tend, therefore, to agree with Schnaiberg's conclusions that "we should not overstate the unity of the modernizing process as some single unilineal evolutionary development taking place across all behavioral and attitudinal spheres . . . . Therefore, we must question the conceptualization of modernism as some unified entity, and continue to explore the *range* of content of 'modernism' in various societies, attempting to account for the variation as well as the similarities."[8]

As we have already described it, an individual's responses to the set of questions in each institutional area could vary from 6 to 12—from traditional to modern as we have defined these terms. The following graphs and tables present the results for each group of persons we interviewed in the two countries.

Before we interpret the significance of these relationships, let us briefly summarize the unmistakable patterns shown in the graphs and tables:

With but two minor exceptions, there is a consistent pattern among the institutional perceptions held by all groups. The family and religion, in that order, are ranked as the most traditional by all groups, while the economy and education are ranked as the most modern. Squarely in the middle lies the polity.*

There is a clear pattern of differences among the groups, with but few

---

*The only minor exceptions are that the Chilean secondary-school students equate the family and religious institutions as the most traditional, and the Chilean university students see education, the economy, and the polity as equally modern.

Figure II - 1   MEAN INSTITUTIONAL SCORES—CHILE

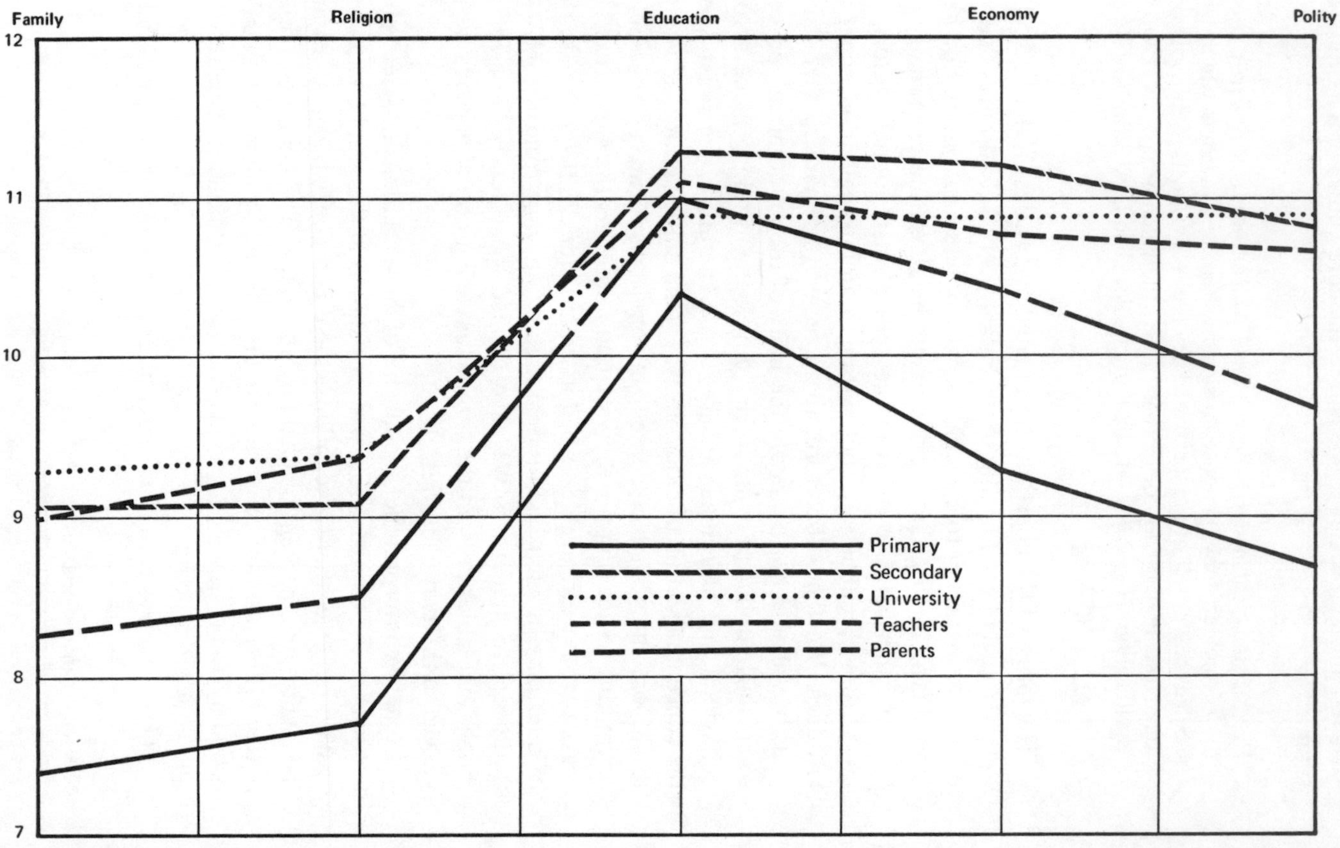

Primary
Secondary
University
Teachers
Parents

Family   Religion   Education   Economy   Polity

12 11 10 9 8 7

Figure II - 2   MEAN INSTITUTIONAL SCORES—VENEZUELA

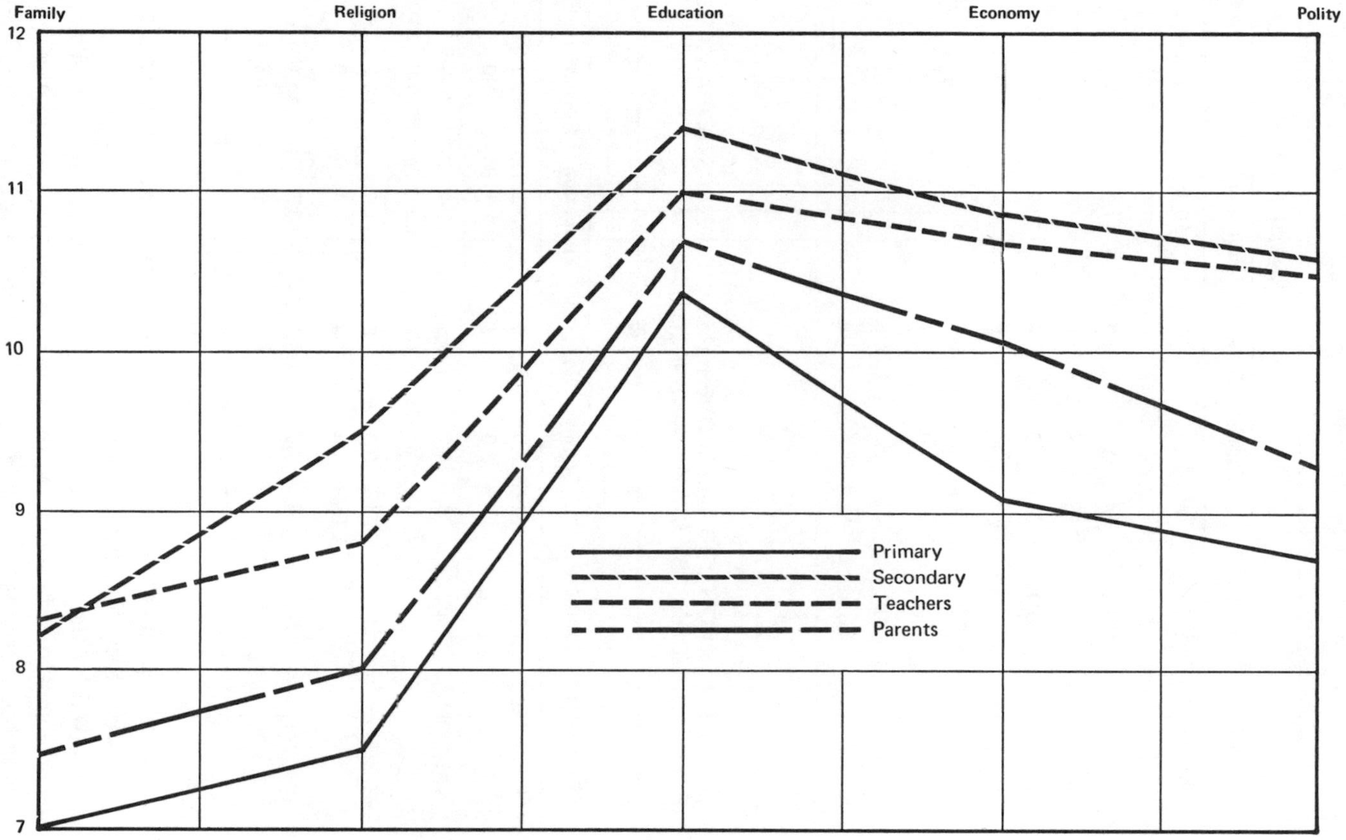

27

Table II-1   INSTITUTIONAL SCORES: MEANS AND STANDARD DEVIA-
TIONS, BY SAMPLE—CHILE

Sample	Number		Family	Religion	Education	Economy	Polity
Primary	1279	M =	7.4	7.7	10.4	9.3	8.7
		S.D. =	1.1	1.2	1.2	1.5	1.5
Secondary	1068	M =	9.1	9.1	11.3	11.2	10.8
		S.D. =	1.2	1.2	.8	.9	1.1
University	284	M =	9.3	9.4	10.9	10.9	10.9
		S.D. =	1.2	1.0	.9	1.0	1.0
Teachers	322	M =	9.0	9.4	11.1	10.8	10.7
		S.D. =	1.3	1.1	.9	1.0	1.1
Parents	481	M =	8.3	8.5	11.0	10.5	9.7
		S.D. =	1.2	1.3	1.1	1.1	1.5

(Column group header: INSTITUTION)

Table II-2   INSTITUTIONAL SCORES: MEANS AND STANDARD DEVIA-
TIONS, BY SAMPLE—VENEZUELA

Sample	Number		Family	Religion	Education	Economy	Polity
Primary	1624	M =	7.0	7.5	10.3	9.1	8.7
		S.D. =	1.0	1.1	1.1	1.6	1.5
Secondary	1302	M =	8.2	8.5	11.4	10.9	10.6
		S.D. =	1.3	1.2	.7	1.0	1.2
Teachers	331	M =	8.3	8.8	11.0	10.7	10.5
		S.D. =	1.4	1.3	.9	.9	1.3
Parents	520	M =	7.5	8.0	10.7	10.1	9.3
		S.D. =	1.2	1.3	1.1	1.3	1.6

(Column group header: INSTITUTION)

exceptions. In both countries, the primary-school students are the most traditional in their perceptions of each institutional sector. They are followed by the parents in both countries, except for the Chilean parents' view of education. At the other end of the spectrum, compared with other groups, the secondary-school students in both countries are the most or nearly most modern in their perceptions. In Chile, the secondary-school students alternate with university students as being the most modern in all areas except religion. In Venezuela, the secondary-school students are most modern of all in their attitudes toward the educational, economic, and political institutions, while they are a close second to the teachers, who hold the most modern attitudes regarding the family and religion.

The comparisons between Chile and Venezuela reveal yet a third pattern. With but two exceptions, the Chileans are consistently more modern than the Venezuelans, group for group and institution for institution. The only deviations appear in Chilean secondary-school students regarding education, and the equal ranking given the polity by primary-school students in both countries.

These patterns of relationships are distinctive and consistent along every possible dimension, whether by institution, sample group, or country. We have our first general confirmation of the cultural similarity between Chile and Venezuela, and of the related hypothesis that Chile, within that cultural realm, is the more developed of the two. That conclusion is so obvious as to need no further elaboration, but two other equally evident findings should be briefly touched upon before we turn to the institutional comparisons, the major theme of this chapter.

First, the order in which the institutions have been listed should be explained as being more than a device of the presentation. Had we been interested in drawing accelerating curves, we would have placed the political institution in the middle, giving us a rather smooth progression from the family at one end to education at the other. But we put the polity last because we wished to represent the institutions in the order in which they are likely to affect persons as they age and mature. The temporal spacing between institutions as they engage persons is, of course, not even. And, obviously, the same order is not followed in all societies or by all individuals. Still the progression we have used is commonsensical and roughly descriptive of Latin American society as well as of Western culture.

A significant theoretical reason also predisposed us to this order. Because we approach the polity as the integrating institution of national societies, we expect attitudes toward politics to reflect ideas about proper relations among all elements of the entire institutional array. If a modern state pretends to a legitimate authority to use its coercive powers in the resolution of intra- and interinstitutional conflicts, then the array of institutional beliefs we have presented should tell us to what degree that role is accepted or rejected. What we should expect, of course, is that to the degree the family and religion are valued, the state's coercive role in those areas will be limited; or again, to the extent to which the economy and education are seen as useful, the state's role in their promotion will be valued. Put in simple arithmetic terms, we should expect that this inherent ambivalence about ends and means will place any institution pretending to decisive power somewhere in the middle range of all other feelings about other institutional activities. And that result is precisely what we found. We shall say more about this richly suggestive finding later in this chapter.

The second point we should now introduce is one that will recur throughout: Why should primary-school students and parents lean so uniformly toward the traditional side of our measures, while teachers, secondary-school students, and the few university students we interviewed lean so consistently toward the other side? To reach for age differences as the explanation immediately runs afoul of the obvious fact that age cannot account for the differences between parents and teachers, who are roughly within the same age groups. Educational differences, the second distinction of the primary-school students, is a possible explanation, for it is a characteristic those students share with most parents. About two-thirds of all parents in both Chile and Venezuela have had no more than a primary-school education, and about half of all parents have not even completed primary school. Hence, parents resemble the primary-school students as far as formal education is concerned. By contrast, the better educated secondary-school and university students and teachers also appear as more modern. On this basis alone, we should attribute a modernizing function to education. Of course, we cannot now go further and specify just *what* components of the educational experience are the most significant. Even so, the simple, quantitative fact of educational exposure itself seems strongly to influence the direction of the responses we obtained. It is a finding that should not be blurred.

INSTITUTIONAL DIFFERENTIATION

There is strong evidence from our data that Chileans and Venezuelans perceive their institutions differently, and that those perceptions are not random but patterned. Specifically, family and religion are in a class entirely apart from education and economics. As shown in the figures, even the *most* modern attitudes about the family and religion still are more traditional than the *least* modern attitudes about education and the economy, with the sole exception of the Chilean primary-school students concerning the economy. Evidently, then, our respondents differentiated between two types of institutions, and, whatever differentiation is recognized among all five institutions, the gulf between the two types is clearly more significant than any conventional statements about differentiation per se. The political institution forms a bridge between these two blocks, and thus occupies a third, and particular, place.

The literature on social institutions contains a long-standing recognition of differences between *expressive* institutions (family, religion), and *instrumental* institutions (education, economy). Indeed, these two terms serve especially well to characterize the several institutions as they are perceived by those we questioned. What differentiates the two categories, we believe, is the basis upon which people make their judgments about values and behavior in the several institutional contexts. In the expressive sphere, individuals believe that their actions are ends in themselves, without any added purpose in mind. Behavior is less subject to rational considerations than it usually is in other contexts. Hence, one's religious or familial behavior is self-justifying, affectively or emotionally satisfying in itself.

In the instrumental sphere, by contrast, individuals act in terms of some further goal, to achieve some added objective. Such behavior, then, typically is open to rational considerations, even though many people will not always or even frequently act rationally in economic and educational endeavors. Activity in the economic or educational sectors carries a presumed purpose that gives shape to the immediate behavior itself, and individuals tend to explain their behavior in such terms. It is rarely asked, for instance, why one is, or is not, devoted to one's family. But, one would ask why one is going to school. Few would ask the purpose of a person's religious beliefs, but many dedicated Protestants used to aver that they sought economic success to achieve salvation.

These are, of course, idealized examples; not everyone is necessarily motivated in this manner. Some persons may act in the economic sector expressively, just as some see their family or religion in instrumental terms. Nevertheless, we do not believe that these latter variations are pervasive.

This way of looking at institutionally shaped behavior draws considerably from Max Weber's classification of human action. Specifically, Weber distinguished four types of motives: affectual, traditional, value-rational *(Wertrationalität)*, and end-rational *(Zweckrationalität)*. It is the last two types that are relevant here, which, Runciman notes, correspond to the distinction between "expressive" and "instrumental" action.[9]

Our use of these two categories of "expressive" and "instrumental" actions is meant to be a classification of utility and of insight to explain the responses of the Chileans and Venezuelans. In their most general context, we would interpret those responses to mean that our respondents permitted themselves a relatively greater choice in assessing the values of the economic and educational institutions, as compared with the narrower choice in the case of religious and family institutions. In line with our conception of modernity and traditionalism, to carry this interpretation a step further, it is a mark of the modern man that he is predisposed to be relativistic and individualistic about the family and religion in some of the same ways that he is about economic and educational purposes. Hence, he sees that not only will there certainly be changes in family relations and religious belief, but also that freedom for individual choice should be recognized in these two sectors.

Traditional man, by contrast, extends his values and beliefs from the family and religion outward to affect even his attitudes about education and the economy. Where he is absolutistic and tightly identified with a familial or religious group, he is also prepared to endow education and the economy with similar qualities and beliefs. That is, he is prepared to view his institutions as organized around a core, ultimate values which he must accept on their face.

Naturally, these characterizations are overdrawn in order to highlight the differences in an ideal-typical way. Human beings are neither so consistent nor so stylized, as is evident from the data we have presented, which show that most of the people we questioned make a clear distinction between the instrumental and expressive institutions. It is not the satisfaction of doing in itself which is their criterion: it is the combination of the immediate satisfaction and the *search for no other goal* that truly distinguishes the expressive from the instrumental function.

This approach to differentiation has richer implications than one which merely observes a growing functional specificity surrounding families of activities. The suggestion of qualitative difference carries with it implications of conflict. It hints when differentiation is held dearly, when held lightly, and which spheres of activity will be cherished more than others. Our respondents have told us that, relatively speaking, they are much less willing to be relativistic, truly pragmatic, open and changeful about familistic and religious affairs than about economic and educational ones. To put the same theme positively, they have also stated that they are more willing to be open, experimental, individually oriented, and innovative about economic and educational affairs, and they imply that they do so because they expect such openness to produce personal benefit, which they can convert to ends pursued in a far less questioning fashion.

Another obvious conclusion from these configurations is that traditional and modern persons in Chile and Venezuela are alike in that they see total institutional orders as differentiated. *The traditional person is just as able to think of a disjunctive, pluralistic, and differentiated institutional structure as is the modern one.* Perhaps traditional men in other societies cannot see social differences for the cultural sea in which they swim. But the persons we studied, whether modern or traditional, plainly do perceive clear difference—even though the *positions* from which they see vary widely—and thus they understand very differently. More importantly, they show the antagonism of their views in the ways in which they would politically reconcile the plural situation they all recognize to one extent or another. It is in the political sphere, where perception may be converted into empowered aspiration, that the recognition of the significance of the expressive-instrumental dichotomy becomes of critical importance for the analysis of development and modernization.

The fact that the family-religion and education-economy blocks do not touch in our graphs underscores the importance of the intermediate position of perceptions of the polity. In the light of the sharpness of the distinction between expressive and instrumental institutions, it is a logical inference that the expressed indetermination about the polity has to do with disagreement concerning whether politics is a means to other ends, or whether political activity somehow reflects the belief that community action is a good per se. The statement, to repeat, is only an inference from the relationships revealed by our information, not a direct description of those data. The questions concerning politics which we are using for this discussion are narrowly within the motivation-standards-change trinity already described. As a sample of these questions, one from each category is paraphrased below:

- Is it your principal function as a citizen to defend the national honor and sovereignty, or to be concerned with the progress of the country?
- Is a good law inspired by human nature, or is it related to ongoing and changing social needs?
- Should political activity have as its goal the maintenance of public order, or should it be oriented toward the development of the country?

33

All of the responses we have labeled as modern (the second alternatives above) have to do with an increase in effective participation in a political process that can serve to increase control over the social as well as physical environments. All of the traditional responses have to do with defending status (such as "national culture," "sovereignty," and "honor,") and with justifying action as an obligation. At first blush, it would appear that it is the traditional man who sees political activity as tantamount to religious behavior—one does it for its own sake, for the defense of what is, or out of obligation. It is then the modern man who would use the state instrumentally, to achieve development, to respond to the decisions of citizens, to achieve a "better" social life, to influence social events.

But we need to remind ourselves of certain theoretical precepts in order to understand the meaning of the responses in the context of the entire set of institutional perceptions. If the traditional man sees politics as a goal in itself, then why does he not put politics, in his responses, on the same level with the family and religion? The same question can be posed similarly for the modernist responses. The question we must ask ourselves concerns the intention of the political response *with respect to the other institutions*. Traditional defenses of status and behavior out of obligation relegate the state to a position of powerlessness relative to religious and family affairs. The role of the state as interinstitutional arbiter is specifically denied; the attitude is *anti*national. The modern response makes the state instrumental for the purpose of mediating among other institutions in the employment of its monopolistic powers of coercion; it is a *pro*national attitude. The data about the *single* institutions of the polity *describe* to us attitudes about nation-building. The data about *all* the institutional orders taken together tell us about national community, and have to do with action in an expandingly participant order. The implication, then, is that this kind of instrumentalism, for those who hold it, assumes the characteristic of being an end in itself. The pronationalists seem to be striving for a reduction of alienation within a general community; the antinationalists seem desirous of maintaining communal alienation in favor of the more intimate ties of family and church.

As of this moment in the discussion, however, we should leave this point as what we have said it is: an inference. Elaborations on this theme will occupy us as we proceed, for it is one of our central concerns. For the time being, however, let us explicitly state that the suggestion we wish to carry forward is that modern attitudes toward the national state eradicate the apparent contradiction between expressive and instrumen-

34

tal functions: participation in the national community for the purpose of reducing alienation turns appropriate functions and procedures into ends to be sought in themselves. The doing is its own reward, for the *practice* of effective participation in order to *increase* effective participation resolves contradictions between public and private ends, and between instruments and goals. These statements can be made of no other institutional order, for in complex societies only the polity can synthesize total institutional situations, providing the realm in which the clash between individual and public interests can be dissolved in an accommodation of micro- and macro-social values.

In summing up this discussion of institutional differentiation, there are many obvious conclusions that can be cited. We have learned in which areas certain Chileans and Venezuelans will tend to resist social change and in which they will tend to accept, if not welcome it. We see that great faith is placed in education as an instrument of individual and social change, and only a little less is put in the economy. But we also see that religion and the family are the most cherished institutions. Politics is a subject of ambivalence for all groups, although for many individuals it is the repository of hope for change, and for others only a warehouse of the symbols of faith. While such conclusions are not to be shrugged off—indeed, we shall return to them for greater elaboration—they pale in significance before the overwhelmingly most obvious and singular of all the conclusions one must draw: these data in their total configurations are inescapably regular, internally coherent, and logically clustered, whether we consider them by sample groups, by institutional sectors, or by country.

A weakness of much social theorizing about institutions and institutional differentiation is that primary attention is put on the growth of social division, while only lip service is paid to the emergence of the new syntheses which must glue together the emergent patterns of differentiation. This failure to see systems of cohesion is true even of Marxist thinkers. The class struggles of capitalist society seen by most Marxists are not adequately framed within the synthesizing institutional mechanisms of capitalist nation-states, raising for them the "national question" usually in a negative way. Among Marxists as well as "bourgeois" social scientists, insufficient attention has been paid to the role that a differentiated institution may itself play in promoting social synthesis. To put it another way, little or insufficient organized thought has been given to the idea that, as the institutional growth of the Western world occurred, it became the specialized role of the increasingly differentiated polity to provide for synthesis. Or, much more accurately stated, within the cultural continuum of the Protestant capitalist world, a primary idealized role of the Liberal state was to provide the systems of equality and access that permitted national community to cement together the divisions occasioned by a proliferating class order and the mincing of institutions that accompanies specialization, roundabout production, impersonal market mechanisms, public educational systems, impersonality in work and other public relations, and the concomitant growths of urbanity and urbanization. *This response was a cultural one, and is not necessarily to be shared in its entirety by the specialization, differentiation, and autonomous structures accompanying development in other cultural milieux.*

The suggestion we advance at this point is that the holistic orderings of the responses we have so far described are reflective of fundamental cultural predispositions. It is for that very reason that they are so regular, that they cross national borders so easily, and that they possess internal logic. When we employ such words as "internal logic" and "coherence," we do not mean that the response patterns are even, dependent upon each other as though they were marks on a ruler. Quite to the contrary, the regularity is found in the ordering of breaks. Our critical point of interest, then, must revolve about how sets of Chileans and Venezuelans perceive the ordering devices that give overarching sense to their evolving societal differences. Toward that end, we must turn to a direct examination of world views, and their relation to views of the polity either as the institutional expression of national community or as merely another in a series of specialized instruments for the realization of private and sacred goals.

three / Views of the World

In this chapter we intend to examine closely and individually the persons we have studied, but we wish to do so without risking psychological reductionism either in ourselves or the reader. We therefore must confront more directly than before the relation between attitudes and behavior. One of the techniques we have used to erode the assumption that institutional and class positions narrowly determined behavior, or the converse fallacy that action streams directly from attitudes, involved asking about attitudes that refer to institutions. Another mitigation of such simplistic determinism is threaded through the analysis by our persistently stated assumption that attitudes imply only latency in the search for preferred solutions, the potential ability to act in certain ways if the social context as a whole establishes the sufficient conditions for appropriate and effective behavior. A third method will appear only in later chapters, when we seek to explore social activities in Chile and Venezuela through historical analysis and interpretation.

There is yet a fourth set of ties we have built, binding social structure, institutions, and attitudes. Those links order our view of causality, without which discussions of the relation between individuals and social orders tend to become arid, leaping over the synapses connecting persons with the components of social organization. The literature on development and social change reveals how difficult it is to start from individual attitudes and motivations without slighting institutions. The distinctions commonly drawn between macro- and micro-theory stand as a monument to this chronic problem. By way of illustration, we wish to quote from two authors whom we have chosen precisely because both are very sensitive to the consequences of explanations other than their own. Yet, each clearly stresses a particular perspective, only implying causal links which remain unexplained. First, here is how S. N. Eisenstadt explains institutional changes:[1]

The passage of a given society from one stage of differentiation to another is contingent on the development within it of certain processes of change which create a degree of differentiation that cannot be contained within the pre-existing system . . . . The extent to which these changes are institutionalized, and the concrete form they take in any given society, necessarily depend on the basic institutional contours and premises of the pre-existing system, on its initial level of differentiation, and on *the* major conflicts and propensities for change within it . . . .

[A]t any given level of differentiation the crystallization of different institutional orders is shaped by the interaction between the broader structural features of the major institutional spheres, on the one hand and, on the other hand, the development of elites or entrepreneurs in some of the institutional spheres of that society . . . .

For his part, Alex Inkeles, beginning from the individual perspective, is interested in the attitudes of persons and their behavior as the source for change even as he recognizes the force of institutions.[2] As we have quoted him in Chapter II, Inkeles believes that a modern man probably possesses a syndrome of personal qualities which distinguishes him from a traditional man. But he also recognizes, beyond this psychological statement, that, "Men change their societies. But the new social structures they have devised in turn shape the men who live within the new social order . . . ." Inkeles acknowledges that major social forces do exert a "determining [sic] influence on men's life condition and their responses to it. But such macro-structural forces can account for only one part of the variance in individual social behavior."[3]

We have been driven to make explicit some ideas of cause in order to spell out how we see such individual and social interactions, lest we elide the critical limitations on and implications from the data we are presenting. It is not enough simply to state that "men change their societies" and that societies change men. These axioms cannot be treated as though they were independent ideas for the obvious reason that both are continuously effective in social reality. Doubtless, most social analysts of change would agree, but then, as in the two quotations above, many would also contend that they must abstract only part of the total social reality in order to analyze it. This is a legitimate and necessary scientific action, but our objection to its application in the present context is that it implies a linear causality that is misplaced.

As an alternative, we prefer a line of analysis that begins with the recognition of a continuous and simultaneous interaction between people and their societies, and starts from the construction of "ideal types." The ideal type is an analytical form long associated with the work of Max Weber; it is a particular orientation toward the subject matter as well as a technique.* Briefly, the ideal type is a form of deliberate concept development that isolates selected characteristics and those interrelationships among them believed to be of causal importance. These elements comprise a statement about individuals in terms of the values they hold and the social actions presumably related to them. Thus, ideal types contain explicit references to the available social options toward which the actions of individuals are directed. For instance, to speak of a "modern man" without reference to the society in which he lives is to assume erroneously that his values and beliefs are everything when, in fact, his values and his actions have meaning only within their social context.

As applied to our materials, the method consists of constructing types of individuals on the basis of an interlocking set of their beliefs about autonomy in their own actions, in the actions of other persons, and within the institutions of their society. These values, when interpreted together with the available real options for change, constitute the path of analysis that we have chosen to adopt in this study.†

Another characteristic of the ideal-type is its assumption of rationality in the individual's behavior, an element Weber consciously incorporated into his use of the device.[4] Rationality means here that beliefs and values on the one side, and behavior on the other, are tied together into a

---

*Weber's methodology is of a piece with his general orientation toward the social sciences, including history. Therefore, we cannot here undertake a full explanation of the ideal type and its epistemological consequences. The best single source for Weber's discussion of this concept is to be found in *The Methodology of the Social Sciences*, trans. and ed. E. A. Shils and H. A. Finch (New York: The Free Press, 1949), especially the last section entitled, "Objective Possibility and Adequate Causation in Historical Explanation." Weber's classic application of the ideal type is in his *The Protestant Ethnic and the Spirit of Capitalism*, trans. Talcott Parsons (New York: Scribners, 1958). In the latter (p. 47), Weber captures an essential meaning of the ideal types when he states, "If any object can be found to which this term [the spirit of capitalism] can be applied with any understandable meaning, it can only be an historical individual, i.e. a complex of elements associated in historical reality which we unite into a conceptual whole from the standpoint of their cultural significance."

†We generally agree with the point of view expressed by Berger *et al.* except that their emphasis upon individual consciousness is stronger than ours. "Society is viewed in this perspective as a dialectic between objective givenness and subjective meanings—that is, as being constituted by the reciprocal interaction of what is experienced as outside reality (specifically the world of institutions that confronts the individual) and what is experienced as being within the consciousness of the individual. Put differently, *all social reality has an essential component of consciousness*." P. Berger, B. Berger, and H. Kellner, *The Homeless Mind: Modernization and Consciousness* (New York: Random House, 1973), p. 12.

means-ends relationship; that is, persons accepting certain beliefs in given social contexts will be likely to pursue ends related to those beliefs. This point reflects our insistence on seeing attitudes as part of the stock of social latency, as predisposition given direction by rationality, but not infused with the social power to act.

From these comments about our perspective applied to the data at hand, and in further explanation of introductory statements made in Chapter I, we suggest that a causal explanation should contain the following elements:

- An ideal-type statement of the total options open to a society, given its resources, the universal state of the technical, theoretical, and ideological arts, and so forth.
- A real-type statement of the more limited array of options that can be perceived within the given society in all the above dimensions, with the others left implied.
- The options available as they are perceived and understood by discrete sectors of that society, as broken down by such appropriate categories as social class and race (when pertinent), age, sex, educational level, and so forth.
- The potential effectiveness of action based on the selection of alternatives; that is, the *power potential* of individuals and groups to make their decisions effective. Institutional positions at the moment of choice are the most important data required here.
- The making of choices, and the behavior to translate the choice into effective action for oneself and others.

This set of elements should not be thought of as a list, a set of steps in a process. Rather, they describe a set of interactions in which no single dimension should be taken in isolation from the whole. We do not suggest that we can or will consider fully detailed causal contexts in this work. Rather, this exposition is meant to serve the purpose of revealing the limits of our inferences and the boundaries of the subjects we have chosen for emphasis. Thus, we are exploring some of the real-type options of some Chileans and Venezuelans as they perceive them, and we are studying the development and nature of such perceptions through education in interaction with such other structural characteristics as age, sex, urban-rural residence, and so forth. We have much information on what choices would be made under certain conditions, as supposed by our respondents, but we must rely on historical inference and reasonable interpretations to tell us about effectiveness and actual decisions made

40

and pushed into attempted implementation. We have seen the persons we interviewed not merely as holders of attitudes, but also as members of global, national, and local societies; as culture-bound, but also as idiosyncratic; as endowed at birth with a potential for social power, but as related to day-to-day structures which set the limits of their actual power; and as persons who will mix rite and reason in varying degrees to make decisions, but who may or may not wish to act on decisions once they are made. We cannot study the totality, but when we proceed piece by piece, we can also constantly remind ourselves that those who study and those who are studied also create ideas of wholeness. Seeking out the integrating patterns used by some Chileans and Venezuelans leads us to the accent on persons of this chapter, and to this attempt to set the more general frame which gives depth to and yet limits the sense of this discussion.

These comments about holism also serve to reveal the connections between this chapter and the previous one. Earlier, we had tried to learn whether individuals recognize differences among institutions, whether they can accept differing role definitions in each institutional sphere, and whether they see their present beliefs as temporally relative and subject to future change. But we also placed great emphasis on the state as a possible integrating institution. That is, we did not stop short with differing perceptions of the uses of relativism, rationalism, and dynamism in each institution, but sought to learn whether the respondents also saw an *institutional* integrating function. In this chapter, we turn instead to the question of how each individual perceives himself within his social order; that is, we are examining individual attitudinal synthesis, not institutional integration. To stop with the previous chapter would leave an unreal impression that persons maintain compartmentalized attitudes about the family, religion, or education. We assume, instead, that personalities are more unified, that identifying threads run throughout belief and attitude-systems.

In pursuing this tack, we shall also make much more complex our understanding of the syndromes of "traditionalism" and "modernism." As we have said, we reject the simplifications of static, mirror-image oppositions assuming that, if traditional man is a fatalist, then modern man must be a rationalist. Even if one is prepared to accept these contrasting extremes as working definitions, it still remains quite unclear how anyone fits into the intervening categories. What, for example, would a mixture of fatalism and rationalism look like when we try to describe an individual holding such complex views? Generalized attitudes can tempt one into simple dichotomies. But attitudes as they are tied to specific institutions and norms can reveal the complications with whose ordering most people have to deal.

Our problem, then, was a dual one: to find the differences in perceptions as well as the unity among them. Our answer was to organize the analysis around empirically constructed types which were based upon several dimensions simultaneously, and which would allow for asymmetrical variations among sets of attitudes. By so doing, we are able to describe not only moderns and traditionals at the extremes—as even the simplest theory is usually able to do—but also to describe intervening constellations of attitudes to be expected in societies undergoing major social changes.

The central idea of the typology is to learn how persons see the amount of "play" they may have with regard to their own, intimate decisions, the amount of effective room for maneuver that others may have, and the degree to which the institutional order is open and variable, or shut and unresponsive and predetermined. The core notion is clear, permitting an extreme opposition between those who think the total range of social experience is mutable and those who see themselves in an unbending order. The introduction of the three dimensions—the entirely personal, others, and the institutionally general—also permits us to examine the mixes of ideas, with consequences we think fruitful and faithfully descriptive of varied shades of Latin American political thought.

We attempted to get at the individual sense of effective openness by reordering one dimension of the questions asked concerning institutional differentiation. It will be remembered that each institutional sphere was approached by questions having to do with the motivation for behavior in each realm, the expected range of effect of behavior, and changefulness. For the purposes of this typology, we took out only the questions having to do with ritualistic or rationalistic motivations, summing them across the five institutional orders. Therefore, we perceive of these motivational questions as transcending any particular set of individual actions, as embracing an individual orientation toward all social activity.* The unity of and relationship among the responses are supplied by the persons interviewed, not by us. We, of course, supply the inferences and the relationship to other elements of our body of data.

The second dimension of the typology has to do with the appreciation of the individual autonomy of others and its exercise, or with the oppo-

---

*The specific questions asked through the typology, the scoring employed, the justifications for the questions, and other methodological details can be found in the Appendix.

site view that the individual is to be measured only in terms of group attributes or his contributions to the collectivity—by his fruit, and not himself. The idea is well put by Robert Redfield in his discussion of folk culture. "We may understand a society to be individualistic to the extent that the socially approved behavior of any of its members does not involve family, clan, neighborhood, village, or other primary group."[5] Our questions developed for this part of the typology were simple and direct. They are:

- Is the best criterion by which to judge a man his contribution to society, or his talents and capabilities?
- Is the best criterion by which to judge a man his family situation, or his personal accomplishments?
- Is the best criterion by which to judge a man his personal religious conviction, or his morality as regards society?

In each case, we deemed the second answer as the one respectful of individual autonomy. There may appear to be some ambiguity in ascribing meaning to each choice. For example, in the first question, "his contribution to society" is taken to be the organicist answer, and "morality as regards society" in the third question is assumed to be individualistic. It is in the *relation* between each posited pair that we sought our meaning, of course, and not in any single item standing by itself. Thus, in the first question the priority of individual talents and capabilities as the basis for judging a person is an obvious characteristic of the autonomous view. Juxtaposed to this possibility, judging a man by his "contribution to society" stresses conformity to social requirements rather than to individual values and personal freedom. Placed in opposition to another choice, however, the item might well be justifiably judged on the "modern" side.

The second question poses no problems of interpretation, for it opposes family ascription to individual merit as the basis for judgment. The third question, however, may at first glance appear to be assigning "respect for the individual" to the traditionalist, and "social service" to the modernist. The more essential difference between the responses, however, has to do with the recognition of ethical standards outside formal religious ones, with the relativeness of individual morality as against the all-inclusiveness of formal religious belief. The main point, as we see it, is whether the individual may be somewhat free to decide for himself the basis for social morality, rather than being forced to accept a single ready-made standard contained within a religious or political dogma.

The traditionalist, in our view, assumes that convictions based upon religious beliefs are the only acceptable ones, and that without an explicit acceptance of such standards, the morality of other individuals must always be suspect.

First we considered the individual's own room for using his head; our second battery asked whether his judgment of others was based upon the use of their own abilities. The third dimension moves another step away from the person toward the master question of secular relativism in interinstitutional relations. In other words, our concern here is not alone with the differentiation of spheres of action, but with secular attitudes that imply that some functions *should*, ethically, be independent of others. We put a series of questions forcing confrontation among the five institutional spheres, from which we have selected six out of the ten possible sets of choices for the purposes of this typology. The complete number would be somewhat redundant. Instead, we chose to emphasize education, because of its centrality to this research, and added two more facets to learn the relation seen by the respondent between state and family, and between state and the economy. The questions are as follows:

	Organicist Response	Autonomous Response
1. Should the principal functions of the state be concern for the well-being of the family?	Yes	No
2. Should the student's education be free of any political influence?	No	Yes
3. Ought the price of essential goods be fixed by the government?	Yes	No
4. Should the student's education be free of any religious influence?	No	Yes
5. Is it the principal function of education to reinforce the unity of the family?	Yes	No
6. Is it the principal function of the school to prepare individuals to earn a living?	No	Yes

Our intention, of course, was to determine just how prepared the individual was to accord each institutional area its own legitimate identity and independence from other institutional areas. In pursuing this point without regard to conventional wisdom or current ideological conviction, our labeling of responses may seem to run counter to what is commonly called "modern" and "traditional." Socialists would certainly consider themselves as "modernists," for example, and would probably contend that the prices of essential goods should be fixed by the state as a means of achieving income equality. Similarly, a conservative Catholic would demand that education be free of political influence if he disliked the incumbent regime, or argue the opposite under fitting circumstances. In the last question, concerning the role of education in preparing a person to earn a living, the occupational response is taken as modern because the emphasis is upon the individual, and not upon the uses of education to certify one's fixed social position.

The elements of this typology, to conclude this description, are designed to reinforce aspects of the causal conjunction described earlier. In taking a decision, what room is there for the uses of reason? In taking a decision, how much can one rely on the ability of other persons to react as individuals, or must one always seek to manipulate them within extant molds? In taking a decision, how much is one bound by inexorable social forces and the sanctity of all that is, or can one assume that parts of a general structure can be moved? This idea provides the thematic and theoretical unity of the typology.

If each of the three dimensions is constructed by categorizing each person's score as "high" or "low," we derive eight combinations or types as follows:

	INSTITUTIONAL AUTONOMY			
	Low		High	
	Autonomy for Others		Autonomy for Others	
SELF-AUTONOMY	Low	High	Low	High
Ritualism	Type 1	Type 2	Type 5	Type 6
Rationalism	Type 3	Type 4	Type 7	Type 8

Naming the types, instead of referring to them by numbers, will make it easier to discuss their significance and to keep them in mind throughout the discussion. Nevertheless, it should be remembered that a name is as much a summary as is an arithmetic total, and may blur the refined complexity we are examining, as an addition may wipe out its constituent numbers. For this reason, we shall briefly interpret each type in order to suggest the context within which we wish to place the names.

Type 1—*The Organicist*. This person is low on his recognition of institutional differentiation, low in recognizing the individuality of others, and ritualistic in his own motivations for behavior. For organicists other individuals are locked into and recognizable only within their networks of relationships, to be judged on the basis of religion and family, and not on talents and achievements. But the Organicist is consistent, for he makes judgments about himself in the same way, and assumes that the entire social universe is responsive to the same judgments appropriate for himself and others. By almost any definition, this person is the complete traditionalist.

Type 2—*The Conservative Individualist*. Like his Organicist cousin, this type is a ritualist and blind to the distinct functions of the various institutional spheres. But he judges other persons on their merits, rather than as part of a web of social relationships. He seems to fit the pattern of what has often been praised in Latin Americans of the old school— their sense of *dignidad*, an insistence upon the integrity of self and the uniqueness of every man. The Conservative Individualist himself acts in a traditional fashion, and does not extend his recognition of the particularity of others into a principle that would have bearing on the functions of institutions in his society. In other words, he judges individuals as they are, but believes that the family and religion should be given priority over the individual.

Type 3—*The Anarchic Conservative*. Persons in this category see themselves as guided by modern and pragmatic choices in their own behavior, but they are unwilling or unable to extend this principle to other persons or to the society. The Anarchic Conservative would not judge others by their talents and achievements, but he himself strives to get ahead in life and express his own capacities. Persons in this category are either consummate egotists, or else attempting to sustain a construction of great logical fragility. So few respondents could fit themselves into this strained posture that we will drop this type from further analysis. We take the relative emptiness of this category as partial confimation of the validity of our techniques.

Type 4—*The Corporatist Technocrat*. This person is a rational man in his own behavior and an individualist in his judgment of others, but he believes that the structure of society is blurred, that religious and political influences should permeate education, and that secular affairs should be judged by external values which, by implication, it is not his to judge. Such views are very common among Latin America's *técnicos*— "technical men"—who view themselves as apolitical, as accepting of the social *status quo* within which individual ability should play. An Eichmann would probably fit this category. In contemporary Spain members of Opus Dei would sustain this argument. Conservative Christian Democrats and most economist-*técnicos* in Latin America give practical life to such views.

Type 5—*The Corporate Pluralist*. Persons in this set see institutional pluralism, but they themselves act ritualistically and judge others by similarly traditional criteria. They are reminiscent of the Spanish thinkers of the Counter Reformation who postulated the importance of discrete social "pillars," but assumed that institutional difference could be made to grow with a preservation of class hierarchies and other values of the traditional society. Today's conservative Falangist maintains similar views; he believes in the possibilities of industrialization and urbanization and the other fruits of the "modern" formal estate, but without normative and hierarchical change. This type of false modernist is often overlooked in studies of modernization, but he is not a *rara avis*, especially in the Mediterranean world.

Type 6—*The Liberal Abstainer*. Here are persons who can see the potentiality for the reality of changes taking place about them and who judge other persons individually, yet cannot make their own behavior move from ritualistic to more open patterns. We would expect that older persons rather than the young would fall into this pattern. Perhaps because of betrayed hopes, or possibly because of lingering traditional values, these persons cling to custom and habit in personal behavior. But they are able to see into the personal lives of others and to judge them by individual lights, and they assume that society is an open and relative construct.

Type 7—*The Modernist Cynic*. This type sees himself as pragmatic and experimental, and the society as differentiated and hinged together in relativistic ways. But he sees other people as rigid and traditional, and judges them accordingly. Like the Anarchic Conservative, the Modernist Cynic is trying to put together a highly dissonant view of the world, for it must be very difficult to see both oneself *and* the social world as open and everybody else as closed. The respondents agree with the stress involved in taking this set of views, and thus very few of them did so. Again, the numbers are so small as to constrain us to relegate the Cynic to the same oblivion as the Anarchist.

Type 8—*The Autonomist*. Persons of this type think they behave rationally and rationalistically; they judge others as individuals, and they see society as open and secular and with limited and demarcated institutional orders. Were such attitudes universalized within an appropriate institutional structure, then we would have basic elements of the quintessential modern society as defined by us in the course of this study.

Another way of understanding these types is to ask what they would

Figure III - 1 DISTRIBUTION OF TYPES—CHILE (per cent)

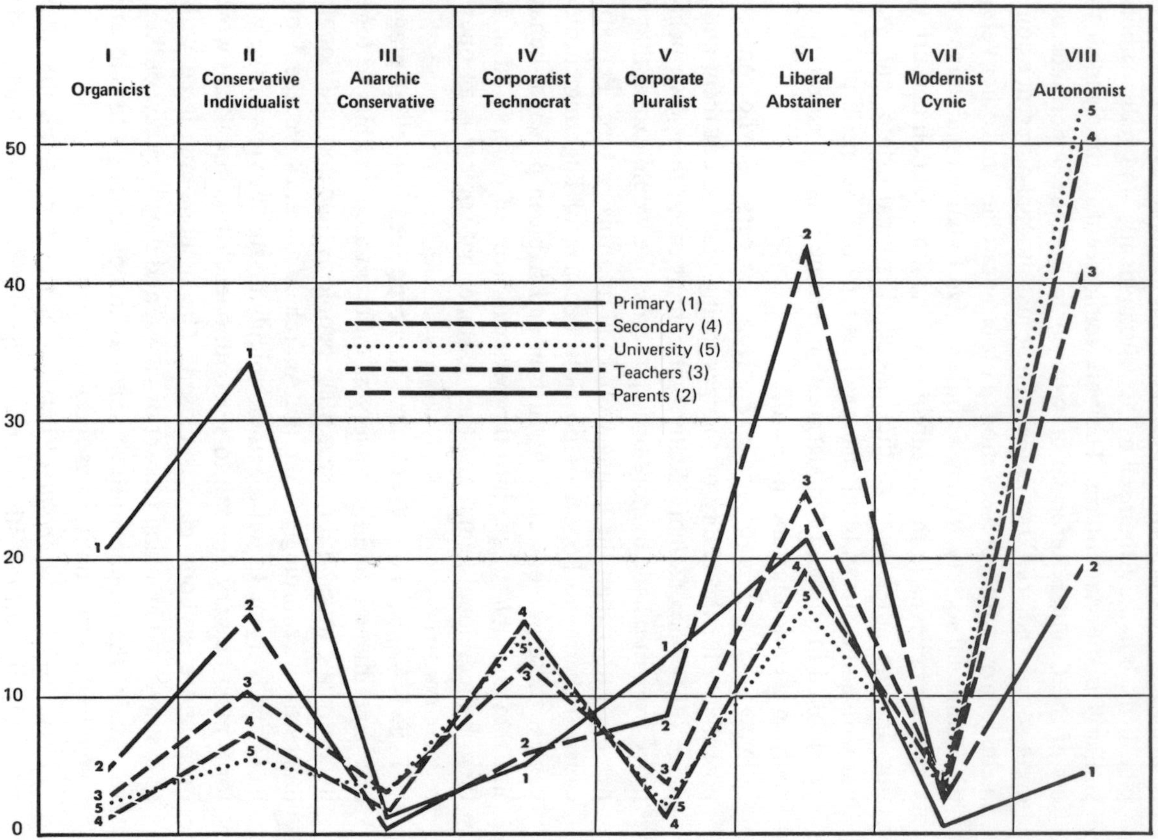
I
Organicist
II
Conservative
Individualist
III
Anarchic
Conservative
IV
Corporatist
Technocrat
V
Corporate
Pluralist
VI
Liberal
Abstainer
VII
Modernist
Cynic
VIII
Autonomist
0
10
20
30
40
50
Primary (1)
Secondary (4)
University (5)
Teachers (3)
Parents (2)

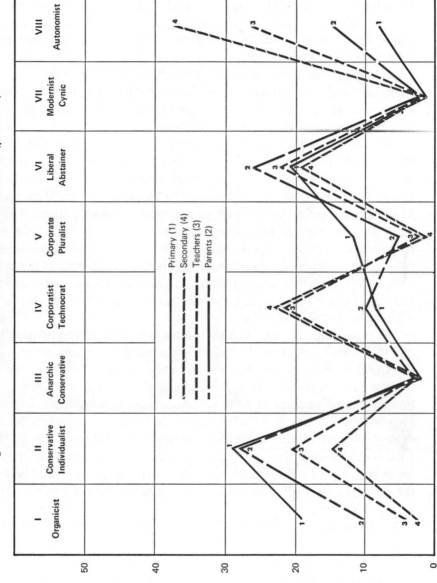

Figure III - 2 DISTRIBUTION OF TYPES—VENEZUELA (per cent)

49

cause to happen were they able to make effective decisions. The Organicist, clearly, would seek to build a sacred, hierarchical order, feeling sanctimonious justification in destroying opposition. The Conservative Individualist would do the same, but with a greater sense of mercy for his opponents and probably greater respect for law as an impersonal instrument. The Anarchic Conservative would model himself on Louis XIV. The Corporatist Technocrat would work hard to rationalize procedures within whatever structure he finds, in order to make it work smoothly and with stability. The Corporate Pluralist would impose hierarchy, order, and stability while promoting the formalistic aspects of development, such as cities, automobile factories, and national airlines—but all within the fabric of captive trade unions, a traditional church, and familistic localism. The Liberal Abstainer would hope for an open society, prepare his children to participate in one, and quietly go about his own personal conservatism. The Modernist Cynic, if he could hold himself together long enough to act, would probably stumble over his blind opportunism; his openness coupled with his view of the autonomous society cannot permit him adequate predictability concerning fellow citizens whom he measures ascriptively. The Autonomist would seek to extend human control over his complete social environment, convinced that rationalism and rationalization can be broadened to the entire sphere of secular action.

The regularities in this typology are aesthetically, methodologically, and theoretically pleasing. If findings here were to be consistent with those of the previous chapter on attitudes toward institutional configurations, then we would expect distributions at the poles to be evident: the primary-school students and the parents clustering among the Organicists and the Conservative Individualists, and the secondary-school students joining with the teachers in the ranks of the Autonomists and the Liberal Abstainers. However, the results are not so tritely expectable, for the polar positions are given sense and shading by the spread across the six types we shall discuss after having discarded the two virtually empty categories.

The most apparent ordering of these findings should be inventoried:

•In Types 1 and 2, the rank order in both Chile and Venezuela runs from primary-school students as the most traditional, to parents, teachers, and secondary-school students, in that order. Among the Autonomists, the order is exactly reversed in both countries.

•In Type 6, the Liberal Abstainers, in both countries the parents fall out of the expected order with the highest percentages, followed by

Table III-1 DISTRIBUTION OF TYPES: CHILE (per cent)

Sample Group	Organicist	Conservative Individualist	Anarchic Conservative	Corporatist Technicrat	Corporate Pluralist	Liberal Abstainer	Modernist Cynic	Autonomist
Primary-School Students (N = 1511)	20.8	34.1	1.2	5.1	12.5	21.2	.8	4.3
Secondary-School Students (N = 1203)	1.3	7.2	1.8	15.5	1.6	19.1	3.2	50.4
University Students (N = 509)	2.2	5.5	3.0	14.8	2.2	16.7	3.0	52.4
Teachers (N = 629)	2.5	10.4	3.0	12.1	3.9	24.7	3.0	40.4
Parents (N = 620)	4.8	15.7	.5	5.6	8.8	42.7	2.3	19.5

Table III-2 DISTRIBUTION OF TYPES: VENEZUELA (per cent)

Sample Groups	Organicist	Conservative Individualist	Anarchic Conservative	Corporatist Technicrat	Corporate Pluralist	Liberal Abstainer	Modernist Cynic	Autonomist
Primary-School Students (N = 1896)	19.2	28.8	2.1	8.8	11.6	20.8	.9	7.8
Secondary-School Students (1454)	2.2	14.3	1.9	23.0	1.7	19.0	1.3	36.5
Teachers (N = 573)	3.1	20.7	2.1	22.8	2.1	22.0	.8	26.4
Parents (N = 875)	10.1	28.5	2.5	10.9	4.8	26.5	2.2	14.5

teachers and primary-school students, with the secondary-school students—the firmest believers in the efficacy of personal autonomy in an open situation—ranked last. The seeming identification of parents with primary-school students now comes into clear perspective. Parents' personal motivations may well indicate a withdrawal into tradition for themselves, but unlike the majority of primary-school children, they perceive an open world. Note also that Chilean parents are almost twice as frequently found in this type as are Venezuelan parents. The latter, like the Liberal Abstainers, see Conservative Individualism as a viable choice, whereas Chilean parents do not. In methodological terms, the single difference between Types 2 and 6 is the recognition of institutional autonomy. In theoretical terms, the difference is created by the nature of the two societies and the options they present—a case in point for our contention that individuals choose within a socially real context, not an abstract, a-historical situation.

•There is predictable order in the neighboring categories of Corporatist Technocrat and Corporate Pluralist. In both Chile and Venezuela, relatively small numbers of respondents put themselves in the latter set—from primary-school students at the top through parents, teachers, and secondary-school students at the low point. The order reverses itself among the Corporate Technocrats. The secondary-school students, university students, and teachers bunch together so closely as to be almost indistinguishable at the top of the category, and the younger students and parents group at the bottom.

•The order of distribution of the samples of individuals among the several types is exactly the same in both Chile and Venezuela. Yet, it is equally clear from the troughs and peaks of the distributions that Venezuelans are more traditional than are the Chileans. For instance, there is a spread of almost 50 points between Chilean primary-school students on the one side, and Chilean secondary-school or university students on the other. Among Venezuelans the ranking is similar, but the difference is only 30 points. We have, therefore, two different sets of intensities of difference among the options perceived by our Chilean and Venezuelan respondents. Understanding these findings requires discussion of some major trends in Latin American Ideological and partisan development.*

---

*An analysis of these data from a slightly different perspective will serve to highlight some of the differences between Chile and Venezuela. Recall that the central characteristic of

52

the typology is autonomy; each ideal-type is a unique variation on this theme from the Organicist at one extreme, who would deny autonomy in all spheres, to the Autonomist at the other, who accepts autonomy as an over-all guiding value. The types believing in some measure of autonomy vary among themselves as follows:

ONESELF	OTHER INDIVIDUALS	SOCIETY
TYPE		
3—Anarchic Conservative	2—Conservative Individualist	5—Corporate Pluralist
4—Corporatist Technocrat	4—Corporatist Technocrat	6—Liberal Abstainer
7—Modernis Cynic	6—Liberal Abstainer	7—Modernist Cynic
8—Autonomist	8—Autonomist	8—Autonomist

If our questions had evoked random answers, the number of individuals in each type would be more or less the same, of course. But the strong clustering we have actually found supports the validity of the questions and their answers: the similarity of ranking of students, teachers, and parents in the two countries; the generally higher scores of Chileans over Venezuelans that fit in with our knowledge of those countries; and the very low frequencies in Types 3 and 7, which were unlikely psychological constellations. Therefore, we feel justified in taking another step in our analysis by grouping the types together in the manner enumerated above. See the Appendix for the percentages and the graphic results. This procedure reveals the following:

- In both countries, the secondary students and teachers rank relatively higher than parents and primary students in the extent of autonomy permitted in each of the three spheres. This finding, of course, recapitulates much of the previous data we have analyzed.
- Except for the Venezuelan secondary-school students and teachers, all others grant greater autonomy to other individuals and to their societies than to themselves.
- Except for primary-school students, who are very much alike in both countries, the Chileans cluster more tightly than the Venezuelans in the autonomy accepted in their social institutions and in other individuals. By contrast, the acceptance of autonomy in one's own behavior is markedly differentiated among the several groups of persons in Chile as in Venezuela.

The distinctive profiles of Chile and Venezuela that emerge are revealing, not only about individuals but also about the social environments they perceive. Like the modernity of which it is a mark, autonomous views are a complex and variable characteristic. Chilean society clearly is more accepting of institutional autonomy than Venezuelan society, both in the degree of agreement among its citizens as well as in its relatively high level of acceptance. For whatever reason, Venezuelan society still has not approached a similar level.

By contrast, the differences between Chile and Venezueal with regard to self-autonomy and autonomy for others are less dramatic than is the case for societal autonomy. In both countries, there is a ready willingness to extend autonomy to the behavior of others, although Chileans express a much higher consensus about this matter than do the Venezuelans. Similarly, in both countries there is less willingness to apply rational rather than ritualistic standards to one's own behavior, although the Chileans again are more accepting of rationalistic standards than are the Venezuelans.

53

There is as much historical regularity as the statistical order we have found.* In brief, the last century in Latin America saw a temporary liaison between Conservatives and classical Liberals for the purpose of gaining independent republican status for the political entities that eventually emerged. After winning independence from Spain, all these countries (Brazil and Cuba were not to gain formal independence until the last decades of the nineteenth century) underwent a time of trouble, followed by the ascendance of Conservatives. Clericalist, ruralist, anticosmopolitan, and anti-Protestant, the Conservative leadership sought to maintain the *anciens régimes* in patterns that ideologically fit what we have called Organicist views. The Liberals, who seemed to gain unequivocal victory over the Conservatives by the end of the century everywhere but in Colombia, espoused secularism, promodern European attitudes, an urban life style, and early forms of industrialization. Many become Neopositivists when the philosophical view swept Latin America in the second half of the last century. As Liberal dominance became established, however, the movement had to face pressures toward social and political integration coming from slowly expanding middle groups, and from newly organized skilled labor in the few countries building an industrial and modern urban structure. In one degree or another, the Liberals failed the test everywhere. If they could extend political rights downward to middle groups as in Chile and Argentina, they were unwilling or unable to continue the process economically, or at all in political-economic terms for the lower groups. Thus, by the end of the first quarter of the twentieth century, Liberalism everywhere had degenerated into conservatism—a class-bound politics of holding the line. Characterological differences still distinguish Liberals from Conservatives, however, much as the typology distinguishes between Organicists and Conservative Individualists. But the loss of identity was probably deeper, and the scattering wider, for the libertarianism of the classical Liberals drove many of them into widely diverse partisan stances, as the Liberal institutionalism they postulated could not be made to work. Some Liberals joined with neofascist military governments, in the hope that the use of force to establish a simulated "free" market was a worthwhile interim (if not opportunistic) procedure. Others became Christian Democrats, and still others sacrificed their idea of free and self-regulating institutions for the sake of political libertarianism, becoming right-wing socialists. In any event, wherever Conservative

---

*Documentation will be found in Chapters V and VI.

and Liberal parties still exist formally, their ideologies are close together, and on the traditional right.

Middle-class, secularist, developmental parties modeled on French Radical Socialism also began to grow in the last century, and became dominant in many Latin American countries by the 1920s. Where successful, they served the purpose of reinforcing secularism, national awareness, and the idea of equality before the law. In their wake came social-security legislation and other attempts to ameliorate the negative social effects of the monopoly industrialism and capitalism that had begun to grow even in such economically rudimentary countries as Guatemala. But the Radical parties, like the Liberals, eventually lost their thrust, unable to reconcile the contradiction between full nationhood for all persons in the society and the persistence of class and racial exclusionism. Thus, by the middle of the century, the Radicals had become insignificant almost everywhere (Argentina is the major exception), and again an ideational and identity scattering took place. Some Radicals, swallowing the bitter pill of identification with quasi-clericalist groups, became Christian Democrats. Many espoused simple *tecnicismo* as best they could, while others became members of one or another left group, but remaining as far to the right within that category as possible. A few gamely struggled to keep their traditional parties alive. They can be found, thus, among the Corporatist Technocrats, but their deeper inclinations probably lead them to cluster among the Autonomists. In other words, they have not yet been able to follow most of their antecedent Liberal cousins into full partisan and normative conservatism.

In the meantime, beginning in the early years of this century, parties of the left began to appear in those countries heavily influenced by European ideas and migration. By the 1920s in some countries, and by the 1930s in virtually all, distinguishable groups of Marxist and non-Marxist leftists were in existence. Their national histories are extremely varied, depending upon patterns of repression, foreign influences, the existence and nature of trade-union movements, the accidents of leadership, and so forth. Socialist and Communist groups have had a long and sometimes distinguished history in Argentina, Chile, and Uruguay. In the recent past they have been of significant importance in the happenings of Mexico, Guatemala, and Venezuela, although now they have receded into relative obscurity in those countries. And, of course, a Latin-oriented Communism took power in Cuba in 1959.

The summary statement about Latin America's far left is that it has been extraordinarily fragmented and highly sensitive to ideological disputation among left groups in Europe and the United States. Some leftists espouse the reduction of alienation as the most important and immediate political task, to be pursued through direct political action. Others strive for national independence and assume that the economic system must be attacked first, holding that politics remains mere superstructure. Others, in Social Democratic fashion, argue for "working within the system" to gain economic socialism by making real the ideals of political democracy that have had such historical strength among major elite groups in Latin America. Most persons of the left would probably put themselves into our typology as Autonomists. In their partisan practice, however, many are Abstainers (ritualistic for themselves, open for others and the society), and others are found in the Corporate Technocratic group—the occupational haven for many left-leaning social scientists, for example.

Even greater confusion was added to the scene with the appearance of Fascist, Falangist, and Nazi movements in the 1920s and 1930s, and then with the developmental military regimes and the right-wing populist movements whose best exemplar remains Argentina's *peronismo*. Although spurred by Portugal's Salazar, Spain's Primo de Rivera, and Italy's Benito Mussolini, their emulators in Latin America during the 1930s came to grief. Their arguments had little popular appeal, and they threatened the institutional and ideological integrity of the ruling Liberal and Radical sectors. But with the emergence of right-wing populism, supported by military machines equipped with the discarded arms of World War II, a way emerged of providing rightist privileged groups with mass support. The alliance came to full bloom in Argentina during the Perón era, with the appearance of Corporate Pluralist leaders, supported by Organicists, engaged in mobilizing popular support which was told to be ritualistically obedient in order to further the tasks of nation-building. In short, right-wing nationalism had come to bloom.

Still, the redistributive dangers involved in mass participation loomed as a threat to the ruling groups. The first authoritarian populist movements died, but they hastened a realignment of middle and upper groups in patterns that have become familiar in contemporary Argentina and Brazil. The Onganía regime which took office in Argentina in 1966 best exemplified the pattern. Organicists (Conservatives) were given education, religion, and diplomacy to administer. Corporate pluralists (out-and-out *franquistas*) were allotted the presidency and the ministries of force—interior (including the police), and the armed services. And the management of the economy was assigned to the Corporatist Technocrats. Expelled were those persons who believed in civil liberties, equality before the laws, and the other essential elements of a *participant* national community, instead of in mere nationality as filtered through class and occupational affiliations, and as ratified by appropriate ideological beliefs—including the willingness to be silent. Naked class interest was not in play, but rather class interest ostentatiously robed in culturally acceptable values.

Confronted with this dissociation of class and single understandings of class interests, Latin America's left has been driven into even deeper confusion. Should one support a lower class even though it is motivated by "false consciousness"? Or, should one accord primacy to ethical beliefs concerning political organization, and decide that even a lower-class fascist remains a fascist? This issue, in numerous ramifications, has weakened and sometimes broken the cohesiveness of Latin America's left. It has also served to force Latin America's rightists to confront themselves, probably for the last time. Will one be a Liberal in the political as well as economic sense, or only in the economic sense? If the way of economics alone is chosen, can one remain a Liberal at all?

Despite these confusions, most Latin Americans attempt to maintain their habitual use of terms signifying "left" and "right." But to do so seems to demand a double scale. That is, we must postulate two scales running from left to right, one for traditional parties, and the other for modern ones. In the case of the former, then, the scale would run from Conservatives on the right through Liberals and some Radicals to some Christian Democrats and technocratic organicist movements on the left. For the modern parties, the scale would run from some classical Liberals on the right through some Radicals and on left through standard socialist, communist, and *fidelista* groupings.

The distribution of responses on the typology fits this biscalar view of the present ideological situation in Latin America. (Although both Chileans and Venezuelans behave in essentially similar ways, it is somewhat easier to read the Venezuelan graph in illustration of this point.) The relationship among the sets within which the responses are ordered breaks between Types 4 and 5 in both countries. That is, unity is given to the other variations in terms of the organizing concept of institutional autonomy in opposition to diffuseness of institutional functions. The most important manifestation of this regularity is that the order of responses reverses itself between Types 1 and 2 (the Conservatives) and Type 4 (the Technocrats). Then, the order seen in Types 1 and 2 reasserts itself in Type 5 (the Falangists), only to be strongly reversed in Type 8 (the Autonomists). Type 4 would appear to be the most "progressive" of the institutionally organic views, the left of traditional politics, if you will. And Type 8 appears to be the grab-bag of progressivism among the institutionally autonomous set, with Corporate Pluralists providing the right wing of the "modern" sector. Put another way, those with the greatest attachment to education rise to their traditional peak in technocratic approaches, and in their much higher modern peak with attachment to a generally open universe. Those groups with the least education rise to their "modern" peak in Type 6, unable to shed their personal ritualism but recognizing openness elsewhere. Of all the types studied, the Corporate Pluralist gains the least acceptance, although at its low levels the distribution replicates the order of the two most conservative groups.

This typology, then, has given us another way of thinking about the varying patterns of social synthesis employed by Latin Americans. As we saw in Chapter II, their views on interinstitutional organization clearly reveal that attachment to or rejection of the integrating function of the political institution is a critical element in understanding the nature of the expressive-instrumental differences all groups see in institutional orders. But from those data we learned little about the state's specialized role as a synthesizing institution that carries with it either authoritarian or democratic nationalism. The inferences to be drawn from the typology, however, provide important insights on this very point.

Autonomists, Liberal Abstainers, and Corporate Pluralists share a belief in interinstitutional constraints permitting each institution to operate with a measure of autonomy. Thus, for them the proper ordering functions of politics are limited. This view of differentiation logically accompanies a more general distinction between instrumental and expressive views of the state, as we have said. For their part the traditional types tend to emphasize expressivism and downgrade instrumentalism in the state. The questions that must be put, of course, are what is the state expressive about, and toward what ends is it instrumental?

In seeking an answer, we have chosen four questions about the polity to run against the six types we are employing.* In paraphrase, the questions are:

- Does one comply with the law because it is an obligation, or because doing so helps people live together?

---

*These four questions are among the six unused questions about the political institution described in the preceding chapter. The remaining two were employed in the construction of the typology.

- Does a good law reflect human nature, or the changing needs of peoples?
- Does one vote because it is an obligation, or in order to influence social events?
- Is the goal of political activity the maintenance of order, or the promotion of a country's development?

The "pure" traditionalist maintains that voting and complying with the law are obligations, and therefore one does it; and that law should reflect the implied stasis of human nature and promote order above desired change. The "pure" modernist believes in "togetherness" and participatory politics in a worldly system that seeks to satisfy the evolving perception of needs. The instrumentalism of the modern responses is in the direction of effectively belonging to a community and consciously working change. The implied expressivism is, then, for a secularly changing and participant social life.

Now, in order to relate the concepts of institutional differentiation to the typology, we should cross these four questions with the six types. In doing so, however, we should ask whether we seek an even distribution among all types, or whether we expect that the very *nature* of each type should suggest to us great variation in the degree of relation between each ideal type and its members' likelihood of holding appropriately "consistent" ideas. If we are to integrate our premise about disjunctive social relations and the ability to perceive them, then we should assume that the more traditional types will be tightly constrained in expressing other political attitudes, while the more modern person will reveal variation and ambiguity. The results can be seen in Figures III-3 and III-4.

The most traditional of all groups are the Venezuelan primary-school students, whose responses provide an almost perfect relation between the types and the attitudes contained in the four questions: i.e., traditionalist types give traditional answers to these four questions, modern types given modern answers. Chilean primary-school students are only a little less decided in this matter than the Venezuelans. The expressive-instrumental relation we expected holds clearly: the more traditional types see the state's proper role highly affectively, while the more modern clearly lean toward an instrumental state serving changeful ends, and the personal participation of individuals in those ends. Also, the sequence of rankings among the four questions fits our expectations, running as they do from an accent on obligation as the most cherished for traditionals, with the least weight given to order over development. Also, the bimodal distribution of responses we have grown to expect

Figure III - 3

"TRADITIONAL" RESPONSES, FOUR QUESTIONS ON POLITICS (per cent)

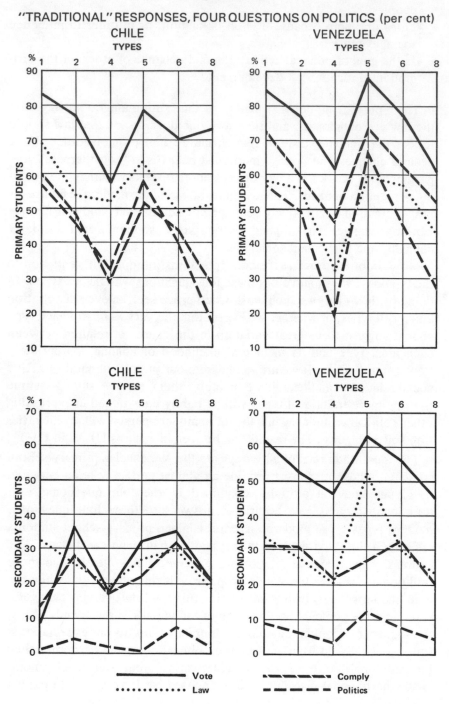

CHILE
TYPES

VENEZUELA
TYPES

PRIMARY STUDENTS

SECONDARY STUDENTS

CHILE
TYPES

VENEZUELA
TYPES

Vote
Law
Comply
Politics

60

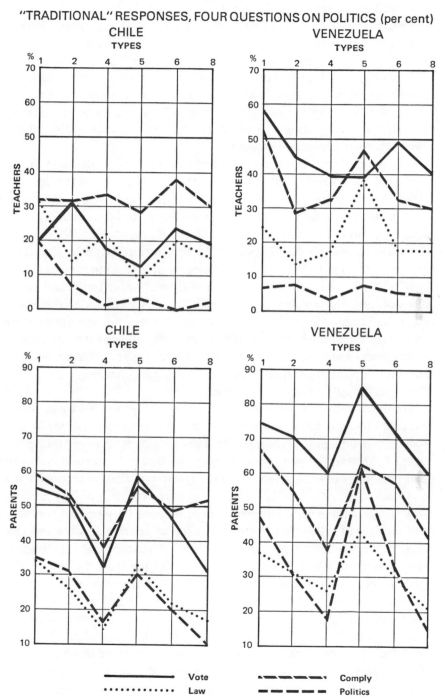

Figure III - 4

"TRADITIONAL" RESPONSES, FOUR QUESTIONS ON POLITICS (per cent)

CHILE

VENEZUELA

CHILE

VENEZUELA

Vote ——— Comply ⟋⟍⟋⟍

Law ••••••••••• Politics ━ ━ ━ ━

61

reappears, reinforcing our observation that we have lefts and rights of both modern and traditional coloration.

But, at the other ends of the distribution among the types, there is almost no reaction to the typology. Secondary-school students seemingly think as a group about these four political questions, not as a group split among six types. The Venezuelan secondary-school students, somewhat more traditional than their Chilean counterparts, show a bit more sensitivity to the typology, principally in the general shape of bimodality. As is fitting, the teachers and parents once again fall between the two families of students.

The general profiles, whether sharply etched as among most of the Venezuelans or gently graded as among the Chileans, reveal the intrinsic sense of the typology as discriminating between those who seek (and at least in attitude, actually find) unitary coherence, and those who see and actually express distinctions, differences, and ambiguities. We also see that *within each group*, Corporate Technocrats respond in almost as modern a fashion to these four questions as do the Autonomists. Similarly, *within each group*, Organicists and Conservative Individualists on one side, and Corporate Pluralists and Liberal Abstainers on the other, share traditional views. These two comments are not merely another way of revealing the bimodal distributions; they suggest the importance of intimately knowing the content of expressivism and instrumentalism, and they further suggest that the typologies gain meaning only within their specific cultures and subcultures.

We think that what we are seeing in these graphs is a way in which national cultures, basic attitude sets, and the conventional wisdom of social groups mingle to produce varied patterns of normative predispositions. To repeat, the more general traditionalism of Venezuela works to pull responses toward greater internal coherence than is true with the more generally modern Chileans. The patterns of the typology interact with this general bent, sharpening the consistency between the typology and the four questions we related to it. But at another level of association, the predominantly modern posture of teachers and secondary school students overrides most of the effects of the typology and general traditionalism in Venezuela, and virtually all of it in Chile, to produce modernist responses to the four questions even among most persons in the traditional types. From the data so far presented, persons with the longest experience of formal education seem able to separate the conventional wisdom of their reference groups from their more profound world views. At this point, then, we should introduce a modifying hypothesis of great importance. It is, simply put, that the tendency toward attitudinal coherence among traditionals appears to be susceptible to breakdown as a function of membership in groups associated by age and tenure with the formal educational systems of the two countries we are studying. We cannot yet make this statement definitively, for we must first look into such other social factors as sex, urban-rural residence, and social class, before any unitary influence or cluster of influences can be singled out as stronger than others. Still, the suggestion is strong that formal education is somehow critically associated with a learned ability to hold highly differentiated sets of secular ideas about oneself, one's fellow citizens, and one's society, no matter what one's basic world view. The burden of the next chapter will be upon a search for the factors other than education which influence the creation and distribution of those social talents.

Another question whose resolution will have to await further analysis is the centrality of the polity to public and personal discord concerning overarching social purposes and organization. The factual content of the four questions we crossed with the typology serves to illustrate some of the dimensions of the patterns of agreement and disagreement. For example, we have seen that the obligational character of voting is given more weight by all groups, except Chilean teachers and parents, than is any other traditional choice. But the percentages vary extremely widely *within* types, ranging from 85 percent of Organicist Venezuelan primary students down to only 7 per cent of Organicist Chilean secondary-school students. At the other end of the traditional-modern division, the classical political function of maintaining order is seen as much less important than the modern response of governmental promotion of national development. With the sole exception of Venezuelan parents, all groups across all types give political order the lowest priority among the four sets of individual and societal political actions. Although variations in response are again wide, only primary-school students in Chile and Venezuela give wide approval to order over development. The numbers of secondary-school students and teachers opting for order exceeds 10 per cent among persons in only two types of the possible twenty-four.

Speculative subtlety is required when we consider the ideas that may lie behind typologically traditional persons selecting modernist responses to these questions, and conversely the traditionalist responses selected by modern types. Two types of explanations suggest themselves. First, some persons undoubtedly understand the alternatives differently from us and, as we shall see, they may well have gone legitimately far past us in political sophistication in certain respects. Another possibility is that the expressed attitudes toward the polity have a predictive quality, suggesting directions in which other attitudes might move.

The most suggestive example of the first possibility of reinterpretation by the respondents of the given choices is provided by the striking clustering of responses among Chilean secondary-school students in the Liberal Abstainer and Autonomist types. About a third of the former and a fifth of the latter agree that law should be obeyed as an obligation, that a good law reflects human nature and not changing societal needs, and that one votes because one must. (There is virtual unanimity among them that the maintenance of order is not to be preferred over development.) Turning these answers into a modernist frame is not difficult intellectually. For example, it is often argued that in a good and just and democratic society, law must be considered temporarily absolute—to be obeyed in order to hold community together until a "bad" law can be changed. Indeed, the question of when illegality is legitimate is a matter that exercised such early Liberal thinkers as Locke and Hobbes, a conflict they resolved by evolving a theory of natural rights whose violation was the only permissible grounds for refusing to obey the sovereign. By the same token, voting may be taken as an obligation representative of the critical importance of participation, and not as a routine acceptance of a ritualistic chore signifying nothing in the way of effective expressions of opinion. The question of more philosophical bent in this group concerns the nature of a good law as reflection either of human nature or of changing societal needs. A Marxist, a Kantian, and a Thomist could all agree that a good law must reflect human nature. The Marxist could well argue that the reduction of alienation is a universal goal, and that laws are good only if they contribute to man's ability to control his labor and its product. The Kantian could expound his version of the golden rule, and add Cassirerite prescriptions concerning man's nature as a symbolic creature, which could serve as a practical measure of the goodness of a law. The Thomist, of course, would argue for the wholeness of the mundane and sacred experiences and orders.

We recognize, of course, that virtually all questions one poses in a survey can be subjected to sophistical wrangling. In this case, however, we think the exercise not misplaced. The consistency of response among the more traditional types and groups suggests that relatively obvious and simple interpretations of the responses are warranted. But the very nature of the more modern groups suggests their greater knowledge of and ability to discriminate among the subjects at issue. Such a capacity should in itself be taken into account in understanding the responses.

64

The partisan complexity among such groups, already referred to, also reveals itself in attitudinal complexity.

All the evidence we have so far underscores the critical position of the polity at the core of social uncertainty. The placing of the state at the midpoint of all other institutional responses was the first major clue. The second was the bimodal distribution in the typology, revelatory of the two highly divergent and qualitatively different scales of beliefs. And the third is the complex institutional and attitudinal ambiguousness of center and left groups in Latin America. For them there is no single, accepted ideological North Star, as most evidently there is, in very large measure, for the hierarchically minded on the traditional and modern right wings. In this respect, Chileans and Venezuelans would appear to be little different from their ideological fellows in North America and Western Europe.

Another possible inference is that the specific responses to the four questions are evocative of past attitudes or predictive of future ones. Although our study does not run through time, it is apparent that attitudes change among many persons with their life experiences. Some present Autonomists will obviously give up on their own effectiveness and become Liberal Abstainers; others will give up on the system and become Technocrats. Some Organicists will see the social system as open and become Corporate Pluralists, while retaining their static notions for self and others. Others will make the transition from closed views of the world to open ones, discarding religious belief and narrow familistic notions as they go. Thus, the complexity introduced into the analysis by crossing the typology with these four questions is not a mere methodological artifact. Rather, it hints at the patterns of doubt and resolution which characterize the minds of people living in social situations of conflict, inequality of condition, rapid change, disappointment, and promise.

four / Situations, Power, and Beliefs

Where and how to begin the exposition of research is not solely a matter of taste. The point of departure always implicitly carries with it a taint of first cause, a matter which we have several times taken some pains to discuss. The issue arises once again because in this chapter we turn to the social situations of the persons we have studied—to their ages, sex, economic and familial settings, occupational aspirations, and other related matters. Most studies typically begin with such information, either for simple descriptive purposes or else to establish the basis for the argument that situations spawn understandings in fairly narrow and determinate ways. This book, conversely, has begun with the idea-worlds of certain Chileans and Venezuelans within only one institutional context, the formal educational system. The addition of other situational factors at this point is for the purpose of relativizing the attitudinal-structural net that has already been woven, to test its efficiency as a sieve, so to speak. We shall find that no other filter we have been able to devise works with such correlational force as what has already been described. We wish to reiterate, however, that if correlation is not equal to cause, a lack of correlation similarly does not equal insignificance. In other words, we shall find in the succeeding pages many failures of statistical significance, but we ascribe high theoretical significance to the *actual* but not *correlative* juxtaposition of ideas and situations.

A preoccupation with the "proper beginning" is common to all persons who worry about methodological rigor. Our task is not ontological, metaphysical, or otherwise philosophical, so that we will not delve into epistemological and related questions, although they must remain implicit to this, as to any, discussion. A starting point can range from an axiom to a specific single occurrence, but it will have implications no matter what it is. The question was very worrisome to Marx, who is described as going through the following train of thought in deciding how to begin his *Grundrisse:*

66

At the outset . . . Marx describes two journeys, or paths, which political-economic inquiry has taken. The first takes "living wholes" as its point of departure, for instance a given nation-state . . . and finishes "by discovering through analysis a small number of determinant, abstract, general relations such as division of labour, money, value, etc. . . . The other journey moves in the reverse direction, beginning with the simple, abstract, general relations, and arriving at the "living wholes" at the end. "The latter," Marx concludes, "is obviously the scientifically correct method."[1]

However, this conclusion conflicted with Marx's own desire to be historically specific, to avoid beginning with the wellsprings of all things. "The proper beginning," he wrote, "is not with the dawn of history, but rather with that category which occupies a predominant position within the particular social formation being studied" (p. 37). Then, he reversed himself as follows (p. 38):

> That the start of the *Grundrisse* Introduction had been a false one, Marx acknowledged about a year and a half later, in 1859 . . . . The notion that the path of investigation must proceed from simple, general, abstract relations towards complex particular wholes, no longer appeared to him, then, as "obviously the correct scientific procedure." In his justly famed "Preface" to the *Critique of Political Economy,* written to replace the *Grundrisse* Introduction, he writes as follows:
>
> > I am suppressing a general introduction which I had thrown on paper, because on closer consideration . . . any anticipation of yet-to-be-proved results seems to me a distraction, and the reader who wishes to follow me at all must resolve to climb from the particular up to the general.

Our starting point has not been an event, a general principle, or a logically constructed or dialectical category, but rather a relationship between beliefs and the experience of living in a particular institutional setting. Put another way, our concern is with the way institutions and beliefs interact, and with how beliefs affect institutional behavior. Another facet of the same question is the relation between preferences and the power to *act* upon them, and how that very power affects the preferences. Our data demonstrate that education is accompanied by profound attitudinal changes. We also know, from general as well as more formal observation, that some power to make those beliefs effective resides within the educational institution itself. However, when we turn from concentrating on ideas as they relate to formal education to ideas as they relate to other structural characteristics of individuals, different questions arise. The reasons have to do with the varying nature of power generated in the other major institutions, with the necessity to distinguish between the latency of class position and the actuality of institutional roles as expressive of manifest power, with the often contradictory purposes of the varied behavior patterns in which we all engage, and with the complex nature of peer-group relations, conventional wisdom, and individual idiosyncracy as they play out within broader patterns.

We should not proceed to introduce these other situational factors until we have speculated more fully about the implications of our findings as they relate only to education. If we do not open broader possibilities, we may lose the richness of inference which we shall need when exploring the more tenuous relations linking attitudes to class and urban-rural difference, for example, or those tying the generations. To this point, we have said the following about how our respondents think of their general social situations:

- All groups, taken as a whole, see *differences* among institutions.
- The more traditional groups seek to *resolve* difference in favor of sacred, private, and familistic purposes.
- The more modern groups seek to *organize* difference through secular and relativistic devices, and to reconcile the simultaneous pursuit of differing objectives.
- Thus, the more modern groups recognize *ambiguity* as well as difference, as is evidenced by the only weak tendency of their world views to determine their specifically ideological attitudes.
- The *recognition* of ambiguity on the part of the more modern groups is accompanied by an ability to *tolerate* ambiguity, as is clearly demonstrated by the factual content of their answers as well as the patterns into which they group themselves.*

---

*We often forget that in real-life situations, as distinguished from constructed situations in research, human beings live with ambiguity and even conflict among the values they hold. Weber, for example, was especially sensitive to this human condition, making it an integral part of his view of behavior. "In almost every important attitude of real human beings, the value-spheres cross and interpenetrate. The shallowness of our routinized daily existence in the most significant sense of the word consists indeed in the fact that the persons who are caught up in it do not become aware, and above all do not wish to become aware, of this partly psychological, part pragmatic conditioned motley of irreconcilably antagonistic values." ("The Meaning of 'Ethical Neutrality,'" *The Methodology of the Social Sciences,* trans. and ed. E. A. Shils and H. A. Finch [New York: The Free Press, 1949], p. 18.)

68

These conclusions are constrained inferences, closely derived from the data and passive in connotation. They carry the suggestion that schooling "acts on" persons to "make" them able to see and choose in ways otherwise denied them. More active inferences can infuse the analysis with the suggestion that education has to do with the positive *creation* of ideational skills that permit not only the passive recognition of ambiguities, but also the ability of individuals to create them, and to see and act upon contradictory elements in social life.

We have already suggested that the neat coherence of the data we have presented is about to fall apart. This shredding is not an artificial device of our method; it is, in our view, an accurate reflection of contemporary Chilean and Venezuelan life and, as a matter of fact, an accurate rendition of what the modern estate is all about—the promotion of diversity, the opening of options and the breaking of deterministic ties, the positive uses of disorder held within a consensual synthesis. The statistical nonrelations we are going to examine are, then, a necessary social product of "development" as it has been taking place in Chile and Venezuela, and they are related to the attitudes and behavior of educated persons. To take from modern and educated persons the ability to recognize, tolerate, and create diversity, ambiguity, and contradiction is to strip them of their modernity, to press them back both conceptually and behaviorally into the poverty of a wholeness without seams. In pursuit of this question, it is useful to examine one's theoretical predispositions in order to make explicit how we choose to give sense to varied patterns of relations and nonrelations.

It would be burdensome to review the entire array of schools of thought about education and society and development in general. But a summary examination of the implications of three milestones in the evolution of such theory may provide a useful sampling, and additional perspective on the approaches we employ. Three exemplars of diverse views are Rousseau, Marx, and the contemporary functionalist school. Rousseau, because of his *Emile*, is viewed as the father of child psychology. He was also an early intellectual anarchist, for his emphasis on reason and the goodness of the natural order led him to a disdain for worldly institutions, and especially politics as practiced in his time. Marx, while also highly respectful of the social import of reason, was more acutely aware of institutional, class, and power factors as they affect perceptions and behavior. For their part, the functionalists raise psychological motivations to a central position, and tend to slight specifically historical conjunctions of institutional arrangements. While each school would have little difficulty in adjusting to the findings so far presented, great divergence would appear in subsequently relating the educational-attitudinal nexus to more general questions of social being and social change.

The sharp differences found between primary and secondary school children would have surprised Rousseau not at all. "Childhood has its own ways of seeing, thinking, and feeling," he wrote in *Emile,* and added that "nothing is more foolish than to try to replace them with ours."[2] He thought that early education must loosen children from their parents, but can only hope to bring them into "the world of things." The education of adolescents, however, is another matter, for they are able to reason. Consequently, secondary education must deal with moral matters. Religious belief must not be confused with moral understanding, for the former is the product of dogmatic devotion, and the latter of reason infused with the passion for self- and social realization. Moral beliefs must be related to fitting man's social situation to his nature as free being, an adjustment that can be achieved only through the use of reason. Rousseau specifically rejected the mechanistic thought of such other Enlightenment figures as Diderot and Voltaire, whose views formed the foundation for the later emergence of Positivism and Utilitarianism. From Rousseau, however, the line of philosophical inquiry opens directly into Kant and a much more voluntaristic philosophy than that of the Utilitarians, Positivists and other heirs of the mechanistic tradition.

Rousseau saw the reasoned search for moral knowledge as the goal of social life and the yardstick by which to measure day-to-day political acts. The major impediment to the realization of the goal, however, is the very set of political and social institutions through which men must work. The impassioned use of insight and reason in the search for a moral life must be directed toward removing those impediments to understanding "original man," for which term one should understand "human nature." Rousseau stated it thus:[3]

> The very origin of the study of man, of his real wants, and the fundamental principles of his duty, is besides the only proper method we can take to obviate a number of difficulties, which present themselves on the origin of moral inequality, on the true foundations of the body politic, on the reciprocal rights of its members, and many other similar topics equally important and obscure.

The implications of this line of reasoning are that our findings to date reflect an increase in the ability to reason, which in turn leads to an appreciation of moral and ideological problems, although not to their resolution. The anarchistic root of this approach would explain confusions in attitudinal and structural relations as the result of accepting the structure of privilege and its attendant patterns of repression, instead of seeking to realize the promise of human nature. No clues inherent to the theory explain *particular* patterns of inequity and the uses of power to maintain them, and the possible relation between those patterns and the distribution of understandings concerning them. Were Rousseau here to see our data, he would certainly applaud the move of secondary-school students away from sacred to secular belief, probably be ambivalent about the increase in secular nationalism that accompanies higher levels of education, and assume that the positive effects of education on the ability to reason would override inhibitions upon reasoned morality arising from class and other social factors.

Marx, as befitted his times, was both more explicit and complex in his views of social organization. But he, like Rousseau, also made assumptions about man's essential nature. The search for control over one's activities and over the products of one's labor comprises Marx's operational definition of the essence of humanness. Therefore, alienation—the removal of man from control over the fruits and effects of his work—is the literally dehumanizing result of inequitable social organization.

> Since alienated labour: (1) alienates nature from man; and (2) alienates man from himself, from his own active function, his life activity; so it alienates him from the species. It makes *species-life* into a means of individual life. . . . For labour, *life activity, productive life,* now appear to man only as *means* for the satisfaction of a need, the need to maintain his physical existence. Productive life is, however, species-life. It is life creating life.[4]

A Marxist approach to our data would start with the assumption that we are examining education, attitudes, and political changes within the context of two particular adaptations of the general, Western, capitalist experience. Consequently, one would expect in both countries to find myths and the practices of freedom in interaction with myths and the practices of alienating maldistributions of power related to an underlying class structure.

Democracy and capitalism go hand in hand when capitalistic free markets are forming themselves—when an industrial labor force needs to be created from a peasantry, when broadened consumption is demanded to absorb the new industrial productivity, when the mythology that contributes to the "freeing" of a bourgeoisie is not yet overtly denied a proletariat. Formal education is, of course, the prime social

71

instrument for loosening the ties of ascription and creating persons individually ready for incorporation into the new tasks and the new orders.* The contradiction, however, is that the bourgeois social order seeks to defend its privileges, and thus inhibits questioning of the entire structure which has been built, or its extension downward to include all social elements. Capitalism, in this construction, is erected upon the organized use of surplus value—the difference between the value a worker creates and that of which he disposes. Thus, capitalism is *in its nature* an alienating system, built on the very necessity of denying to some social sectors control over the products of their work, and transferring that advantage to others on an organized basis backed by the might of the state. Under such conditions, education frees persons from medieval ties only in order to bind them to capitalistic ones.

The contradiction between the limited freeing of individuals and their more general social captivity was later underscored by Weber, as he evolved his view that the "iron cage" of bureaucracy was an unavoidable consequence of the rationalization accompanying industrial capitalism. This theme has since been consistently worked by writers on technocracies and "postindustrialism." Contemporary thinking on this subject is influenced by the new industrial techniques and organization, which seemingly void the necessity for a complex set of intermediate labor skills. Thus, automated industries need only a few, strategically placed, highly trained engineers for their installation and subsequent technical management, and consequently education loses its former direct relation to occupational success for the great mass of the citizenry. In other words, the freeing of individuals for participation in production and the creation of surplus value is not necessary on a mass basis as it was in days of cruder techniques. Still, consumption functions remain critical. But the link between production and consumption must be distribution—the point at which power most clearly enters the marketplace and removes it from the mythical purity posited for it by Manchesterian political economists, a process which ultimately strips capitalistic economics of its claims to the existence of a free market.

A Marxist view of the data could then tenably agree with a Rous-

---

*One radical exploration of this Marxian position on education is expounded by Paulo Freire, *Pedagogy of the Oppressed* (New York: The Seabury Press, 1973). Freire argues that bourgeois society emphasizes the "banking function" of education by which students are turned into "containers" to be "filled" by teachers as a means of adapting individuals to the required tasks and values of that society. He argues that it is the humanistic consciousness of individuals that should have first priority, so that education is directed toward this goal.

seauian view that education increases the ability to reason, but the Marxist would go on to say that the reasoning concerns dialectically related social contradictions. A sophisticated Marxist would assume that the traditional views we have detailed reflect a particular kind of false consciousness—a view of interest not appropriate to one's own class position and the desire for a reduction of alienation fitting to that position. But such a Marxist would also assume that the diverse sets of attitudes reflected among those we have called more modern similarly reflects false consciousness, although of differing content. In addition, a Marxist would long since have been clamoring for an explanation of the class situations of the countries concerned and the persons we have studied; his analytical starting point would certainly have been social class. The Marxist would also expect conjunction between structural and attitudinal factors. Or, if reliable data indicated little or no conjunction, then he would tend to see the educational institution only as a major force in propagating the dominant myths that comprise the false consciousness of the unwittingly alienated.

The functionalist would take as his point of departure neither an idealized state of naturally free man, nor a historically rooted system betraying man through alienation, but rather an imputed psychological loathing for discomfort. As the heirs of nineteenth-century Utilitarianism, modern functionalists assume that imbalance and disjunction are socially necessary discomforts, for in fleeing from them societies cause social change to occur. The functionalist, thus, would ask of Organic men whether their value-sets explain social happenings well enough to permit reasonable predictability of the results of their action. If not, then a disjunction sets in between perceptions and societal effects which must lead men to change one, the other, or both. Similarly, the attitudinal complexity of teachers and secondary-school students would be labeled "dissonance" by the functionalist, and not "ambiguity," the emergence of reason, or the recognition of contradiction. Like "ambiguity," the word "dissonance" carries much less emotive freight than do "reason" and "contradiction"; it also is not attached to a theoretical system that has as much to say about social structure as the round rejection of Rousseau, or the painstaking attempts of Marx, Weber, and others of historicist bent to explain the intricacies of families of institutional situations.

In moving from attitudes per se to situational characteristics of the Chileans and Venezuelans, functionalists would seek as many cross-tabular relations as possible, so as to prove that where there were relationships there would also be consonance and, by implication, stability;

where such relationships were absent, there would also be disjunction and disfunction and, by implication, instability and the possibility of unrest leading to change to redress the disturbed balance.

In linking this chapter to the foregoing ones, we shall omit all questions referring to a state of nature, man's inherent and universal characteristics, or psychologically rooted cause. The reason for this forbearance is that our analysis will not be served by making any assumptions at that level. In scientific work that which is not needed should not be employed. This single abnegation eliminates for us any possibility of employing a functionalist approach, for its premise stains all further thought. The same is not true of Rousseau-like and Marx-like interpretations. Thus, we will feel free to say, first, that the data clearly indicate an increased measure of the ability to reason independently among those persons with higher levels of schooling. They cling much less to all-encompassing and extramundane systems of explanation. They are clearly able to see their fellow men with fewer systematic preconceptions than their less educated compatriots, and their political attitudes are diversified, as befits their actual national situations. We also feel that the move from ambiguity to reason can be extended to permit the working hypothesis that some of the Chileans and Venezuelans of this study are perceiving contradictions in the world about them. We have already stated, as a theoretical postulate so far uncontradicted by our data, that social normality is described more accurately in terms of lack of coherence and neat fit among social elements than by the opposite. Such disjunctive relations must, in part, include directly contradictory factors. If there is one finding in which contradiction and puzzlement show with naked clarity, it is in the political dimension. There our respondents clearly see a confrontation between sacred and secular objectives, between instrumental and expressive purposes, and between political community as necessary evil or as potential source of social satisfaction.

Past this point we must also abandon the Rousseau-like approaches, for they will not guide us into seeing how reason and the perceptions of social conflict interact with social class, institutions, and the other means used by persons in all societies if they are to reconcile aspirations with the empowered behavior needed for their satisfaction. The idea of contradiction then remains as our guide when we examine intergenerational differences, aspirations, and possibilities, and the varying springboards provided by class, type of school, and urban-rural as well as sex differences. We will not build dialectical frames for the examinations of these contradictions, as would a Marxist, but we will see contradictions as becoming recognizable through education, and as posing problems perceived in differing ways by given sets of Chileans and Venezuelans. In this fashion, we will once again seek to meld attitudes and institutions, for we are saying that education both creates problems and affects the ways in which persons define problems into perceived existence—with how individuals see and judge conflict and contradiction, and with the kind of solutions they are able to envision to problematic relations.

EDUCATION

As befits our theme, let us turn first to the educational attainments of the groups we have chosen. Where the students are, we of course know. As a group, they will far outdistance their parents educationally in both Chile and Venezuela. In the former country, about half of the parents of children in the public and private school systems have gone no further than primary school. About another quarter have had some or have completed secondary schooling. Only 3 out of 100 have completed university training. Chilean parents of children attending Catholic schools, however, have had more formal education, three-quarters of them having gone beyond primary school. As is to be expected, parents living in rural Molina are much less likely than urban parents to have achieved either secondary or university levels.

The urban-rural difference in educational attainments also is apparent among Venezuelan parents; some two-thirds living in rural Ocumare have gone no further than primary school. Aside from that coincidence of findings, the Venezuelan and Chilean experiences are quite different in ways that begin to suggest the workings of social class in combination with education. While in Chile parents with children in Catholic schools have the highest attainments, in Venezuela such parents, and an even higher percentage of those with children in private schools, tend to have some measure of education beyond secondary school. And further, many more Chilean parents have attended or completed secondary schools than have their Venezuelan counterparts. There are two aspects to the reasons for these distributions. The first is that private schools in Chile include prestige institutions, as well as some of low status—i.e., schools underwritten by the state for less privileged students because of a shortage of public facilities. The next chapter will explain the origins of this private system for the underprivileged. In Venezuela, on the contrary, private schools are exclusively for the better-off. And the second, and more important, part of the explanation for the more even spread of

75

the Chilean parents is that Chile's educational system is older, and that educational opportunity has for a longer time been more broadly available than in Venezuela.

The relation between type of school and the educational level of parents does not hold when comparing school type with the educational levels of the teachers. In Chile more than 25 percent of the teachers in every type of school system have completed their university work. In the public system an additional half have completed normal-school training, and a third have done so in the private schools. In the latter two systems, conversely, only 10 per cent have secondary-school training or less, while over a third of the teachers in the Catholic system are at those low levels. The lower levels of preparation are predominantly seen in the rural schools of Molina, as well as in the lower status levels of the Catholic schools.

The Venezuelan teachers are less well prepared than the Chileans, but much more directed towards university training than are the Chileans with their greater attachment to normal-school preparation. Solid majorities in all three Venezuelan systems have had some university training, but only 7 per cent in the public and private schools have completed such work, as compared to almost a fifth in the Catholic system. Again, this datum underscores the difference between the Chilean and Venezuelan Catholic schools and adds to estimates of the status of such schools in Venezuela. It should also be noted that Ocumare, unlike rural Molina, is not notably different from Caracas or Barquisimeto in terms of teacher training, while Maracaibo is far ahead of the other places in this respect. We have no explanation for the latter phenomenon.*

---

*We are not working on the basis of national samples, of course, so the figures given in this chapter should not be taken as representative of all of Chile and Venezuela. Still, it may be of some interest to have some comparative national figures. The educational categories used officially in each country differ, and neither set of criteria fits our own categorization. Still, for the vague comparability it affords, the following information may be useful. In Chile in 1962, a year roughly similar to 1966, when the Chilean data in this study were gathered, the educational levels of primary classroom teachers were as follows: 67.2 per cent of the state teachers and 19 per cent of the private teachers had some or completed normal-school training; 1.4 per cent of the state teachers and 5.6 per cent of the private teachers had university teaching degrees; 29.4 per cent of the public and 20.1 per cent of the private teachers had completed regular or commercial secondary-school training; and 2 per cent of the public and 55.4 per cent of the private teachers had religious instruction or fell into a miscellaneous category. There were 24,987 primary-school teachers included in these categories in that year. The totals for all secondary-school personnel, including administrators, were as follows: 43.5 per cent of the public-school teachers and 19.4 per cent of those in the private schools had a teaching degree at the university level; 32 per

Whatever the spottiness evident in the education of teachers, they have achieved striking educational gains when compared with their own parents. Even granted the possibility of some overestimation by the teachers of their parents' attainments, in Chile only about 13 of every 100 parents of teachers got as far as the university, but it was very rare for them to graduate. Again, the urban-rural difference appears very sharply. And, as is to be expected, even more dramatic gains were made by Venezuelan teachers over their parents than by Chileans. Only rarely (6 per cent) were the Venezuelan parents of teachers able to complete secondary school, let alone go on to incomplete attempts at higher levels. For most of them regardless of the school system in which their children teach or their place of residence, the completion of primary school was a major accomplishment and entry into secondary school a giant step forward. We may deplore the fact that so few Venezuelan teachers have managed to complete their university work, but given their familial starting points, the fact that so many have had some university experience reflects the ramification and "popularization" of secondary and higher education which will be examined in succeeding historical chapters.

Poor as the Chilean teachers' parents may have been in educational achievements, they were nevertheless quite advanced for their generation. Hence, where 13 out of 100 of the teachers' parents went on to university, only 4 out of 100 of the grandparents of today's school children did as well. In Venezuela, neither the teachers' parents nor the children's grandparents went very much beyond the primary school.

---

cent of the public- and 41.8 per cent of the private-school teachers had a secondary normal-school degree; 6.8 per cent of the public- and 6.5 per cent of the private-school teachers had other professional university degrees, and 17.7 per cent of the public- and 32.3 per cent of the private-school teachers had religious or other training. The total number of persons involved was 13,144. [Source: Comisión de Planeamiento Integral de la Educación, *Algunos antecedentes para el planeamiento integral de la educación chilena* [Santiago: Min. de Educación Pública, 1964], pp. 282-83.)

The Venezuelan figures are less detailed. For primary-school teachers the available data are broken down by those with a primary-school teaching license, which requires completion of the equivalent of normal-school training at the high-school level. For the year 1963–64, 66.5 per cent of all primary-school teachers had such a license. There were 39,629 primary-school teachers. There were, in that same year, 6,825 teachers in the public secondary-school system. Some 20.7 per cent were graduates of the Pedagogical Institute at the university level, 14.4 per cent had primary-school teaching degrees, 8.8 per cent were university graduates with the degree of "doctor," and 4.5 per cent had the university degree of *"licenciado,"* while 27.9 per cent had other secondary-school degrees (*bachilleres*), 12.7 per cent had other degrees, and 11 per cent had earned foreign degrees not validated in Venezuela. (Source: Ministry of Education, *Memoria y Cuenta, 1964* [Caracas: 1965], II, ix and xvi.)

Venezuelan teachers undoubtedly represent the first generation of a significant educational advance.

The conclusion is obvious that, if we are to judge by educational attainment alone without regard to implications concerning other social opportunities, we are, except for Venezuelan parents and grandparents as a group, studying people in ascendancy. The mere situation of the primary and secondary students with respect to their parents and teachers strongly suggests that the probabilities of their reaching higher educational levels than their tutorial and parental elders are greater.

The actual educational progression we see shines through student aspirations for and expectations of very high future attainment. The majority of Chilean primary school students and a quarter of the Venezuelan students at that level see themselves as completing university training. Parental educational levels affect these findings, of course, as does residence, so that urban children, as well as children in favored private and Catholic schools, have higher aspirations. And, as is to be expected, the clear class factor among Venezuelan private-school students shows itself in educational expectations which top those for any other set of primary-school children.

By the time one reaches the last year of secondary school, the possibilities for a university education become more real, and the aspirations rise even higher. Again except for Molina, three-quarters of the public school students and all the private school students in Chile either want to begin or to complete university training, and the expectations are similarly high in Venezuela. Realistic or not, these hopes suggest that students wish to transcend the general level of education of their families of origin, and the students assume both a personal and a societal ability to fulfill their ambitions.

OCCUPATION

These students also expect to enter prestigious occupations after completing their studies. We asked whether students wanted to be laborers, skilled workers, farmers, white-collar employees, professionals, businessmen, technicians, or members of some other occupation. About two-thirds of all Chilean primary-school students stated they wanted to be professional—an aspiration shared even by almost three-fifths of the rural children of Molina. The second most popular choice was to be a technician, an engineer, or perhaps an economist or planner. In Venezuela, many fewer than in Chile wished to become professionals, although their number still included two-fifths of all the primary-school students. The major part of the difference is made up of those who wish to become technicians. And in Venezuela as in Chile, the occupational aspirations of rural children do not lag far behind those of their urban brethren, even though their educational aspirations do. Naturally, there will be much slippage between the aspirations of a twelve-year old and his actual attainments at maturity. There should be less when dealing with eighteen-year old secondary-school students, who have already demonstrated financial and intellectual abilities far above the average for their countries.

Fully 85 per cent of all Chilean secondary-school students want to become professionals. The figure is almost exactly the same for Venezuelan students. The few university students we were able to interview (155 in Santiago and 359 in Antofagasta) similarly chose the professions. Of those two groups in Chile, 88 per cent expected to enter the professions, and an additional 7 per cent said they expected to enter a white-collar occupation. The steeply graduated educational pyramids in both countries graphically illustrate the difficulty of traversing the entire educational route from first grade to a university degree. However, movement into a profession is not an unrealistic aspiration for last-year secondary-school students and university students in economies that, at the time this study was done, were both expanding, although the Venezuelan growth was much more marked than the Chilean.

As students' actual and hoped-for educational and professional attainment outstrips that of their parents, so also do their aspirations for occupational prestige. We take such prestige simply as a clue to one's standing in the community, not as a synonym for social class. We also take prestige ranking not as an absolute, unequivocal quality, but only as a means of contrasting one group of persons with another within a relative framework. Hence, those whom we will denominate as being occupationally of "upper," "middle," or "lower" prestige should be considered always in relation to one another and not as possessing any inherent qualities by virtue of their position. Thus, "middles" may or may not have bourgeois virtues and defects, and "lowers" may or may not be proletarians in the sense of being marginal to their society's institutions.*

---

*The original information we gathered from parents concerning their occupations was coded into 65 categories based on the following 10 occupational situses: arts, communication, and entertainment; business; political; military; religious; agriculture; service; manual work; and "others"—a category including the retired, housewives, and those not working for any reason. Within each situs, occupations were further specified by such

Because educational attainment and occupational prestige are invariably highly correlated, we must expect to find a gap between students' occupational aspirations and their parents' actual situations, as we did between students' actual and anticipated schooling and their parents' achievements in that respect. We also should expect to find the same inferences concerning the status of parents as their children attend schools in one or another part of the educational system. In Chilean private schools, for example, two-thirds of the parents are in lower occupational ranks, but almost half of the parents whose children are in Catholic schools are in middle positions, and another 13 per cent in the upper category. In public schools about one-half are in the lower bracket, 40 per cent in the middle, and just about 4 per cent in high-prestige occupations.

Location also reveals variations, with the lowest-prestige occupations naturally in Molina, and the highest in Chillán, followed by Antofagasta, and Santiago. These figures are not a valid profile of the entire populations of these locations, of course, for we stratified the schools in which we chose to conduct interviews on the basis of social-class judgments. The propositions presented here corroborate that judgment to the extent of providing us with a range of prestige responses. They also corroborate reasons for choosing the four locations, for one would expect low attainment in rural areas, a high proportion of lower-status students in an industrial city like Santiago, and the highest proportion of prestigious occupations represented among students' parents in a provincial capital like Chillán.

The Venezuelan responses mirror the ratification of the prestige representation in private schools, but the data are skewed by the very high numbers of parents who did not respond to the occupational questions. The distributions of "no responses" suggest that they came largely from lower-prestige occupational groups, for 40 per cent of parents with children in public schools and 37.4 per cent of those connected with the Catholic school system did not answer. Fully two-thirds of persons in Barquisimeto did not reply, and a third each in Caracas and Maracaibo also refused, whereas only 6 per cent in rural Ocumare did so. This

categories as "free professionals," "national big-business men," "subsistence farm workers," "skilled mechanics," and so forth. For the purposes of the analysis presented in the text, we regrouped occupations from all these categories into three prestige groups, which form the basis of this discussion. This tripartite classification was based on our own general knowledge of occupations in the context of the three countries. Although there might be some slight differences between our classification and one created by others, we believe that such differences would not be significant. The reduction of 65 categories to only 3 also sharply reduces the effect of possible variations in judgment.

failure to reply did not reflect itself in any great reticence concerning other portions of the questionnaire and, as a matter of fact, most persons who would not speak about their own occupational situations were, as we shall see, quite willing to speak about their parents'.

An explanation may well lie in the marital and sexual status of the respondents in Venezuela as contrasted with the more informative Chileans. The interviewers were instructed to speak with the head of each family, and they returned with 79 per cent of the Chilean interviews conducted with the father, and 56 per cent of the Venezuelan interviews with the mother. Interviewer bias is almost certainly not at issue here, for more than 23 per cent of the parents with children in Venezuelan public schools whom we interviewed were unmarried mothers. Since the public-school parents were the largest group of all parents interviewed (587 persons), the reason for a majority of women in the total for parents is clear. In Chile, to the contrary, fewer than 6 per cent of the parents were unmarried, so that the head of the household was much more likely to be the father. An unmarried woman acting as head of a household is generally unlikely to respond freely to questions concerning the sources of her livelihood. She may well be receiving public charity, or funds from a present or former common-law husband, working irregularly in unskilled occupations, sharing with neighbors, receiving assistance from relatives, and possibly occasionally visiting friends and relatives in the countryside.

Unfortunately, these gaps in the responses prevent us from comparing the present situation of Venezuelan parents with that of their own parents. We can say with certainty only that the vague comparisons we can make strengthen the suggestion that low occupational prestige and nonresponse go hand in hand. We see, for example, that the responses for upper occupational groups remain the same for the two generations. And, when more responses appear for the grandparents of today's students, the lower ranks fill for public school and Catholic school grandparents but the middle ranks fill for those from private schools. Whatever a full explanation might turn out to be, the Venezuelan data suggest an educational system that in the past was closed to persons in lower occupational positions, but that is now opening to them, primarily in the public-school system, and secondarily in the Catholic schools.

The Chilean data superficially suggest a slight increase in occupational prestige among parents as contrasted with their own mothers and fathers. But such a conclusion is too tenuous to invite discussion, for the major gains have been made among small groups, and the nonresponses could well wipe out what other differences appear. The safest conclusion would be that there is little or no change in occupational prestige from parents to grandparents, a conclusion which fits other studies reflecting low mobility among Chileans.

The situs concept we have employed would blur subtle prestige shifts involved in moving from one set of occupations to another—for example, from agricultural to industrial work settings. Thus, much lateral mobility could well have taken place to accompany Chile's slow industrialization and urbanization processes, without being reflected in relative prestige as such. Subtleties aside, however, the major conclusion is unequivocal: the realization of the aspirations of students would remove them educationally and occupationally from the worlds which most of their families have inhabited for at least two generations. They already have removed themselves in their hopes and world views.

Contrasted with their students, Chilean and Venezuelan teachers generally come from much more favored backgrounds. Naturally, we should expect this situation, given the required educational levels of teachers and the relation between the general family situation and the ability to continue schooling. The confirmation is strong, for almost two-thirds of the teachers in the three Chilean systems come from parents of middle occupational prestige, and almost one-tenth from upper-prestige-occupation families. While the distributions are somewhat different in Venezuela, the strength of the conclusion holds. But another phenomenon, of equal interest, also appears: about a quarter of all teachers in the public and Catholic systems come from families of low occupational prestige. The use of clerical personnel in Catholic schools explains much of the case for those schools, for many priests and nuns are of relatively low social origins. To some extent teaching functions as a stepping-stone to upward mobility, especially in the public schools. If points of view are shaded by family experience, then Chilean and Venezuelan students are exposed to teachers of sufficiently varied backgrounds to provide diversity and a pedagogical reinforcement of the variety found among the students themselves. However, this effect is blunted (but not negated) when students are sorted by the prestigious Catholic schools in Chile, and the private ones in Venezuela.

SOCIAL CLASS

The discussion of occupational prestige has brought us perilously close to implications concerning social class, even though we have cautioned against such an extension of our intentions. Our shying away from a class discussion may seem strange, especially given our political theme and the obvious links between class and politics in terms of power and its application. Rousseau and Marx were not alone in seeing the state as a partisan defender of the rights and interests of some groups over others. All scholars who consider social class an important variable do so as a result of studying power relationships. For example, Weber's famous construction of social class as a compound of economic, social, and political power has served ever since to inform class analysis with an understanding that the sources of power and its applications are many and varied.

There have, however, been two persistent and fundamental problems connected with class analysis. One has to do with the relation between situation in a class, and an appreciation of that situation. That is, one issue has to do with the origins of beliefs, the relation between setting or position and belief, and with the nature of community and subcommunities, as values are distributed through the strata that may characterize a given society. The other concerns the distinction between class position and the particular institutional locations which individuals may occupy at specific times. For example, a wholesale withdrawal of upper-class persons from military positions and their replacement by members of the middle class cannot easily be dismissed as mere "upward mobility." Such a vacating and replacement, which takes place institutionally, does not reflect a static life-chance situation for the new military men. Rather, it serves to change the meaning and amount of class power held by the upper groups.

Explanations are neither difficult nor mysterious—that is not our point. What we wish to underscore here is that making a clear and crisp analytical distinction between institutional and class position indicates that the former can be examined at any particular point in time, while the study of social class must necessarily be done historically. Institutional roles, the actuality of power, are substantively different in concept from social class, which is the potentiality for power. To pick up Weber's idea, social class refers to "life-chances," the sets of possibilities—all other things being equal—that inhere in the positions of discrete clusters of persons on the basis of historically cumulated group characteristics. A social survey at a single point in time such as we are examining here can tell us about institutional positions. But it cannot provide the longitudinal dimensions required for class analysis. A single survey can tell us only what people *think* about social classes, and how they place themselves at that moment into a class hierarchy. At best, then, it can provide class-relevant information, from which inferences can be drawn about the potential power of their groups of origin and of subsequent identification. Class is a subtle and complex phenomenon that will not be revealed by simple prestige rankings, indexes of socioeconomic status, or occupational position.

Our queries about class are not to be taken as a substitute for other data, but rather as another way of understanding the situational complexities in which our respondents place themselves. We have considered the patterns of educational achievement, occupational location, occupational prestige, aspirations of the students, and an indication of intergenerational relations. We have seen the connections between education and occupation, and that this relation persists through generations. That is, the classlike hint, so far, is that the combination of education and occupational level among parents clearly affects the distribution of students' educational and occupational chances. But we have also learned that educational opportunity is opening up, offering students much broader chances than their parents and grandparents enjoyed, and we also know that student aspirations far outstrip a class-bound set of hopes.

The patterns of conjunction and disjunction can be pushed a step further by looking into a series of questions we asked concerning self-appreciation of class position. We sought to get at the matter through three ways of ranking groups: first, a simple, unfreighted listing going from "very high" to "high" to "intermediate" to "low" and then to "very low"; second, an income-status ordering, running from "rich" to "well-to-do" (*acomodado*) to "modest" and finally to "humble"; and, third, a political-ideological distribution, going from the "ruling class" to the "traditional class" to the "middle class" and, finally, to the "common folk." In the last ranking, "ruling class" (*clase dirigente*) was divided from "traditional class" (*clase alta tradicional*) because of the clear distinction drawn between the two in Chile. A distinction is obviously being made in terms of what Weber called "status" and "power"—with the traditional uppers having the status, and the new *clase dirigente* having the political power.

Let us look first at the parents, for it is their social position from which the children begin. In the first listing, three-quarters of all parents in both countries chose the intermediate position, and an additional 15 per cent denominated themselves as "low." Shying away from the sharp distinctions of "high" or "very low" sets a pattern of "middlingness," in line with the sense of the descriptive words used in the questions, and holds through the other two sets of categories. The income-status ranking permitted respondents to range through the categories more fully than did the "high" and "low" inhibitors, and the results show interesting intercountry differences. Only a very few count themselves as "rich" in either Chile or Venezuela, but a fourth of the Chileans do consider themselves as well-to-do, against only a twelfth of the Venezuelans. About the same number (almost two-thirds) in each country count themselves as "modestly" set. The difference reappears in the "humble" category, of course, with a seventh of the Chileans and a quarter of the Venezuelan parents placing themselves there. These replies echo those in other areas, for the Chileans were generally better educated and of higher occupational prestige than the Venezuelans. With these confirmatory exceptions, the second set of class self-rankings falls into general concurrence with the first—the bulge is in the middle and toward the bottom of the distributions, the Venezuelans revealing that they trail Chile socially and educationally, as we earlier found that they concomitantly are closer to attitudinal tradition than the Chileans.

The same findings reappear in the political-ideological set of questions. The consistency is striking on several counts.* First, the accommodation among the responses suggests the stereotypical view of Latin Americans as being very conscious of class position to be an accurate assessment. In other countries, major differences appear in accordance with the choice of terms offered respondents. For example, "working class" is a more amenable term in the United States than is "lower class." Despite such possible differences in verbal affect among these rankings, the consistency of response holds. Second, there is a shying away from words referring to *relatively* extreme positions, but seemingly a willingness to accept a full range of other, *absolutely* descriptive

---

*To determine the extent of relationship among the three sets of questions, we calculated tetrachoric correlations for the parents' responses, as follows:

TETRACHORIC CORRELATIONS BETWEEN FAMILY POSITION MEASURES: PARENTS

Family Position	CHILE		VENEZUELA	
	2nd Set	3rd Set	2nd Set	3rd Set
1st Set	.70	.78	.84	.82
2nd Set		.70		.71

The results obtained through the cross-correlational use of any one of these measures are likely to be duplicated through the use of either of the remaining two. We will employ this conclusion in our later analysis.

alternatives. After all, it is to be expected that only very few persons are actually members of the most powerful groups in any society, and that in Latin America not many parents of the lowest occupational and income levels will be able to afford to send their children to school.

The responses of the teachers are much the same as those of the parents. In the first set, the simple hierarchy, 9 out of 10 teachers in both countries place themselves in the "intermediate" category. In the second set, 57 per cent of the Chilean teachers put themselves down as "modest," and another 33 per cent place themselves a step higher, among the "well-to-do." But Venezuelan teachers place themselves overwhelmingly (83 per cent) in the "modest" category, with only 12 per cent seeing themselves as better off. The two country groups converge again in the political-ideological list, with 86 per cent of the Chileans and 81 per cent of the Venezuelans considering themselves members of the middle class.

For teachers and parents in both countries there are some differences in these class-influential responses by type of school and by locality. Most noticeably, parents from rural areas tend to see their status as being slightly lower than those from urban areas. Even though the clear majority of parents in Molina and in Ocumare place themselves in the middle, like parents in the larger cities in both countries, the former are also more frequently in the next lower class category in each of the three sets of responses. Among teachers these patterns are less attenuated, probably because they are a more homogeneous group than are the parents.

When parents in both Chile and in Venezuela are compared by the type of schools their children attend, there is a pattern for those parents connected with the Catholic schools to peg their class status as slightly higher than those whose children attend the public schools. This difference would seem to have an objective basis, for we have found Catholic parents to hold better occupations and to have had more schooling than other parents. Even so, clear and large majorities in all instances choose the middle position in each of the subjective class measures. Again, teachers in all school systems in both countries responded very much the same to the subjective class questions, overwhelmingly in the middle position.

Primary- and secondary-school students tend to magnify the slight differences exhibited by their parents. Hence, both these groups from Molina and from Ocumare judge their family's position as relatively lower than do those living in urban areas. When the comparisons are drawn in terms of school systems, students in the Catholic and private schools judge their family's status as relatively higher than those attending public schools.

Throughout this discussion we have relied upon parents to make the judgments about the class positions of their families, and to indicate their occupations and how much schooling they have had. But we also asked the students to tell us about these parental characteristics. We already know how optimistic most students are about themselves. They also seem to view their parents with a similarly elevated perception in matters having to do with status and class. All students—primary and secondary, regardless of school system or locality—judge their parents to be better educated, in a higher prestige occupation, and in a higher class position than do the parents themselves.* In virtually every such comparison, the students' appraisal of their parents' position almost invariably was higher than the parents'. Not that these differences were always large, but the pattern that emerged 95 times out of 100 is in itself highly significant statistically.

Generally, such overestimation by students appears to be a function of age, not of school system or locality. Primary-school students tend to make greater errors of judgment about their parents' occupation, education, and standing, than those in secondary schools. No such definitive pattern emerged in comparisons by type of school system or locality, however, nor were there sharp or consistent differences when Chilean and Venezuelan students were compared.

Aside from the general optimism of the students, the differences between Chile and Venezuela, and the tendency for secondary students to begin to approximate their parents' estimates, the other overarching regularity of these data is that the optimism is visible but relatively light concerning the topmost and the lowest categories, but intense in the students' move away from the array between the borderline connecting upper lowers with lower middles, and toward solidly upper-middle-class positions. Majorities of all parents in both countries and in all schools see themselves as modestly set, while their children—and especially the primary-school youngsters—push toward being *acomodados*. But certainly there is no pure and simple explanation which can hold that these students have already translated educational and occupational aspirations into elevated family class position. That element certainly plays

---

*This conclusion is based on comparisons of group means for the smallest identifiable samples of persons. For instance, primary-school students in Santiago attending a public school were compared with the group of parents having a child in precisely this same group of students. See Appendix V for the data on these comparisons.

some part, but it should not be forgotten that primary-school children have lower aspiration levels than secondary-school students, and yet higher class positioning of their families. Primary-school students who, it will be remembered, tend to see society as closed, with the family and religion as the most cherished institutions, may well be protecting themselves through family estimation, while tentatively beginning to think about social roles in their ambitions. Secondary-school students tend to see an open world of opportunity; they are hopeful for themselves in that world, and they begin to share their parents' self-estimations, although still permitting a flush of enthusiasm to spread over their origins.

This picture is an interesting one, complex as befits reality, revelatory of youthful enthusiasms and perhaps innocence, descriptive of the attitudes of older persons and suggestive of the complications of class, educational, regional and national, and occupational interactions.

WORLD VIEWS AND OTHER SOCIAL CHARACTERISTICS

So far in this chapter we have used our information only to describe the groups we have studied. Consistent with our methodological views, we have not attempted to build a correlational set that would make out the attitudes we have isolated to be firmly a function of characteristics other than the level of schooling of a person. The data simply will not perform effectively and consistently in that way. However, we need to make the attempt to search out such patterns in order to know to what extent such manipulation may indicate that school system, residence, family position, and similar characteristics "explain" attitudes held. This procedure should be seen as the ultimate test, within our available data, of the idea that has slowly been maturing throughout this study of the underlying effect of education as contributing *by itself* to changes in the normative political postures of individuals. It will also tell us about the degree to which this study is truly useful as a comparative tool, for random irregularities between Chile and Venezuela in this kind of statistical confrontation will severely damage claims to the validity of the generalizability of our ideas and methods. In order to prepare the harshest test possible within the limits of our information, we have taken the typology presented in Chapter III—the most complex grouping of attitudinal data that we have, and one whose intra- and intercountry regularities have been established—and we have crossed the types with eleven independent attributes for the parents, and a slightly smaller number for the other groups, depending on their applicability.*

Interspersed throughout the following text are graphs illustrating this section. It will be recalled that we constructed the eight-part typology as a linked series, each category being seen as an ideal-type—intrinsically different from every other one, although conceptually joined. Our procedures now are designed to tell us to what extent these types are different in terms of the eleven "background" characteristics listed in the preceding footnote, and the measured extent of those differences. We expected to gain little explanatory power directly from these manipulations, for we know from numerous other studies that such relations are highly tenuous. That is, we did not expect the data to "tell" us what was "causing" the breaking-down of our groups into their types. We already know the highly significant effects of educational level on the distributions by types. In this analysis we are seeking not merely confirmation of previously suggested weak associations, or of the strength of the educational association we already know, but much more importantly, we wish to inquire further into the matter of constraints and freedoms within specific national contexts, this time with respect to situational attributes instead of the patterning among attitude sets already established. We have already seen a gross and unmistakable difference between Chileans and Venezuelans precisely in terms of ranges of differ-

---

*For each group—primary, secondary, and university students, teachers and parents in each country—we performed a multiple discriminant function analysis. As the name implies, this analysis permits the simultaneous consideration of all attributes or variables for their combined effects in discriminating between the six types of belief-sets we have identified. In addition to this decided advantage, the analysis assumes that these types are discrete rather than continuous; that is, these types are different from one another and are mutually exclusive.

The multiple discriminant function analysis provides us with several relevant summary statistics that provide the basis for our description. First, we can determine which of the attributes or variables are statistically significant in distinguishing between types by means of a multivariate F ratio. Second, an F matrix that compares each type with every other type reveals the pairs of types that are significantly different from each other. Finally, a U statistic indicates the degree of equality between means of the types, or the proportion of the variance that is "explained" within the kinds of data being employed. The relevant section of the Appendix contains the specific statistics, and we limit our discussion in the text to general summaries.

The eleven independent attributes were as follows: school system, sex, urban-rural residence, parents' education, father's occupation, level of political activity, respondent's education, respondent's occupation, and three subjective measures of family class position. We acknowledge the assistance of John H. Reed in this analysis.

89

ence within both the typology and attitudes toward differentiation. We also have seen that the typology acts to describe a sharp decrease in attitudinal constraint with the move across the sweep from Organicists to Autonomists. The form in which we are about to present the data should reveal a third aspect of constraint: the relation between world view and situation.

The reader should have little difficulty in immediately comprehending the figures. The line in a figure between any two types represents a statistically significant *difference* between those types by the total set of social characteristics enumerated in the last footnote; the larger the ratio—the number expressed—the greater the difference. The "U" statistic for each graph represents how much of the differences between all the types is statistically "unexplained" when all the relevant independent attributes are simultaneously considered. As is evident, this explanatory power is generally low: the best we have been able to do with these operations is to account for 19 per cent of the variance among parents in both countries (100 per cent −81 per cent) and, at the other extreme, only 8 per cent among Chilean primary students (100 per cent −92 per cent). But this kind of "explanatory power" is not the point; the clusters of difference between types, however, is.

We shall later look at all the data taken together. Let us at this point examine some of the discriminations that appear within each sample group. We shall learn a little about stereotypes and the degree to which they have validity, and put to rest any lingering doubts about the degree to which certain factual details may need further exploration. Because this kind of data presentation is usually confounding and demands close attention, we shall engage only in very summary and discursive description, with few percentages, proceeding by group and country.

Primary-School Students. Being similar in their distribution among the six types, Chilean and Venezuelan primary-school students differ in terms of the relative weight of the attributes attached to each type. In Chile influences are felt, in order of strength, from family class position, type of school, parents' education, sex, and urban-rural residence. In Venezuela the factors were, again in order of weight, urban-rural residence, father's occupation, parents' education, and type of school. In Chile the triadic Autonomists, Liberal Abstainers, and Corporatist Technocrats are more likely to be found in public than Catholic schools. But in Venezuela, Autonomists and Corporatist Technocrats are more common in Catholic schools. (We have already seen that in some measure the two types of schools perform reverse status functions, in the two countries.) As for urban-rural differences, Organicists are more likely to be found in rural Ocumare in Venezuela than in the cities, and Autonomists in the cities rather than Ocumare. *But no other types respond to this difference.* In Chile, however, Organicists and Autonomists are more prone to be found in rural Molina than in the cities, where Conservative Individualists are found in slightly greater numbers than in the countryside. The suggestion we may derive is that urban-rural differences are less sharp in Chile than in Venezuela, and that the conventional wisdom about Catholic schools holds true for Chile, but not true for Venezuela.

We already know that the parents of primary-school students, taken as a group, have little education on the average. Therefore, this datum "pulls" little against the typology. What slight influence appears, however, shows that in Venezuela, the parents of Autonomists and Corporatist Technocrats are more educated than those of other types, while in Chile the Technocrats share the same favored parental educational levels, but the Autonomists, as well as the Corporate Pluralists, have parents of very low educational levels. Subjective class measures and occupational prestige similarly show mixed and differing results in the two countries. As for sex differences, they did not appear as important in Venezuela, but in Chile girls were more likely than boys to be Corporatist Technocrats; the males were more likely to be Liberal Abstainers.

Clearly, there is no obvious and consistent set of characteristics distinguishing the types among primary students. Taken together, however, there is a sharp difference between Chile and Venezuela in the degree to which these background characteristics help describe each type. In Figure IV-1, it can be seen that eight lines distinguish the six types, indicating that significant differences exist between those types. In Venezuela, however, there are twelve such differences. In addition, the ratios of difference are considerably higher in Venezuela than in Chile. For example, the background characteristics dividing Chilean primary school Organicists from Autonomists is only 2.0; in Venezuela, the same distinction has the very high ratio of 7.7. We may conclude that the typology of belief-sets implies a deeper division among Venezuelan students than among Chileans, to the extent to which type-differences are reinforced by other social characteristics.

Secondary-School Students. It will be remembered that half of all Chilean secondary-school students interviewed typed themselves as Autonomists, and another fifth as Liberal Abstainers. The Venezuelans were much more evenly distributed among four of the six types, with very few Organicists or Corporate Pluralists. The number of distinguish-

92

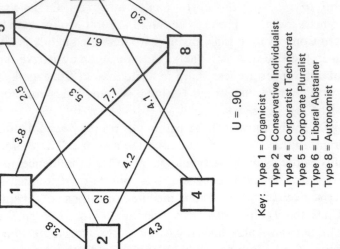

MULTIVARIATE F RATIOS BETWEEN VENEZUELAN PRIMARY-SCHOOL STUDENT TYPES

U = .90

Key: Type 1 = Organicist
      Type 2 = Conservative Individualist
      Type 4 = Corporatist Technocrat
      Type 5 = Corporate Pluralist
      Type 6 = Liberal Abstainer
      Type 8 = Autonomist

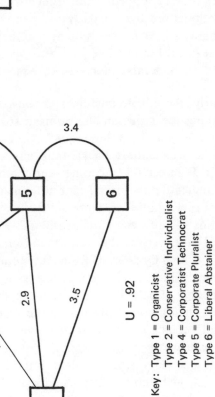
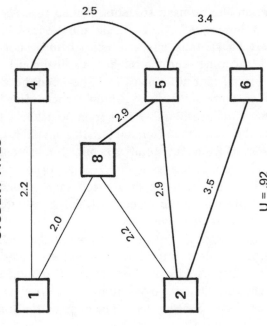

MULTIVARIATE F RATIOS BETWEEN CHILEAN PRIMARY-SCHOOL STUDENT TYPES

U = .92

Key: Type 1 = Organicist
      Type 2 = Conservative Individualist
      Type 4 = Corporatist Technocrat
      Type 5 = Corporate Pluralist
      Type 6 = Liberal Abstainer
      Type 8 = Autonomist

Figure IV-1

ing characteristics among the types ir the two countries is much smaller than for primary-school students, but their relative import tends to be greater. Chilean types are distinguished by school, family class position, and one of the self-estimates of class. Venezuelan types are distinguished by school and sex. The common element for both—kind of school—however, distinguishes the types in the same direction in both countries, unlike the case of the primary-school students. In both countries the more rational Abstainers and Autonomists are to be found in the public schools, and the Corporatist Technocrats decidedly predominate within the Catholic schools. (Other types are not distinguishable by the kind of school.) Where the sex difference mattered in Venezuela, Conservative Individualists tended to be males, and Autonomists predominantly females. Liberal Abstainers were more often male in the public and private schools, more often female in the Catholic schools.

More important is the degree to which the types are distinguishable when all the characteristics are taken together. In Chile we find that only the Technocrats are distinguishable from the Abstainers and the Autonomists (see Figure IV-2). In Venezuela, however, the distinctions are much more frequent.

Teachers. It will be remembered that teachers were distributed among the types more evenly than secondary-school students. In Chile about a third are Autonomists, a quarter Abstainers, and an eighth each placed themselves as Technocrats or Conservative Individualists. Among Venezuelans the distribution is more even, with a quarter to a third in each of those types. But the characteristics distinguishing the types are even fewer than those dividing the advanced students, coming down only to kind of school and school level in Chile, and kind of school and sex in Venezuela, exactly the same as for the secondary-school students. Classlike characteristics do not function in either case.

In both countries Corporatist Technocrats were more likely to be teaching in Catholic than public schools, and Liberal Abstainers were predominant in public schools. Otherwise, the effects we found were scattered, with Chilean Autonomists more likely to be in public primary than in secondary schools, Abstainers distinctly underrepresented in Catholic schools, and Conservative Individualists in the Catholic primary and the public secondary systems.

The sex differences that appeared in Venezuela ramify the differences found among secondary-school students, but are in the same direction: Autonomists are more likely to be women than men, whether in public, private, or Catholic schools. Abstainers tend to be women in the public schools, and men in the private and Catholic systems. Conservative

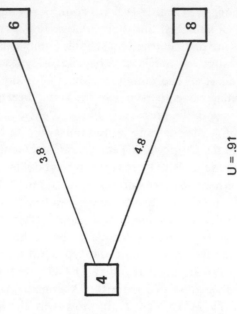

MULTIVARIATE F RATIOS BETWEEN CHILEAN SECONDARY-SCHOOL STUDENT TYPES

U = .91

Key: Type 1 = Organicist
Type 2 = Conservative Individualist
Type 4 = Corporatist Technocrat
Type 5 = Corporate Pluralist
Type 6 = Liberal Abstainer
Type 8 = Autonomist

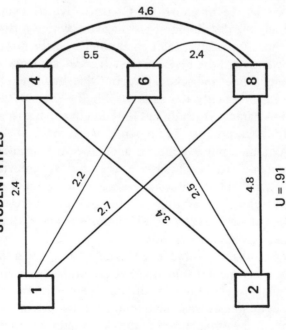

MULTIVARIATE F RATIOS BETWEEN VENEZUELAN SECONDARY-SCHOOL STUDENT TYPES

U = .91

Key: Type 1 = Organicist
Type 2 = Conservative Individualist
Type 4 = Corporatist Technocrat
Type 5 = Corporate Pluralist
Type 6 = Liberal Abstainer
Type 8 = Autonomist

Figure IV-2

Individualists tend to be male in the public and private schools, female in the Catholic schools.

Again, consistent with all our comparative data, the differentiation among Venezuelan types is much stronger than among Chileans. As in the case of the secondary-school students, Technocrats are distinguishable only from Abstainers and Autonomists among Chilean types. But the greatest relative freedom from the effects of background characteristics among Venezuelans shows up for these teachers, there being only four differentiating lines to be seen in Figure IV-3.

Parents. Our interest in parents is intense for, as we have pointed out, they act as a special kind of control group, being the only one with the full range of educational experiences. Thus, it is of more than passing interest that in relatively developed Chile, the only statistically significant attribute in differentiating among the types is the parents' level of education. This finding means, of course, that the generational differences of educational attainments we found in Chile (but not in Venezuela) override the effects of other attributes on the holding of world views. The association that is found is exactly what should be expected, a replication within parental groups of the divisions characterizing primary-school students, secondary-school students, and teachers— three ascribed levels of education. The better educated among the parents tend, of course, toward the more rational types. Half of all parents who have attended a university are Autonomists. Liberal Abstainers come next, with somewhat lower educational levels than Autonomists, but relatively more than any other type. The ritualistic Conservative Individualists have the least education, with greater numbers than any other type never having attended school at all or having incomplete primary education. In their educational attainments, Corporate Pluralists tend to resemble the Individualists more than the rationalistic types.

Venezuelan parents do not respond similarly to the educational variable. Remember that their educational levels tend quite uniformly to be low, and that both the students and teachers we have studied represent the first great push into higher educational attainment for their families. Chilean educational levels, on the contrary, are continuations of family trends that seem to cover at least three generations. For Venezuelans, then, sex, school, and one of the subjective class measures have influence. The preponderance of women among Venezuelan parents is, as we have already pointed out, also a partial reflection of poverty and irregular unions or broken homes. Thus, the sex ratio is nearly equal for parents with children in Catholic schools, but many more female heads

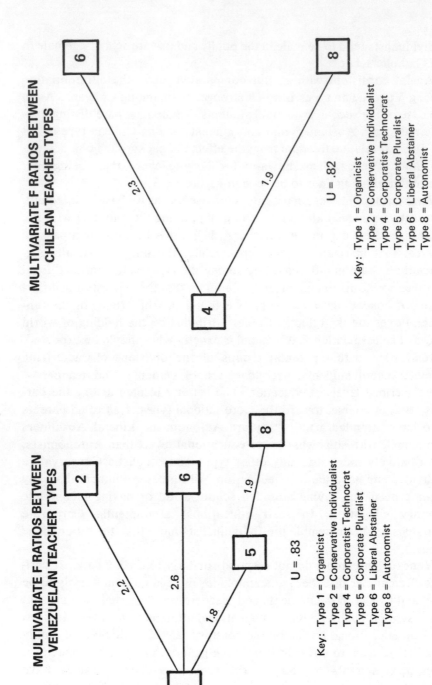

MULTIVARIATE F RATIOS BETWEEN
CHILEAN TEACHER TYPES

U = .82

Key: Type 1 = Organicist
Type 2 = Conservative Individualist
Type 4 = Corporatist Technocrat
Type 5 = Corporate Pluralist
Type 6 = Liberal Abstainer
Type 8 = Autonomist

MULTIVARIATE F RATIOS BETWEEN
VENEZUELAN TEACHER TYPES

U = .83

Key: Type 1 = Organicist
Type 2 = Conservative Individualist
Type 4 = Corporatist Technocrat
Type 5 = Corporate Pluralist
Type 6 = Liberal Abstainer
Type 8 = Autonomist

Figure IV-3

of family have children in public schools than do male heads of family, whose children attend private schools in higher proportions. When we analyze sex ratio by the typology alone, many more women than men are among the Conservative Individualists and Corporatist Technocrats, regardless of school system. The Abstainers are predominantly male types in all schools. Among Organicists, women predominate in the Catholic schools, men in the public schools; the relationship is reversed for the Autonomists.

The sex variable, as we have pointed out, has a built-in artificiality. Therefore, the distribution of parental types by the school system attended by their children is of more pertinence to our immediate purpose. Here, it is the level of school that is important, permitting an inference concerning occupation and education. Autonomists are underrepresented at primary levels in all school systems, but overrepresented in secondary-school systems. The inference is that parents able to maintain their children through secondary school are more likely to be well off than others, a success which usually implies educational achievement. Occupation and educational level differences were obviously not sufficiently great to appear as statistically significant, but nevertheless a shadowy inference lies behind these data.

This suggestion gains strength from the division by class indicators. Most Venezuelan parents judged their position to be a "modest" one— better than "humble," but neither "comfortable" nor "rich." The Conservative Individualists, Abstainers, and Technocrats are very solidly in the "modest" category, but the Autonomists turn up more frequently than others in the next-higher category of "comfortable." The Organicists and Corporatist Pluralists, on the other hand, are overrepresented in the lowest category. In other words, Venezuelan parents act by classlike measures, Chilean parents by educational level. The inference is obvious; the fact will have to wait on time for testing.

The discrimination among Chilean pairs is uncluttered (see Figure IV-4). Organicists are differentiated from Abstainers and Autonomists, while the latter are also distinguished from Abstainers and Individualists. But the Venezuelan differences are 13 in number, indicating great heterogeneity among groups by these attributes of about the same nature as was found for Venezuelan primary-school students.

As we have said, it is not the degree of correlational strength that is important here, but rather the meaning of the much more salient nonrelations and the degrees—even when the relations are weak—to which some situational characteristics influence some groups but not others.

97

MULTIVARIATE F RATIOS BETWEEN
VENEZUELAN PARENT TYPES

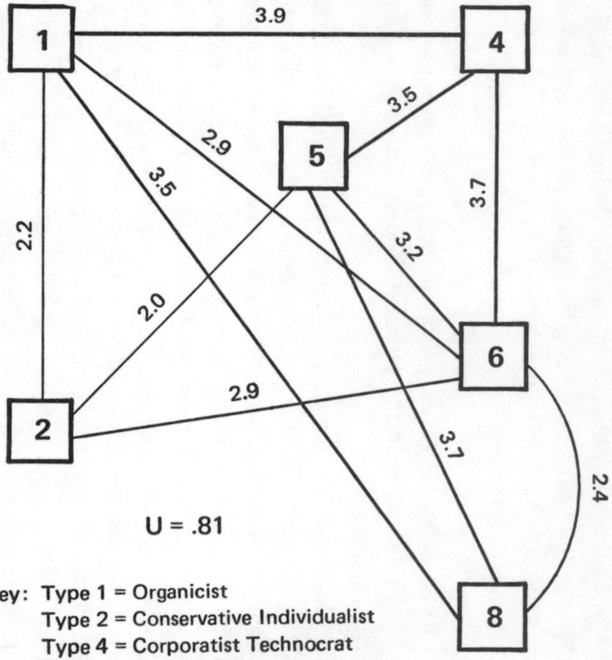

U = .81

Key: Type 1 = Organicist
Type 2 = Conservative Individualist
Type 4 = Corporatist Technocrat
Type 5 = Corporate Pluralist
Type 6 = Liberal Abstainer
Type 8 = Autonomist

MULTIVARIATE F RATIOS BETWEEN
CHILEAN PARENT TYPES

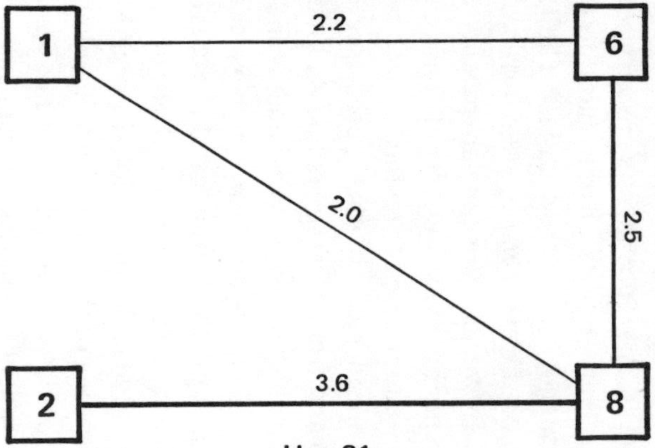

U = .81

Key: Type 1 = Organicist
Type 2 = Conservative Individualist
Type 4 = Corporatist Technocrat
Type 5 = Corporate Pluralist
Type 6 = Liberal Abstainer
Type 8 = Autonomist

Figure IV-4

98

The conclusions we draw recapitulate points made elsewhere, but they are given strong added confirmation through this analysis:

- •The greater traditionalism of Venezuelans than Chileans is confirmed.
- •The concepts of tradition and modernity are definitionally enriched, for now we can speak not only of a lack of constraint among components of an idea-system or an attitude-set, but also of an increased freedom among the more developed persons from the effect of mundane situation on world view.
- •None of the background characteristics we have analyzed has even remotely as much influence on type of world view as has educational experience, whose effect is overwhelming.

The processes of development through which Chile and Venezuela are moving create two overriding organizing structures: the social nation and the class system. We have made this statement before, but it needs reiteration here, when we are quite specifically dealing with education and ideas, and when we have established a strong case for assuming that Chilean and Venezuelan educational institutions effectively predispose persons to lead an empathic, secular, and relativistic existence within a multiclass community. If modernization has something to do with secularization of thought, with freeing minds from rite and judgments from ascription, if it has to do with enabling men to engage in intellectual life free of the accidents of their social origins, then—whatever else they may be doing—Chilean and Venezuelan schools are producing a goodly number of intellectually free persons. The occupational and class facts of the matter are that the two educational systems are used to certify the class positions of some and to promote the mobility of others. The class aspects of capitalistic development are respected; so, too, are values of democratic equalitarianism.

Obviously, the Chilean and Venezuelan societies will not be able to deliver fully on their political and economic promises. Class lines will be blurred by individual occupational mobility and by the very skill of educated persons in seeing across the lines. But the ability to live in a fully participatory national community will be reinforced simultaneously with the shaping and reinforcing of a modernized class structure. Therein lies the essential contradiction with which the students we have studied will have to live. How or whether they will recognize the conflict, and whether or how they will be prepared to act on their possible recognition, are questions that our data cannot answer. But they do suggest a pattern of diagnosis.

The discontinuities revealed in the latter part of this chapter should not be read as chaos. Taken whole, they tell us where families of political approaches are to be found, and how to relate those families to structural characteristics within each society. We should not search for an "upper-class mentality," or feel democratically secure with the personal autonomy and optimism evinced by advanced students, or dismiss corporatists because their numbers are small and associated either with underprivileged persons or the graduates of professional schools. Adequate diagnosis will depend on constructing understandings of sets of persons—for example, the well-to-do persons of Autonomist persuasion, in specific institutional situses, and their interaction with other well-to-do persons who espouse open and secularist views of the social world in their institutional settings. This way of proceeding is clumsy in the sense that it demands highly specific information that must be ordered without the ease of scalar inference and with the difficulty of typological construction. We have no recourse but to engage in such efforts, however, if we are to understand countercurrents as well as currents. Certainly the part education plays in the contradictory tasks of nation-building and system-maintenance will not be revealed by a search only for accommodating patterns.

five / The Ideology of Education in Chile During the Nineteenth Century

The increasing strain between the "all" and the "some," and between "right" and "privilege," has led to a growing concern with the classical issue of equality in the United States, and in 1973 caused a breakdown in the constitutional process in Chile. The question of equality, which is as old as democracy, capitalism, and nationalism, has created problems that have been with us for some two centuries. Neither age nor usage have blunted the sharpness of the issue. Indeed, it has been growing more acute, honed by the view that inequality is a more "natural" human condition than is equality. In the time of the French and American revolutions, it could be argued that these middle-class revolutions would liberate all persons, not only the *mezzi,* from the grip of the aristocracy. Laws, public freedom, citizenship, the nation were to be the blessed fruits for all men, now proudly called *citoyens*. Equality was the touchstone of acceptance within the social community and a condition "natural" to all men, not by conferral but rooted in the fact of existence. Belonging was then both an individual right and a group attribute.

But the stress between nation and class showed itself early and it was seized upon by those who were aggrieved by the human costs of early capitalism.

> . . . Marx contends that in modern society man is cut into two distinct persons—into the "citizen" *(citoyen)* and the *"bourgeois."* Within the state man is expected to live up to universal criteria; within civil society, he is supposed to behave according to his egotistical needs and interests. Thus the state, which should have incorporated the universality of social life, appears as one partial organization among the other powerful interests of civil society. . . .

> This confrontation of *bourgeois* versus *citoyen* is not confined to Marx's thought. Some of his contemporaries, drawing as he did on the Hegelian heritage, used it as well. Max Stirner, for example, made the same terminological distinction, but his conclusions diametrically opposed Marx's. . . . Stirner said about the French Revolution:

> Not individual man—and it is only as such that man exists as a real person—has been emancipated; it is merely the citizen, the *citoyen*, political man, that has been liberated; and he is not real man, but just an exemplar of the human species, to be more precise, of the genus *citoyen*. It is only as such, and not as man, that he has been liberated . . . . In the French Revolution it is not the individual that is world-historically active: only the nation.[1]

In the early days of thinking about universal national communities, the role of education was to prepare the citizens in the exercise of Reason. Man's intellect was to make him understand that the private and the public interest were both maximized by a reconciliation between them. The concept of natural law made men equal before God, regardless of sectarian religious beliefs. A free and competitive market made him equal before the economy. The nation made him equal before the laws. And education became the equalizer, the universal mechanism to free man from the accident of his status at birth, to make him rational in the use of his skill for overcoming other economic differences, of his reason to guide him to secularism, and of his participation to make his citizenship effective. This nexus, which united group and individual, broke down as economic specialization and social differentiation grew, and as new patterns of privilege were hardened by the evolving economic mechanism.

Three main currents of thought developed to explain the stresses that unexpectedly arose between the public and private good. Marxism, as is well known, seeking to resolve the differences, predicted an end to class privileges through the downfall of capitalism with its dependence upon surplus value in the process of capital accumulation, a factor that made social class an ineluctable accompaniment of capitalist development. The Mediterranean response was corporatism, a rejection of the social scrambling and exploitation accompanying capitalism in favor of fixed class orders that still permitted some institutional differentiation and occupational specialization.

However, the explanation most familiar in the Protestant West was that of the Utilitarians, Positivists, and Social Darwinists. They resolved the contradiction by denying the reality of class, accenting individualism instead. It was they who substituted the idea of "equality of opportunity" for the simpler term but the more difficult accomplishment, equality per se. Thus, for them education did not in the first instance serve a macropolitical purpose; rather, education was to assist individuals in finding their "proper" place in society by promoting individual mobility. Mobility thereby made class *conflict,* but not classes, inane and "proved" that the fixed, pre-established hierarchy of corporatism was an anachronistic hindrance to the advantages of recognizing "natural" merit triggered by universal, public education. The movement of individuals throughout the social strata would produce the benefits of equality by guiding persons into a hierarchy of occupational categories and lifetime settings, unhindered by the influences of class privileges extending across the generations.

The Utilitarian-Positivist-Darwinian postulates assumed linearity: (1) education acted as the selecting mechanism for the meritorious, resulting in (2) their mobility through occupational placement, and leading to (3) income and consumption habits that shaped other aspects of the individual's participation in social life. The contribution of this school of thought to educational analysis came to fruition in manpower studies that analyzed labor-demand conditions to determine policy for the educational institution. Developing countries, in particular, were encouraged by manpower experts to link education directly to the requirements of the economy, for resources, being scarce, should not be wasted by training people for unneeded jobs. A closely related idea often pushed by the same experts was the "multiversity," a university engaged in all aspects of social life, from the creation of ideas, making a choice among them, implementing some of them, to teaching others how to implement all of them.*

However, the theory founders on the commonplace: occupational success is not an inevitable fruit of educational attainment even in developed states. Although we view this finding as a happy one and base our theory on the naturalness of such disjunctiveness, others who are steeped in the conventional wisdom are dismayed by this knowledge. A major debate has been taking place in the United States on this very issue of the apparent noncorrelation between education and economic success. The initial findings of James Coleman in 1966, and the reanalysis by Christopher Jencks and his colleagues in the early 1970s,

---

*"The multiversity is an inconsistent institution. It is not one community but several—the community of the undergraduate and the community of the graduate; the community of the humanist, the community of the social scientist, and the community of the scientist; the communities of the professional schools; the community of all the nonacademic personnel; the community of the administrators. Its edges are fuzzy—it reaches out to alumni, legislators, farmers, businessmen, who are all related to one or more of these internal communities. As an institution, it looks far into the past and far into the future, and is often at odds with the present. It serves society almost slavishly—a society it also criticizes, sometimes unmercifully. Devoted to equality of opportunity, it is itself a class society," (Clark Kerr, *The Uses of the University* [New York: Harper & Row, 1963], pp. 18–19.)

point up the difficulties in translating statistical predictions across the major facts of institutional life, and specifically, into matters concerning education and economic behavior.[2] Jencks and his associates sum up the matter as follows:

> The basic strategy of the war on poverty during the 1960s was to give everyone entering the job market or any other competitive arena comparable skills. This meant placing great emphasis on education. Many people imagined that if schools could equalize people's cognitive skills this would equalize their bargaining power as adults . . . .
>
> This strategy rested on a series of assumptions which went roughly as follows:
>
> 1. Eliminating poverty is largely a matter of helping children born into poverty to rise out of it. . . .
>
> 2. The primary reason poor children do not escape from poverty is that they do not acquire basic cognitive skills. . . .
>
> 3. The best mechanism for breaking this vicious circle is educational reform. Since children born into poor homes do not acquire the skills they need from their parents, they must be taught these skills in school. . . .
>
> So far as we can discover, each of these assumptions is erroneous.
>
> 1. Poverty is not primarily hereditary. While children born into poverty have a higher-than-average chance of ending up poor, there is still an enormous amount of economic mobility from one generation to the next. . . .
>
> 2. The primary reason some people end up richer than others is not that they have more adequate cognitive skills. . . . There is almost as much economic inequality among those who score high on standardized tests as in the general population. . . .
>
> 3. There is no evidence that school reform can substantially reduce the extent of cognitive inequality, as measured by tests of verbal fluency, reading comprehension, or mathematical skill. Neither school resources nor segregation has an appreciable effect on either test scores or educational attainment.

We present this long quotation not to criticize it at this time, but simply to describe the common stereotype of the efficacy of education as well as its refutation developed from findings which show how tenuous are the relations between schooling and economic life. Jencks concludes, "We have not . . . been very successful in explaining most of these inequalities [among educational opportunities, cognitive skills, educational credentials, occupational status, income, and job satisfaction]. The association between one variety of inequality and another is usually quite weak, which means that equalizing one thing is unlikely to have much effect on the degree of inequality in other areas" (p. 253).

Although the data we have used are much more restricted in scope than Jencks', we have found apposite results *methodologically*. That is, we found relatively weak relations between strictly educational variables on the one side, and other factors such as sex, type of school, social class, and urban locale on the other. We expected that finding, of course, deeply rooted as it is in our approach to social organization and change. But, unlike Jencks, Coleman, and others, we chose *not* to study education as instrumental to other, principally economic, facts. We did *not* ask how education helps persons earn a living, but rather, what it does to persons in forming their own political perceptions. Here our findings were strongly positive and tightly related to the educational experience. In the political sphere, education does make a *cognitive* difference, for it is legitimate to view the development of secular, relative, and empathic views as skills useful in modern society. *But, we do not presume that by holding such views persons will act on them effectively. On the contrary, the mere possession of modern political skills and attitudes cannot be translated into effective behavior without support from extra-educational institutions.* Indeed, it is reasonable and provable to conclude that institutional atrophy is a precondition for student activism, for attempting to make the university or even the high school a surrogate for the parties, congresses, and associations that are unresponsive to the very skills learned in school.

As we have said, the political attitudes whose growth we have studied both generate and identify the clash between state and civil society, between nation and class, which underlies modern national histories. We suspect that resolution of the conflict between the two ideals cannot much longer be postponed in mature societies because the changes we see are heightening that conflict instead of resolving it. The contemporary situation, including its idea systems as well as its mechanical technology, permits change to become encysted without necessarily or automatically altering all aspects of society. As we said in the previous chapter, cities can grow without urbanity, industries can be built without cities, and industrialization can occur in any given national setting with a minimal increase in trained workers. In fact, even the product of industries can be distributed and consumed in the absence of an educated populace: goods and services can be given away through such devices as negative income taxes, guaranteed annual wages, and the dole. The productive system no longer demands a trained mass labor force; it can get along with a few technicians, some skilled workers, and a small troop of unskilled workers. The prime economic reason behind the development of national community is gone; only the political-ethical reasons remain. We are back to the naive political questions of the days before the Industrial Revolution, and we must learn to discard both the euphemisms of self-interested nationalism and the mechanistic social science which supported it. We must ask whether we wish citizenship and national community for *their own sakes,* and whether we want to continue the process of formal education within which the skills of citizenship are patently learned.

The national history of Chile is poignantly appropriate to the theme of this book, for there in September, 1973, the confrontation between particular and general interest became absolute—evidenced in violence, revolution, and a profound change in political organization. For more than a century and a half of national life, Chileans had pursued both the building of a formally democratic society and the creation of a complex class structure supported by commerce, commercial farming, mining and, later, industry. Firmly a part of the Western cultural world and in close and affectionate normative touch with Western Europe, Chilean intellectuals and political figures managed for many years to combine the libertarian, democratic thought of England, France, and the United States with some of the ideas of hierarchy typical of the northern Mediterranean rim. That is, in political terms they managed to reconcile imported elements of the Protestant ethos with their patrimonial heritage of the Catholic ethos. The Protestant ethos is not merely a matter of reverence of work, nor a collection of aphorisms by Benjamin Franklin. In its political sense, it is profoundly secular, establishing a worldly basis for social and political responsibility, as well as for the work ethic. Its emphasis upon the secular here-and-now underlies the Hobbesian nation of the social contract and obedience to the sovereign even in conditions of great (but not limitless) authoritarianism. But it also is the underpinning of the idea of responsible and autonomous individualism and the self-governance of men sufficiently enlightened to order their mundane lives in accord with a natural law equal for all.

The Catholic ethos insists, however, on the seamless joining of the sacred with the secular, and underscores the naturalness of imposed order instead of the naturalness of intellectually inspired, individual, self-ordering. If the Protestant ethos lends itself to the acceptance of secular law as temporarily absolute, it also introduces the idea that violent resistance is legitimate when an individual's natural rights are violated. The Catholic ethos, however, predisposes its adherents to see mundane phenomena as the direct working out of the will of God. States are fatally flawed by an aspiration toward universal representation, for such a task can be accomplished only by subsuming the sacred—a violation of the role of the Church. *Social* particularization, and its accompanying personal privatization, are *necessary* facts of human organization, for the proper universalism can occur only within the realm of the sacred. The ideal-type authoritarianism of the Protestant model is a Nazi-like totalitarianism—the individual standing naked before the all-powerful secular state, bereft of institutional and class protections. The ultimate authoritarianism of the Catholic ethic is corporatism—the ordering of *institutions* (not of individuals) through which hierarchy is manifested and preserved within an organic whole. Conversely, the most open Protestant society approaches ideal anarchy, a *laissez-faire* community of the self-governing. The most open Catholic society is not based on individualism, but rather on the small group, a persuasion increasingly called "communitarianism."

This listing of ultimate situations is not a mere exercise in political theorizing. Rather, it is intended as an introduction to the limits of the actual thinking that has taken place in Chile concerning the good state, and the proper role of education in attaining that state. The focus of this essay into Chilean history of the last century will be formal ideology, the express justifications and hopes of the political men and educational leaders who built the Chilean educational system. These views will be taken here as the rationalized counterparts of the attitudes to which we have given structure in the previous analysis. Our purpose, of course, is to work out through ideology the same creation and perception of conflict that we have seen as the outcome of prolonged participation in the formal educational process.

Like France, Chile is often taken as a historical archetype, even though its colonial period reflects nothing of the grandeur that characterized colonial Peru and Mexico. Instead, the distant and unattractive Captaincy-General that was Chile during the colonial epoch was able to emerge into the day of independence relatively untrammeled by imposing colonial institutions. The approximately half a million persons who lived in Chile's central valley at the turn of the nineteenth century were able to enjoy their isolation in the form of relative freedom to experiment as they wished, secure in the knowledge that they were protected from foreign hostility by desert, sea, and mountain.

Innovation was early attempted in both politics and education. Chile's postindependence time of troubles was rapidly overcome; within a decade, a strong, integrating dictatorship of the Conservatives was established, and a tradition of civilian rule began. Similarly, the educational system was quickly ramified beyond its Hispanic antecedents. Colonial education had its base in the Church or, more specifically, in the reli-

107

gious orders organized in monasteries, convents, and parishes which had as their purpose the training of members of a Christian community. The educational curriculum centered on the teaching of Church doctrine in an atmosphere of strict control of books and other printed matter by the Spanish government acting as the defender of faith and morality. This control persisted until the end of colonialism; indeed, it was not until 1803 that the first printing press was brought to Chile. As a well-known Chilean historian of education has put it, "Since priests or, exceptionally, lay teachers were in charge of training the youth, they thought the primary purpose of their task that of developing a sense of the fear of God and of obedience to that double majesty: the priesthood and the king."[3] There were three types of colonial schools. The primary level was served by *escuelas de primeras letras* (literally, schools of first letters), dedicated only to reading, writing, and speaking.[4] For older children, these same primary schools taught grammar, spelling, writing, arithmetic, and catechism.

The second type of school was the grammar or "Latinity" school which taught Latin and prepared students for higher education. During the first two centuries of the colony, the highest education was provided by convents and seminaries which taught Aristotelian and Thomist philosophy as well as theology, but no other humanities or any sciences.

True university education came in 1757, when the Real Universidad de San Felipe opened its doors. The process of establishment of this university began in 1713, with a declaration of the *cabildo* (town council) of Santiago that ". . . the task of greatest utility in the service of both majesties [Church and state] is the erection of a royal university. . . ."[5] The university's charter was granted in 1738, and nineteen years later instruction began in the philosophy of St. Augustine and St. Thomas, in Justinian and canon law, Latin language and rhetoric, mathematics, and medicine. The program of study was for three years in philosophy, and four in theology, law, and medicine. By the time of its closing by decree in 1839, the university had produced 1,788 graduates, 620 of them in philosophy, 569 in theology, 526 in law, 33 in medicine, and 40 in mathematics.[6] This distribution of graduates makes evident the religious character of the institution, for even the law graduates were trained in canonical and ancient law only, with the public and private law actually used in the colony not a subject of instruction.*

---

*The law of the colony began to be taught only in 1778, with the establishment of the Academy of Laws and Forensic Practice by the attorney general of the Real Audiencia. (See Bascuñán, *op. cit.*, p. 66.)

The colonial era left as an educational heritage a primary school in every parish of the country, a handful of secondary schools, a school for the training of upper-class Chileans (the Conventorio Carolino), an advanced seminary for the training of priests (the Seminario Concilar), and a university oriented to the teaching of medieval theology and ancient philosophy. But in the last years of the colony, there also appeared the ancestor of a long line of schools devoted to commerce and manual skills, the Academia de San Luis, founded by one Manuel de Salas on September 18, 1797. Such schools were evidence of the reactions of Latin America's elites to the mercantilistic Liberalism beginning to affect Western Europe. Salas expressed this view bluntly, seeing his school as a reply to the scholasticism and otherworldliness of the other colonial institutions of higher education. He commented:

The abstract faculties . . . will find their realization in applied faculties, if first one is taught through them to seek, in a practical and progressive order, the useful and solid information of which the human wit is capable. Thus one can correct himself by becoming accustomed to exactitude in reasoning, and in that way one can purge from his spirit the scholasticism and the partisan spirit which, after warping one's judgment, inspire a denseness . . . which is very different from the sincerity and modesty inseparable from those who study only the truth, who habituate themselves to it by searching for it, and base their most sublime discourses on simple and certain principles.[7]

The Chilean independence movement began in 1810 and ended with definitive victory over Spain in 1823. From the beginning, the nascent state's provisional governments evidenced full faith in the critical nature of education, which, when available to all classes, would provide the means to build a new and democratic society, in direct contrast with the archaic Spanish heritage being discarded. The Enlightenment had come to the new nation.

The first major idealistic expression of faith in education came from the Junta de Gobierno, the provisional group running a country whose independence was not yet assured, on June 18, 1813. An earlier educational census had revealed that in the entire city of Santiago there were but 7 functioning primary schools, with a total enrollment of 664 students.[8] The Junta's statute called for the establishment of a primary school in every settlement of more than 50 persons, to be paid for by the townspeople themselves, and required the free distribution of teaching materials. The announced purpose was to provide education for all persons, without regard to sex or social position.[9] The secular faith of the

Enlightenment, however, was still mixed with the faith of Chile's past. All teachers were required to pass an examination in Christian doctrine, as well as present an affidavit from the local administrative authorities testifying to their "patriotism . . . life and habits" (p. 36). The religious and political components of the Junta's reasoning revealed themselves also in the approved list of textbooks included in the regulation; the volumes consisted of two catechisms, a history of religion, and a history of Chile.

The regulation also sought to ensure the proper education of girls, hitherto largely neglected. So, the law required that there "be established in every town a school for women in which will be taught reading and writing and those customs and duties fitting to their sex" (p. 37). The act further provided that women teachers had to follow a life of the highest quality and virtue; they also needed to pass the tests required of all teachers, and to be given the same written testimonials concerning their Christianity and patriotism. It was further stipulated that boys were to be taught by men, and girls by women.

Obviously, these plans could not come to fruition during the life of a revolutionary government beset by military and political problems, and one, moreover, soon to fall into other hands. But the concepts persisted, as did those concerning the reorganization of secondary and university education. The idea of a National Institute which would assume all secondary and university teaching functions was contained within a draft constitution completed in 1813. Article 215 of that draft read:

> There shall be established in the Republic a great National Institute for the sciences, arts, trades, military instruction, religion, functions which may give occupation, vigor, health, and, insofar as they can cultivate the physical and moral character of the citizen. . . . From primary instruction onward there will be found classes for all the sciences and schools useful for reason and the arts; there will be workshops for all trades whose industry may be useful to the Republic. . . .[10]

The Real Universidad de San Felipe, the Colegio Carolino, the Academia de San Luis and the Seminario Concilar were fused to make up the National Institute, which, from 1813 on, took over the teaching functions of those institutions. The rector of the University was given the task of supervising all education, and degrees were granted by the University, even though instruction took place in the Institute. Although the plan to have the Institute provide all instruction from liberal arts to religious, military, and manual training was not to be realized for more than a decade, the intellectual rigidity and thematic poverty of the Spanish educational system was broken. The Institute's original program was built around sixteen "chairs" (*cátedras*, or principal subjects): introductory "letters," Latin, drawing, French, English, philosophy, physics, theology, dogma, sacred scriptures, "eloquence," natural law, the *jus gens* and political economy, civil law, canon and political law, and chemistry." Degrees were given in theology, natural sciences, law, medicine, and surgery.

Experimentalism was not limited only to form or to uncomfortable attempts to link secular rationalism and Christian piety in the minds of the fledgling republic's leaders. During the 1820s, the Chileans engaged in the first of many subsequent attempts to import teaching techniques—in this case, the so-called Lancastrian system. The idea, brought to Chile by one James Thompson, was similar to the self-help methods sometimes used in the colonial period. The best students were required to teach their less advanced fellows, thus effectively increasing the limited supply of trained teachers. Thompson established a school in Santiago as an adjunct to the University of San Felipe to train teachers in the system. The method remained in use for about fifteen years.[12]

But these developments were merely hesitant stirrings. In the absence of a stable political base, a republican educational system could not be established. The temporary postindependence ascendance of Liberals came to an end in 1830, with a Conservative victory that consolidated its power for the next thirty years. Although it is now fashionable to see little difference between Liberals and Conservatives, the Tweedledee-Tweedledum interpretation of party difference was certainly not shared in 19th-century Latin America. In Chile the Conservatives were clericalist, opposed to European secularizing trends, reticent in matters concerning the development of commerce and industry, and in favor of frankly tutelary government. For their part the Liberals favored separation of Church and state, urban development as a product of commercial and industrial development, and openness to European ideas. They were also prone to see politics as a competitive arena open to the participation of all "prepared" citizens. No important class differences split these partisans, for both Liberals and Conservatives came of socially and economically favored groups.[13] Their differences in approach to education will inform almost all of the following discussion.

The preparation of the Constitution of 1833, which was to endure until 1925, signaled the formalization of firm governmental control. The

111

document contained echoes of the ongoing debate about the establishment of an *Estado docente*—literally, a "teaching state," one devoted to the educational improvement of all citizens, an idea borrowed from the Napoleanic example. Educational institutions were to be national, municipal, and private, the latter term then referring almost exclusively to ecclesiastical schools. The Constitution guaranteed the right to be educated, but did not concern itself with the ability to enjoy such a right. The right to teach, however, and to teach given doctrines, was circumscribed by Article 5, which limited dissidence in a document that also established the Catholic Church. The specific constitutional articles concerning education were:[14]

> Article 153. Public education is a preferential activity of the Government. The Congress shall formulate a general plan for national education; and the Minister of the respective office shall report annually on its state throughout the Republic.
>
> Article 154. There shall be a superintendency of public education which shall be charged with the inspection of national education, and of its direction under the authority of the Government.

It is often said that Latin American constitutions mean little, being honored principally in the breach. The stereotype is false in several respects, but particularly as organic law reflects political values. In this case, these two provisions encapsulated an important political controversy that has lasted until this day. The first concerns the meaning of "public education." Does it refer to *all* education of the public, or only to the establishments run directly by the state? Naturally, Conservatives would have it that the Constitution, via the state, regulates only public (as distinct from private) education, while the Liberals argue that the *Estado docente* has the right, in the last analysis, to govern *all* education. The second controversy has to do with the closely allied question of supervision—the meaning of the term, the closeness of supervision, and the agency that is to be entrusted with the task. The controversy remained latent during the period of undisputed Conservative ascendancy, of course, for the incumbents' interpretation of the law was naturally their own. As an example, one of the first acts of the newly arrived Conservatives in 1830 was to decree the establishment of convent schools, especially in those parishes where Church properties taken by the predecessor Liberal governments were restored to ecclesiastical authority,[15] making them economically capable of assuming educational tasks.

112

Whatever the talk, the truth was that the government did very little for state-run primary instruction. It was not until 1836 that the first allocation for education appeared in the national budget, and then it was for only 7,621 pesos.[16] In 1830 there were only 33 primary schools in Santiago, with but 1,724 students.[17] Eleven years later, there were 79 primary schools in Santiago, but only one of them was national and public—the primary grades attached to the National Institute. Eight were municipal, 7 were established in convents, 3 were organized by parishes, and 60 were private; they enrolled a total of about 4,000 students.[18]

A true educational system did not begin to function until the establishment of the University of Chile in 1842. The significance of the University for national education was, simply, that it, and not the Ministry of Education, was charged with supervisory functions. The growth of primary education from the bottom, and of secondary education downward from the universities, was a natural concomitant of this pattern of development, and in Latin America is not restricted to Chile. (The development from each end even more clearly characterizes the history of Argentine education, for example.) During the two presidencies following the establishment of the University (of Manuel Bulnes from 1841 to 1851, and of Manuel Montt from 1851 to 1861), the educational plant expanded enormously. By 1853 there were 571 primary schools (280 public and 281 private) with a total enrollment of 23,156 students, or 1 of every 10 age-eligible children.[19] By 1861 there were 933 primary schools, 598 of them public and 335 private, with 45,219 students, of whome 23,882 were in public and 21,337 in private schools. The balance had tipped in favor of public instruction, and one of every 6.63 potential students was attending at these beginning levels of instruction.[20]

The original statute of the University was drafted by Andrés Bello, one of a long line of intellectuals, foreign and Chilean, who have contributed to that country's ideological culture. Bello, born in Venezuela in 1781, was deeply influenced by the Utilitarianism of Jeremy Bentham and the libertarianism of James Mill, both of whom he knew during his eighteen-year stay in England at the time of the revolutionary period in Latin America. Grammarian, educational theorist, literary figure—a Renaissance man of the post-Enlightenment, so to speak—Bello managed comfortably to work for Spaniards and revolutionaries, Conservatives and Liberals. Knowing his political leaders well, he designed a university closely linked to the executive authority, and in turn exercising potentially close supervision over all teaching in the country. It was

113

not until 1879 that the university itself assumed pedagogical functions; until that time, the Instituto Nacional remained charged with university instruction.

Under Bello's statute, the rector of the university and the deans of the several faculties were appointed by the president of the republic. In addition, all regulations of the institution were issued by the president in his role of *patrono*. Still, the need for educational expertness and for a degree of autonomy was recognized. Montt, in his ministerial report to Congress in 1844, stated:

> Public education should not be abandoned to chance; it is necessary that it should have a purpose and that there be unity in the measures which are adopted to arrive at it. Therefore, there is the need for a common center, from which will come direction and impulse, and in which may be prepared and elaborated the improvements which will accelerate the advances of one of the most important branches of the administration. Up to this time the Government has been this center, but in no way is it proper to submit the advance of education to the instability of a Minister, nor condemn it, to a certain point, to political oscillations.[21]

The tension among political authority, academic freedom, and university autonomy was clearly felt at this time, just as it was also common to worry the matter of equality and the role of education in securing it. Bello made many an eloquent statement in definition of his idea of political equality and the way in which it could be reconciled to inherent social difference. The following comment summarizes his views:

> The distinctive character of man is his susceptibility of improvement. Education, which enriches his mind with ideas, and adorns his heart with virtues, is an efficient means to promote his progress. . . . But not all men are to have equal education, for each has his own way of contributing to the common felicity. Whatever be the equality which political institutions establish, there is nevertheless in all people an inequality—we shall not say a hierarchy (which cannot exist among republicans, especially in their share in public rights)—but an inequality of condition, of needs, of mode of life. To these differences, education must adjust itself. . . . In a matter of such vital importance, government cannot be too careful. To develop public establishments meant for a limited portion of the people is not to develop education, for it is not enough to turn out men skilled in the learned professions; it is necessary to form useful citizens, it is necessary to improve society; and this cannot be done without opening the path to advancement to the most numerous part of the public.[22]

114

Like the English thinkers with whom he is so closely identified, Bello saw education as helping *individual* men. His support of the equality of citizens did not concern itself with structural inequality, the effects of race and class on social standing, but rather with universalizing education in ways that could adjust equal availability to unequal talent and differing desires. The issue is, of course, part of the problem besetting all societies characterized by the coexistence of class and democratic political aspiration. Whatever the depth of attachment to egalitarian republican principle, however, Bello and his associates lived in a society comprised of a thin upper-class coating, a slightly thicker layer of new middles, and a heavy mass on the bottom. The elite had to act in a tutelary fashion; there was no escape. And, for them, the University of Chile was the instrument for bringing into existence a universal educational system while answering the needs of their own children.

The nonteaching University of Chile was organized into five colleges, or *facultades:* Philosophy and Humanities, Mathematical and Physical Sciences, Medicine, Law and Political Science, and Theology. Each was comprised of 30 members, initially chosen by the government, but thereafter self-selecting. Each faculty supervised its respective disciplines. Faculty members were to comprise a corps of learned men studying problems of their specializations. The Faculty of Philosophy and Humanities was given responsibility for supervising primary education, "proposing to the Government the rules it may judge most fitting for the organization [of the primary schools] and taking charge of . . . the books to be used in them . . . and inspecting the primary schools of the capital and the provinces." [23]

Both the *bachiller* (the degree given at the end of secondary school, the *liceo*) and the *licenciatura* (the highest university degree of the time) were awarded by the university on the basis of examinations made up by the appropriate faculties. Professionalization was furthered by the stipulation that no one could be appointed either to the National Institute or to positions in the provincial *liceos* without holding a *licenciatura*.

If the university was to provide teachers for secondary and higher educational levels, the primary schools needed their own teacher-training school—yet another reflection of the bifurcation of the two subsystems referred to earlier. The need was recognized by Manuel Montt in his message to Congress of 1841, when he referred to disorder in the primary schools, and to teachers and persons of ill fortune who look to teaching as "a means of subsistence, when they feel themselves without aptitude to earn their living in any other way." [24] The decree of January

During this whole period (1842–1872) the University has had very little or no direct influence on the arrangements for primary instruction. Already in his report of 1850, Rector Andrés Bello pointed out that the Faculty of Humanities, in whose care the relevant organic law principally placed this level of education, lacked means to extend instruction and supervision beyond Santiago.[29]

An attempt through a decree of 1854 was made to tie the University more closely to provincial establishments by the creation of provincial educational councils (*Juntas Provinciales de Educación*) but, comments Domeyko, "rare has been the Junta which from the first years of its establishment sent periodic reports to the [University] Council." An anomalous situation then developed: a lack of supervision became combined with an extreme centralization of formal measures of control, leading to delays, the complexities of red tape, and a slowing-down of change. The university concerned itself with the choice of textbooks and curricula, while personnel matters, the location of schools, and budgets were the grist of the ministry. Abdón Cifuentes, a leading educational figure of the time, argued that Chile was still caught in the colonial mentality—"the eternal red tape and the centralized and hierarchical order of the Spanish colony still oppress us"—and in his memoirs he offered the following example:

It was managed that the Government should establish a school in a coastal village of the department of Petorca, called Los Condores. Six months were spent in renting a miserable location for the school, waiting on the reports of the Inspector and the Governor. At last the teacher opened the school, but as there were no benches or furnishings of any other kind in it, the students sat on the floor and the teacher limited herself to the verbal teaching of reading and the catechism from books of her own, and for writing she substituted for the blackboard a plank on which she wrote the letters in charcoal. The teacher complained to the Inspector, when the latter in his roamings through that extensive and mountainous province managed to pass through that isolated village. The Inspector informed the Governor, he transcribed the report for the Intendant, the latter sent it on to the Inspector General and he to the Minister who, in his infinite attention to that office in all matters of public law, forgot about the affair. . . .[30]

To correct this situation, a relatively ineffective act to reform primary education was passed in 1860. It is of interest here because of its statement of aspirations, and also because its class bias shines through clearly. Schools were to be provided at government expense (national and municipal) throughout the country; two primary schools, one for boys and one for girls, were to be set up for each 2,000 inhabitants. In addition, a secondary school was to be established in each department. The qualifications of teachers were also listed in the act, with requirements concerning character and morality that were little changed from those of the first days of the republic. Most important, the act reaffirmed the Conservative meaning of freedom of instruction. Article 11 reads, "Schools paid for by private persons or through emoluments paid by students will be subject to the inspection established by the present law insofar as the morality and order of the establishment are concerned, but not with reference to the instruction therein provided nor the methods employed." [31] One might interpret the law as stating that freedom of choice regarding programs and methods was a privilege open to the favored and not to lower-class groups. Most private schools were, of course, controlled by religious groups, as they had been since the first years of the republic. In addition, the 1860 act stipulated that convents had to continue to provide free education, considered as being public and not private, and hence under state control. Liberals centered their opposition to the act on this point, arguing that the device was merely a way to deliver what should be a state function into the hands of the clergy.*

Whatever the quality of education, a major quantitative expansion occurred. By 1860 there were 625 public primary schools in Chile, as contrasted with 216 in 1852. Total student enrollment was almost 30,000 in 1860, about three times as large as eight years earlier. About 30 per cent of the students in 1860 were girls. In 1861 there were 316 private primary schools, 176 for boys and 140 for girls.[32] This increase almost certainly reflected the beginning of school attendance by persons of lower-class origins, but only in the cities. We found no way to document this statement, basing it on the knowledge that few rural primary schools were actually established, and that an increase in public school attendance of this magnitude could have come only from the increased attendance of less favored students. Then as now, the private schools continued to cater to the children of the privileged.

The class bias of Chilean education of the time reveals itself even more poignantly on the secondary level, an antechamber to higher edu-

---

*The device has been very persistent in Chilean history, the twentieth-century version being the so-called *escuelas primarias gratuitas,* "free primary schools," which are subsidized by the government but operated by religious orders and parishes.

cation open to very few. In 1830 there were ten secondary schools in Santiago, but only three had relatively full curricular offerings—the National Institute itself, the Liceo de Chile, which catered to the children of Liberal parents, and the Colegio de Santiago, directed by Andrés Bello and partial to the progeny of Conservatives. The student total in that year was 772, of whom 486 attended the National Institute, 83 the Liceo de Chile, and 113 the Colegio de Santiago.[33] Public secondary schools also had been established earlier in the towns of La Serena and Concepción; Talca's school opened its doors in 1831, followed by Coquimbo (1834), Cauquenes (1837), and San Felipe (1838). By 1849 the country could boast of ten public secondary schools, including the National Institute. Eight more were established between 1851 and the secondary education act of 1879.[34]

The employment of the difference between primary and secondary education to reinforce class distinctions was a conscious decision. Ignacio Domeyko was one of the principal *pensadores* of the Conservative persuasion. He proposed, for example, that only the children of the governing class be permitted to enter secondary and higher education, although the lower class should be provided with primary schools spread throughout the country. He was in favor of the constitutional provision holding literacy a prerequisite for voting, and argued that certain occupations should be reserved only for those holding secondary-school diplomas. What might be called an "enlightened Conservative," or certainly a Conservative in favor of enlightenment. Domeyko, the son of a Polish nobleman, had fled his country after participating in an unsuccessful revolt in 1830. He went to Paris, where he was educated in the sciences, particularly in chemistry and geology. In 1837 he contracted to teach in the newly opened *liceo* of Coquimbo, and afterwards wrote extensively on the reform of secondary and university schooling. He later was appointed to posts in the National Institute and became rector of the University of Chile. His idea of enlightenment was to spread learning to all classes, although in varying degrees and kinds, for the purpose of education was not to alter the framework of society, but rather to preserve the moral order within a strictly controlled pattern of development.

> Whatever the system which the government adopts to promote public instruction [he wrote], it seems to me that the principal purpose of its endeavors should not be to equal other nations or to surpass them in civilization, nor to spread among the population the lucrative professions that tend to increase their welfare. I think that public education, free of all national vanity and

material purposes, should before everything else take into consideration the moral good of the country, the stability of order and institutions, the formation of the national character and the progressive development of the most noble inclinations of the inhabitants. Only learning can let men know that, beyond natural rights, they also have social obligations which are arranged and determined by the form of the institutions themselves. In this way respect for and submission to laws are introduced, without organizing a spirit of slavery; and man will enjoy his inner liberty, he will know how to aspire to every national freedom without warping existing relations or changing the reality of the world in conformity with utopias. In a word, the true perfection to which a people should aspire through its public education consists in submission to order and law *through conviction,* in a love for humanity on the part of the rich as well as a feeling for the true dignity of human nature, and in the right use of reason by all classes.[35]

It is fair to say that Domeyko was typical of the then leaders of Chile. The de-emphasis on professional training, especially for privileged children, and an emphasis on "right reason" and social stasis have remained part of the thematica of Latin American conservative groups. Naturally, students, according to their Conservative critics, held other ideas; they wanted occupational advancement, and they remained concerned with the material aspects of life. Conversely, students complained then, as they do now, that their professors were without imgaination. Cifuentes had this to say of another distinguished Chilean educator:

I had the fortune of doing almost all my studies of humanities . . . with the most distinguished of the professors of the Institute, Miguel Luis Amunátegui. An intelligence clarified by vast learning, a heart of gold, a most generous character. . . . Unhappily, great science is neither enough nor is necessary to make a good professor. . . .

I studied world history with Mr. Amunátegui, from ancient to Chilean history. How? The class was called to order, the attendance list was passed, Mr. Amunátegui then walked about the classroom and said, "John, read the lesson." The student recited from memory or abstracted the chapter of the text which had been assigned for the lesson, and when he was finished the professor would say, "Next, James," and thus in succession until the hour was used up and, when the bell rang, he added, "Bring the next chapter for tomorrow." That eternal and monotonous recitation which incited the students to distract themselves in some way was interrupted only by the justified scoldings provoked by lapses from science and order of the children.[36]

Whatever the disagreements, the effective demand for education continued to increase. At the start of 1871, the National Institute had 1,162 students, and about 3,000 were in secondary schools in Santiago alone. The year before, 73,926 students were enrolled in primary schools throughout the republic.[37] One of the latter, the School of Arts and Crafts, was opened in Santigo in 1849 to provide "trained, hardworking, and honest artisans, who through their example and skills may contribute to the improvement of industry in Chile and the reform of our working classes." [38] Initially, the school provided all instruction and living costs to the students, as well as housing. But in 1878 various kinds of part-scholarships granting partial maintenance were introduced. The school itself was never well funded, and of course did little to better the conditions of more than a few individuals.

A much more important reform adopted in this period (in 1865, specifically), was a change in Article 5 of the Constitution, which in its original form established the Roman Catholic Church and prohibited the practice of other religions. The change permitted the observance of other religious "inside edifices of private property" and, most importantly, also permitted "dissidents to establish and maintain private schools for the teaching of their own children in the doctrine of their religions." [39] Federico Errázuriz, then Minister of Justice, Religion, and Public Education, and later to be the president of the republic around whom the Conservative-Liberal educational conflict was to break open, presented the official viewpoint in the Senate concerning the amendment:

Once the freedom of dissident cults to be observed in edifices of private property is recognized, what can be raised to oppose those same dissidents the right to educate their children in the religion they profess? Nothing.

Intolerance would be manifest if we were not to recognize that power indubitably guaranteed by our laws.

The civil code guarantees to the Protestant parent the right of educating his children in his religion, and in practice the facts are as in the case of Article 1 [of the proposed constitutional amendment]. . . .

. . . dissidents have had in fact complete liberty to establish and direct schools for their children.[40]

Even though this constitutional change may merely have reflected established practice, as Errázuriz avers, the formal amendment of the constitution in this respect is evidence of the adjustments and compromises taking place throughout this period. Indeed, compromise has been a valued art in Chilean politics, as the adjustments of Liberals to Conservatives throughout this period demonstrate. It must be granted, of course, that in educational matters neither side took steps likely to change the class order or other structural characteristics of Chilean life. But embattled partisans in other Latin American countries came to *golpes* over lesser issues. The test of flexibility and pragmatism was yet to come, for up to this time we have recounted an essentially Conservative approach to education. In the last thirty years of the nineteenth century, the Liberals began to move into ascendance, and so the next phase of this historical study must concern a shifting of weight.

The issue was finally joined in 1872. The previous year Errázuriz had been elected to the presidency as the candidate of a Conservative-Liberal coalition. The two kinds of political rightists had ratified their earlier interaction with a formal association, holding off the party of the new middle groups, the Radicals—ideologically related to the French Radical Socialists, bourgeois, secularist, merchant-oriented. As is usual in such coalitions, the Ministry of Justice, Religion, and Public Instruction was given to a Conservative, Abdón Cifuentes. Cifuentes saw the prerogatives of the public system as a "monopoly" destructive of "freedom of instruction." The obvious point of attack was on the requirement that the Instituto Nacional and other public bodies administer the qualifying examinations for all schools. On January 15, 1872, Cifuentes decreed the abolition of the examination rights of the state system and declared that private schools were free to adopt the study plans, methods, and texts of their choice—a right always granted them, but limited in practice because of the requirement that their students pass the state examinations.[41] In defending this decree before Congress later in the year, Cifuentes argued that the burden of applying the examinations was eating up valuable professorial time and that the maintenance of a state educational monopoly was untenable in a free society. To wit:

That the professors of the State should be judges of the studies carried out in the state schools is entirely natural; but that they should be judges, and absolute and irresponsible judges of the pupils, texts, methods, systems, in a word of the teaching in general of the free establishments, is a system in which neither liberty . . . nor competence is at all possible, but only monopoly, dependence, and servility.

If such a system would be unacceptable in industry and all other spheres of human activity, it is much more so in teaching, for education is of the most noble and elevated, it is the moral and intellectual education of youth, and

123

therefore it profoundly affects the freedom of conscience, the freedom of the family, and the natural and civil liberties of man.

Therefore the freedom of education in a republic such as ours is at once a natural right, the primitive and inviolable right of parents; a political right, the logical consequence and indispensable complement of the other public freedoms; a literary right corresponding to the freedom of intelligence and of letters. To monopolize, thus, directly or indirectly in the hands of the State, to attribute to [the State] the supervision [of education] . . . is at the same time to oppress reason and the conscience of the citizens. . . .[42]

The issue had now reached full bloom. The Cifuentes statement refers to the family, religion, education, the economy, and the proper relations among them *as a matter of politics and natural right*. The argument of this Conservative is that the state should *not* be a universalizing agency. The ultimate and inviolable rights refer to the family and to "conscience." The state, like the economy, must be encapsulated, and made to compete like any other secular agency in a proper marketplace. As for education, let it also be instrumental, and thus a mosaic, serving the more profound natural needs of individuals. Clearly, such a profound challenge to secular nationalists could not pass uncontested. The growing storm of protest centered on Barros Arana, then Rector of the National Institute, and Miguel Luis Amunátegui, Secretary General of the University of Chile and a Liberal Deputy on the one hand, and Cifuentes and his followers on the other. The abolition by Cifuentes of Barros' post was the incident triggering the forging of the secularist opposition, for that move was a direct attack on university autonomy in the name of freedom of instruction.[43]

The decentralized examination system led to the opening of diploma mills and other irregularities, producing scandals and threatening the integrity of degrees earned in standard institutions. Coinciding with heated congressional debates concerning the deposal of Barros Arana, it produced a governmental crisis. Feeling abandoned by some of his most powerful colleagues, Cifuentes resigned, followed by the resignation of all Conservatives from the cabinet. The government reconstituted itself as a basically Liberal-Radical alliance, with the former clearly dominant; a new education minister was named, and less than two years after its imposition, the offending decree was repealed. Once again, private schools were subject to examination by national educational bodies.[44]

The decision was a vote of confidence in secularism and the nation-state, but taken in such a way as to permit continued private education

124

within what had been effectively broad limits of tolerance. Obviously, the postulations of Cifuentes and his associates took little account of the existing social order and the possible role of education in promoting equality, while the opposition emphasized education's putative part in achieving a just society. Máximo Lira, a Conservative deputy, put the particularistic case in crystal-clear terms:

It is certain that children are minors who should be subject to tutelage. But who should be the tutor, the State or the head of the family? Doubtlessly, the latter. The head of the family should be free to give to his child the education he thinks fitting; but that freedom cannot exist without another correlative one: that in which each may offer freely his teaching to the heads of families. . . .

It may be objected that the State does not impede the establishment of private schools which can offer parents an education distinct from that given by the State. But that objection is no more than a sophism, because those schools are not free to provide the education they think best. Since it is the State which grants degrees, and since the students in private schools must submit themselves to the decisions of the State professors, liberty disappears and what remains . . . is the regimentation of intelligences, what remains . . . is the omnipotent infallibility of the State which admits of no learned men other than those cast in official molds.[45]

The Liberal response is best summed up in the reactions of Amunátegui. He did not propose the state as the only teacher; rather, he argued the centrality of the government's role in maximizing the educational level of the population, in imposing education upon those who did not see its purpose, and in responding to self-correction flowing from an enlightened and free citizenry, untrammeled by religious beliefs concerning secular affairs. The Conservative position being preoccupied with religious dogma and not social utility, Amunátegui maintained, at best subordinated, but usually ignored, the question of equal opportunity. At its worst, Conservative doctrine viewed an ordered society as good in itself and beneficial to the lower orders by proposing to keep them in their "proper" place. Amunátegui, using the United States as example, argued as follows:

The best organization of public education which has been established thus far is that which educates in common or together, under the direction and inspection of the [public authority], all students without distinctions concerning the social classes to which their families belong, or concerning the pecuniary fortunes they may enjoy.

That is the organization of education which reigns in the United States of America, where it produces the most advantageous results.

Adopting that system, the education of the poor is paid for at the same expense as for the rich, but without imposing on the former any humiliation, since the funds used for maintaining the schools and colleges are taken not from a private tuition which is collected from each student for his admission to the establishment, but from a special tax, or from the general taxation.

Thus the school ceases to be a kind of hospice in which poor children are given education as though receiving alms, as in other types of charity one gives housing and food to beggars. . . .

As can be seen, a system of that type, in which each person is treated only as befits his personal merit, is the most appropriate preparation that one can imagine for republican life. . . .[46]

Continuing the attack, Amunátegui charged Cifuentes with fearing only that the state would impose doctrinal uniformity, when what he should most fear is "the slumber of that ignorance from which nobody can awaken."[47] But, as a convinced Liberal, Amunátegui had also to shun the authoritarian imposition of dogma. He took refuge, with ideological consistency, in his belief in democratic principles. "The [governmental] authority is impotent to impose doctrines and systems, especially in modern times, especially in democratic and republican nations, in which there is open, constant and general discussion of all matters, whatever they may be."[48]

Amunátegui also addressed himself to the distinction between mundane and secular beliefs and teaching, and to the difference between scientific and normative subjects of study. "There is no known Catholic arithmetic, algebra, or geometry, nor a rationalist arithmetic, algebra, and geometry. . . . I confess that history and philosophy have to deal with religious, philosophical, and political doctrines; but, in line with the method put into practice to teach those subjects, it would be very difficult for a professor to impose [his] beliefs. . . ." The reasons, he went on, are various. First, no teacher of history or philosophy can hide the "facts," and must permit discussion with the students. And second, Amunátegui makes common cause with the Positivist thought that was later to come to full flower. "According to modern methods, teaching tends only to make known the general and positive results of science and to exercise the reason of young people to give them the ability to judge doctrines and fact for themselves."

126

With regard to the highly sensitive questions of religion and the family, Amunátegui also took clearly secularist and national positions. He denied the universality of religious belief: "Religious doctrines are learned in a catechism and not in a grammar or chemistry text. Let us not complicate questions of mundane education with others which do not and should not have anything to do with them." As for the family, he was as plain spoken: "The right of the head of a family appears to me highly respectable, sacred if you wish; but not absolute. The child is not a stick in the hands of his father."

The rationalist faith of Amunátegui and his ideological allies can be summed up in the following epistolary comment: ". . . learning, especially that which is based on discussion and experimentation, is as impotent to enslave minds as it is most powerful in stimulating them to research and reflection."[49]

The result of the controversy, in political terms, was a Liberal victory they chose to share. The primacy of the state system to guide all education was established; the right of private schools to exist was reaffirmed. Religion would be taught in public and those private schools which wished to do so, but students could ask for exemptions from religious training, which could not bar them from entrance into higher levels of education. The result, in ideological terms, was a clear victory for secularist, nationalist views, plus a pragmatic compromise with organized religious groups in a pluralist vein. The toleration which the Conservative believer had hesitated to concede to his opponent was extended to him, often with little more than pro forma requirements for compliance with state-originated educational plans and common examinations. From a social structural point of view, however, little changed immediately. Primary schools in rural areas were still rare, secondary schools nonexistent. Poor children had no effective means of attending school, even when physical access was possible. Primary education was still not obligatory, and was not to be made even legally so until 1920.

Change at the secondary and university levels followed behind the primary school changes with much less fanfare. On January 13, 1879, free education at the advanced levels was provided for. Again, public agencies granted degrees, set standards, and applied qualifying examinations. Further, *libertad de enseñanza* was also guaranteed at this level, permitting private institutions to function as before. In addition to establishing definitively the principle of free university education, the act also extended an important measure of autonomy to the University of Chile and, ostensibly, to any other public institutions which followed it into existence. The rector, secretary general, and the several deans of the university were made public officials whose removal by the executive from office required the approval of the Senate. Instead of being appointed by the President of the Republic, the rector was elected by an assembly of the university comprised of the professional personnel of the faculties. Importantly, the law also established *libertad de cátedra,* or academic freedom within the classroom. As the law stated it, "the moral dignity of the professor [and] . . . his intellectual liberty, indispensable for the satisfactory exercise of any activity of a scientific nature [were secured]."[50]

Within a decade of the passage of this law, the clericalists organized their own university, taking advantage of the doctrine of freedom of instruction. On April 1, 1889, the Catholic University of Santiago opened its doors, with 50 students in attendance, divided into the faculties of law and mathematics. The growth of the university was slow; only 184 students were enrolled in 1894. The Institute of Humanities was founded in the Católica in 1900, and in 1905 special courses for skilled workers were instituted, testifying both to the slow expansion of the academic core of the institution and to a paternalistic approach to blue-collar workers that lingers to this day. In fact, however, the new university was to be an institution for training of the elite in both fact and ideological conviction. Cifuentes, in a speech made at the inaugural ceremonies for the new university, bluntly justified not making of the Catholic University a means for social mobility:

> The children of working people who acquire some literary culture raise themselves to a sphere very superior to the humble one in which they were born, they despise the professions of their fathers, despise their fathers themselves and pretend to a mastery which would not be at all bad if, on the contrary, it would cultivate their sense of dignity . . . if it would not push them to laziness and to vegetate in shady and routine occupations, most of the time contrary to the happy dispositions given to them by nature.[51]

While these pathetic stereotypes—and, it might be added, such common ones across the boundaries of cultures—were the comfort of the Conservatives as they established their new university, the Liberals and Radicals were engaged in importing the latest intellectual vogue from Europe—Positivism as applied directly to the theory of educational practice. The views of Comte and his followers had already come to Chile, of course. But now came application, to be implemented directly not by the importation of ideas, but by teams of practitioners themselves. Thompson, Bello, Sarmiento, Domeyko and many others whom

128

we have not mentioned were distinguished foreigners who contributed importantly to Chilean political, intellectual, and educational development. Now it was the time of the Germans, first to reform the primary teacher training schools but immediately thereafter, and with much more significance for all Chilean education, to work in the newly formed Pedagogical Institute of the University of Chile.

On October 11, 1883, an act was passed in the Chilean Congress authorizing the President to build new primary schools, and to contract teachers abroad to instruct in the Chilean normal schools, as well as send Chilean teachers overseas for advanced studies. One of the first actions taken under this act was the contracting of a group of German professors from the Royal Teachers' Seminary in Dresden to reform the program of the primary teachers' schools. In the meantime, continued attempts were made to organize a teachers' college at the university level for secondary school personnel. Finally, under the reformist presidency of Juan Manuel de Balmaceda, the *Instituto Pedagógico* of the University of Chile opened its doors in 1889, graduating its first meager class of 29 students in 1892.[52]

The design for the Institute was taken from projects prepared by Valentín Letelier, Chile's last famed nineteenth-century educator, and at the time of the Institute's founding a member of the Chilean diplomatic mission to Berlin. While the pedagogical thought guiding the Institute was to be German in orientation, the formal curriculum was modeled after that of the Normal School of Paris.[53] Letelier argued that professional teacher-training was coming so late to Chile because of the earlier dominance of the Catholic Church, and because a universal ignorance of teaching principles made education everywhere a mechanical and routine process. He so persuaded himself of the virtues of teaching technique that he became, in effect, a didactic technocrat. For example, he stated flatly that the best test of a teacher's capability is "not his knowledge, but his didactics. Very often great scholars have failed in teaching because of a lack of pedagogical preparation and it is simple enough for the most renowed literary figure to make himself ridiculous giving the first lesson in rhetoric."[54]

Letelier pushed through his Pedagogical Institute under the proper president. Balmaceda, who committed suicide in 1891 when confronted with revolt from the right and the threatened loss of his program, was an activist Liberal firmly committed to that part of his party's program that had to do with secular nation-building. Addressing a party convention in 1886, he had this to say about the role of education:

Instruction is the law of the spirit and morality applied with discernment to the actions of men. It constitutes the surest foundation of individual rights and the most serious guarantee of general prosperity. Intellectual influence, the advances of the century, experience, and political foresight all single out the field of public education as the cardinal point at which Chilean liberalism will have to prove its intelligence, the superiority of its doctrine, and its positive attachment to the interests of the people.[55]

Balmaceda was expressing a profound ideological division in liberalism, and at the same time taking his side. That is, liberal thought has attempted to encompass two divergent streams of thought—secularism, equality, and nation-building on the one hand, and a *laissez faire*, self-adjusting political economics of the happy mean on the other. This period in Chilean history—from 1888 to 1891—witnessed the unfolding of this ideological schizophrenia, and determined whether liberalism was to be defined as right-wing (as eventually happened throughout Latin America) or as moderately left-wing (as occurred in the United States). Naturally, those liberals—among them Letelier and Balmaceda—who opted for directed reformism incurred the charge of authoritarianism from the liberal opposition wedded to the notion of rational self-guidance within the marketplace of ideas as well as of goods and services. In his *La lucha por la cultura,* Letelier tackled head-on the charge that he was authoritarian:

When we judge it to be necessary, let us make education compulsory, or vaccination, savings, or insurance; let us forbid the employment of children who have not finished their schooling; let us fix the hours of labor, with no considerations in mind other than those of science and hygiene; let us regulate prostitution, intoxication, examinations, degrees, professions . . . let us make the authority of the State prevail over that of the Church; and let us not worry if they call us authoritarians, provided we are by these means giving man more power, making him more master of himself, and endowing him with greater vigor, originality, and independence of mind.

Above all, let the label of authoritarians not bother us so long as the freedom to think, to speak, to write, to read, the freedom of worship, of public meetings, of printing, of teaching, of movement, in short all the liberties that man needs to develop his capacities and society to develop its culture find in us the surest guarantee of their existence.

Let us be men of science and, as such, remember that the aim of government is not liberty, nor yet authority, nor any abstract principle whatsoever, but to satisfy social needs in order to arrive at the perfection of man and the development of society.[56]

Perhaps the most-quoted phrase from Letelier's writing is his argument that "To govern is to educate, and every good political system is a true educational system, just as every general educational system is a true political system." What should be taught is positive knowledge; and such knowledge—scientific truth—is necessarily the same for all men. Hence, the greatest danger to social stability and progress is not ignorance, but diversity of fundamental beliefs, and so ". . . the social purpose of education is . . . the convergence of all hearts on the same proposition and of all understandings on the same faith, with the deliberate intent of producing the harmonious development of all of society's active elements."[57]

Uniformity of doctrine was the ideal, the state was the vehicle for its achievement, and all other institutions were to be subordinated to the state as vehicles of socialization. Modernization was the drive toward brotherhood, whose principal barrier was the existence of parochial doctrines dividing men within political units and in the international arena. Parents legitimately teach children domestic matters and generally initiate them into life. But, beyond that point, *systematic* education must certainly not be left to parents, "the great majority of whom" are "ignorant people as lacking in culture as in letters," so that it would be absured to grant them the right either to educate their children systematically or to allow them to choose the education they favor.[58] Similarly the Church should be barred from formal education, for it is the exemplar of the particularism and the factionalism Letelier found so odious. Thus, in his view, *libertad de enseñanza* took on a new meaning: it was not the right of private groups to establish schools that might dissent from official views, but rather the right of men to make science emerge from the restrictions of religion. "Understood in this way . . . the freedom of education arises everywhere as an indispensable corollary to the freedoms of research and of thought and it has been able to establish itself only at the expense of traditional beliefs, thanks to the continued efforts of the secular spirit, personified by the liberal parties."[59]

Letelier saw his belief in the universality of science, and the corollary desirability of a shared basis of social belief, as promoting the democratic spirit by contributing to the disintegration of ascription and an end to the differences among classes. Letelier, as a latter-day rationalist, assumed that all minds are capable of reasoning, that the form of reason is always the same, and, thus, that all minds are essentially equal. Bringing out this kind of equality was the primary task of education.

We should convince ourselves that in general discrepancies at the intellectual level are so minimal that in practice . . . we can proceed as though in reality they did not exist, as though all intelligences were by nature equal. The greatest elevation, the greatest clarity of perception . . . that some minds reveal does not . . . ordinarily stem from their having been favored with exceptional and privileged natural gifts, but rather because they have observed more and possess more science and philosophy than most. Therefore, to raise the intellectual level of . . . our republics we should not wait for geniuses spontaneously to arise, but rather we should introduce our youth to the sciences which may dignify them and which will nourish their spirits with general conceptions and fire their hearts with the sacred love of country and of humanity.[60]

Thus Letelier naturally reached out to European positivists to build the new *Instituto Pedagógico*; the German teams imported were infused with the didactic theories of J. F. Herbart, who drew his ideas from the Kantian interpretation of Plato's analysis of perceptions. Herbart felt that by means of metaphysical reasoning one could bridge the gap between the phenomenal and the nominal, pass from the perception of shadows to the perception of reality. Translating his philosophy into didactics, Herbart declared that the mind was an empty space at birth, and that all experience served to form images that fill the vacuum. Hence, to teach well was to provide representations which would form true and logical images, or scientifically based ones.[61] The interrelation of representations was seen as mutually reinforcing. Herbart, thus, counseled the use of study plans that concentrated related matters within the same time period. He argued that, above all, the teacher "must be concerned with . . . the way in which the *circle of ideas* is established in his pupil, for from them are born sentiments, and from those, the principles and means of working."[62] From this premise came course programs called "concentric programs." These ideas, and many others, became articles of faith in Chilean educational theory, and served to orient concepts and teaching practices for the next fifty years.

As the end of the century approached, the grand ideological thinking in Chile about education has been done. These ideologies are like the attitudes we have studied; their relationship to deeds is subtle and varied. The quantitative educational job alone that needed to be accomplished remained huge. In 1865 some 83 per cent of the country's population was illiterate. The figure had fallen to 68 per cent by 1895, and it was not to drop below 50 per cent until 1920.[63] In 1865 only 11 per cent of the school-age population was enrolled in primary schools, while in 1895 the figure had gone to 28 per cent. In the former year, 70 per cent were enrolled in public primary schools, the remainder in the private schools. The numbers for 1895 are 80 per cent and 20 per cent, respectively. It is clear that by the end of the century the educational system had begun to touch persons from the least-favored groups, had begun the job of social integration postulated for education by both Liberals and Radicals. For many years thereafter, the problem was not one of ideas but rather of will, means, and the building of capacity. But grand politics, on which education partially depends—but only partially, it should be noted—became uncertain.

With the revolution of 1891, the Chilean government fell into the hands of the so-called Oligarchy, an alliance of rightist Liberals and Conservatives openly protective of the upper class. A "parliamentary" regime was instituted, based on a strong congress that could repel the moves of any president of such reformist persuasion as was Balmaceda. This regime lasted until 1920, when an electoral coalition of Radicals and progressive Liberals took the presidency in the name of strengthening democracy and participation, economic development, secularism, and an expansion of social services. The classical themes were still there, as was the classical opposition. Stubborn congressional resistance hamstrung executive action, as it was meant to do, leading to military interventions, the first overt military moves in Chile's political history since the early days of the republic with its unprofessional military forces. Three years of political uncertainty culminated in 1927 with the military coup of Carlos Ibáñez del Campo, uncertainly pursuing the then current corporatist ideologies, given the appeal for many rightists of the works of Salazar in Portugal, Primo de Rivera in Spain, Mussolini in Italy, and Austrian corporatism with its close links to the Church. But the traditions of Chilean formal democracy were too strong, and with the added impact of the economic crisis of 1929, Ibáñez was forced to resign and, after a year of interim governments and confusion, standard electoral processes returned a Liberal-Conservative coalition to office, headed by Arturo Alessandri, the same man who in 1920 had led the Radical-Liberal coalition to victory.

Whatever the vagaries of politics, the educational institution had taken on something of a life of its own. Obviously, no Chilean government of the time was totalitarian; there was slippage, even within the official institutional family. Thus, through the period of the oligarchy slow extensions of the system continued, generally led in the public sector by persons devoted to center-left politics. Literacy and primary educational statistics most clearly reveal this quasi-independence, inferential as they are of the slowly growing incorporation of poor persons into the society's structure of opportunity. A contemporary Chilean sociologist of education categorizes the historical steps of primary education as follows:

. . . one can distinguish . . . at least three characteristic *moments* relative to the fluctuations in the rate of illiteracy since 1865.

The first *moment* comprises the period 1865–1920 and is characterized by a slow but permanent decrease in the rate of illiteracy from 83 per cent to 49.7 per cent, with a mean annual rate of decrease of a little over 0.5 per cent.

The second *moment*–the most exemplary of our history—extends from 1920 to 1930 (to be exact from 1920 to 1928) and it is the period in which there occurs the most important cultural leap in the transformation of our population from an illiterate to a literate one. The percentage of illiterates in Chile's population dropped abruptly from 49.7 per cent in 1920 to 25.6 per cent in 1930.

The third *moment* is of relative stagnation. The rate of illiteracy *climbed* in 1940 to 27.3 per cent—a fact . . . without precedent in our history—only to drop to 19.8 per cent in 1952. Taking the beginning of the period—1930—we observe that the rate of illiteracy decreased only by 5.8 points in 22 years, that is to say, it underwent an annual decrease of 0.26 per cent, the lowest of our history.

While the exact statistics are in dispute among scholars, the general trend is clear and unquestioningly accepted. The upsurge in the 1920s reflected the legal imposition of obligatory primary education, but it also was a reaction to strong governmental interest in educational promotion. Programmatic and technical innovation, however, was minimal, the efforts made being contained within the frames of pre-existing doctrine and practice. The new constitution of 1925 in its educational provisions, for example, reaffirmed the state's obligation to make educational institutions broadly available, repeated previous statutory requirements for obligatory schooling, and once again guaranteed the right of private schools to exist. The conservative understanding of the doctrine of *libertad de enseñanza* was reinforced in this period with the granting of subsidies to private schools and the similar legitimation of the Catholic University. The Ibáñez period was one of tinkering with the educational structure, since schools are always a preoccupation of authoritarian governments. A commentator has noted of this time:

. . . the educational services were those which underwent the greatest modifications in the period between 1924 and 1932. While other ministries and public services preserved their traditional lines [education] was shaken to its foundations. Decree-laws, decrees with the force of laws, and other decrees whose character is difficult to determine . . . were charged with organizing, reorganizing, and modifying the services in such a way that it is in many cases impossible to establish in a clear and explicit fashion what the Ministry of Education is charged with doing and which services branch out from it.[65]

134

The modernization of the structure and functioning of education in Chile continued through the 1960s, gaining speed with the reforms of the Christian Democratic administration of Eduardo Frei (1964–70), and then tapering off through the Popular Unity (leftist coalition) government overthrown on September 11, 1973. But ideological debate about education in effect repeated the postulates of the nineteenth century with minor modifications to adjust to contemporary events. Thus, the economic consequences of educational progress began to be discussed, and manpower studies to be published. University students began to speak of making the university an active part of social life, and extending the classroom to the arena of "real" social problems.[66] But the same issues remained verbally paramount: equality, social class, democracy, authority, and the nation. In structural terms, too, the growth of primary education from the bottom, failing to meet the developments at the top, went its way. As late as the 1960s, only two-thirds of those children starting first grade reached the second grade. Only a fifth enrolled in secondary schools, and fewer than 5 per cent completed their secondary education. Of all those entering primary school, 0.2 per cent reached the fourth year of university education.[67] The sharp difference between urban and rural populations in their access also persisted. For example, in the province of Chiloé, with over 80 per cent of the population listed as rural, 14.8 per cent of the age-eligible children were in sixth grade; the national average was 29 per cent, and in Santiago 44.1 per cent of the age eligibles were in that grade. The figures at the bottom grades showed slow improvement through the 1950s and the 1960s, but the numbers at the top remained stagnant. Higher education remained by and large a facility for the children of the wealthy from the entire country, and for middle-class students from the cities. The children of a peasant or of an unskilled worker had virtually no chance to be graduated from a university, no matter what the aspirations expressed in the survey data we have presented. The essential problem was not educational or aspirational, but political. Forced to make a choice between equality and privilege, Chilean democracy foundered.

The Conservative-Liberal coalition voted into office in 1932 was succeeded by a Popular Front government representing the Radicals and all major parties to the left, notably the several branches of Chilean socialism and the Communist Party. The election was not surprising in the Chilean context. The art of accommodation, a traditional skill of Chilean parties, was shared by the left as it developed. Further, the practice of coalition governments was well established in the last century, when Chile developed a multiparty system. Proportional represen-

135

tation in congressional elections and the tradition of a strong parliament reinforced receptivity to a government of the left. Another reason was that the Popular Front device was patterned on the French experience of the thirties, and France was and is an admired model in Chile. Lastly, and most importantly, a Popular Front president could be accepted because the Congress remained generally in conservative hands, as had occurred previously with the election of Alessandri in 1920. With changes in party membership, a leftist coalition retained presidential power in Chile through World War II, breaking in late 1947 as the result of Cold War pressures and a slow drag of the Radical Party back to centrist positions. But this shift destroyed the effectiveness of the Radicals, supplanted in 1952 by the electoral return of the former military dictator, Carlos Ibáñez del Campo, who ran independently of the major parties and won on a personalistic appeal. A Conservative-Liberal coalition took office in 1958, to be succeeded in 1964 by the first major victory of Christian Democracy in Latin America.

In the meantime, the social question remained unanswered, while the democratic practice and overt ideology of the Chilean political scene made ever more urgent an incorporation of Chile's lower class into the social nation. Reformism, which had ameliorated the misery of some and opened up limited opportunity for many others, was hampered by habit and custom, economic debilities, and uncertain governmental action. The election of Salvador Allende as head of a generally Marxist coalition was designed not to disturb Chilean democracy but to extend it; not to administer an ongoing economic system but to socialize it. Again, it is not surprising that Marxists should take office in the Chilean executive establishment, especially when the left party leaders shared long experience in Chilean parliamentary institutions and party politics. What was unusual is the clarity of the choice made in 1970, and the equal clarity of the counterchoice seemingly stemming from the military revolt of 1973.

The causes for the downfall of Allende will be long debated, and at the time of this writing it is much too early to forecast the shape of Chilean politics for the years ahead. But an interim and tentative conclusion should not be avoided. The words and deeds of the Allende administration favored equality, a growth of the social nation, universal participation, and democratic practice. Its administration was maladroit, its understanding of economics romantic and limited, its foreign political and economic relations with major powers confused and debilitating, and its relations with its constituent parties confounding and sometimes contradictory. The military junta now governing Chile is antinational in

136

social matters, xenophobic and ideologically nationalistic in a right-wing sense, anti civil-libertarian, corporatist in leaning, opposed to democratic procedures, and determined to institute "order" and hierarchy. The typologies of which we have spoken earlier in this book have come alive across the entire spectrum.

Only a relatively sophisticated and developed country could have moved so far in posing for itself two such contrasting alternatives. Only an insufficiently developed one could have so sadly bungled the democratic alternative and permitted the military-corporate one. The questions Chileans had the wit and courage to pose for themselves, however, are those that must exercise all societies of the Western world, for not one is free of the tensions debated so thoroughly not only by nineteenth-century Chilean intellectuals, but by eighteenth- and nineteenth-century men of conscience across the European cultural continuum.

six / Educational Development in Venezuela During the Twentieth Century

Only pallid vestiges of the grand tradition of Latin American *pensadores* survive into this century. The politician-thinker-activist creators of nineteenth-century ideology were the Latin American counterparts of the North American men of *The Federalist*, who themselves were gone within fifty years of the American Revolution. It seems that once the tasks of nation-creation are concluded, the tasks of nation-building fall to other kinds of minds. Perhaps only when competing grand social designs come into public consciousness, do men emerge who can combine vulgarization of philosophical thought with utopian visions of social construction. Certain it is that the only near relatives to figures like Sarmiento, Alberdi, and Bello to be found in Latin America in this century were similarly involved with attempting to make new public worlds. In Mexico, José Vasconcelos (1882–1959) and Antonio Caso (1883–1946) gained renown for their work in attempting to define the new Mexico, apparently made possible by the sweeping revolution that began in that country in 1910. Both were concerned with problems of melding races, and, naturally, were deeply involved with educational innovation. The later analogue of the Mexican Revolution is, of course, the Cuban movement of 1959; it, too, found its exemplary *filósofos* in Fidel Castro and Ernesto Guevara, whose writings and speeches show the same mixture of philosophical referent, popularization, and exhortation to action for utopian ends that distinguish the men discussed in nineteenth-century Chile.

One can employ the presence of such moralizing activists as an indicator of the time of founding of the nation. The age of the *próceres*—the founding fathers—was clearly over in Chile and Argentina within 75 years of the achievement of independence. This long period spanned the dispute between Conservatives and Liberals, the two factions whose opposing world views were the subjective matter of politics and educational policy making. Once into the twentieth century, and with democratic capitalism in a Latin variant ensconced as the reigning utopian ideal, the victorious Liberals could then become conservative, which they, of course, promptly did. Social thought and action then became divided. Intellectuals, in the Mannheimian sense of that world, increasingly found their only long-term institutional place inside the university. Professional philosophy also developed, although most slowly and hesitantly. By the late 1930s, the modern "empirical" social sciences began to make their appearance, led by economics. Political thought and political action had become separate entities, and social science was added as a third, "objective" branch of social thought. Even more important, questions of change, development, and social purpose became depoliticized. This tendency came to a head in the post–World War II developmental euphoria which swept Latin America, accompanied by the emergency of *técnicos* committed to intrasystemic change. The age of the philosopher-president was over, except in a few countries lagging far behind their sister republics.

We have already mentioned some major "stages" in which one can conceive of the histories of Latin American republics: the division between Liberals and Conservatives in preparation for independence; the temporary coalition of the two for purposes of the wars of independence; the succeeding times of trouble; the appearance of an integrating dictator, sometimes a Conservative and sometimes a Liberal; the emergence into civilian and formal, quasi-democratic civilian rule interspersed with military government in most places; and contemporary versions of authoritarian capitalist developmentalism. As has been said, these "stages" should not be thought of as an inevitable progression; they are not filled with the same content everywhere, and not all countries have gone through them. Every republic, however, has experienced its time of troubles and its integrating dictatorship. If that integration came very late, however, after a long period of caudillistic states, then the ideational content that filled it could not be the same as for those countries that achieved their aristocratic and territorial integrations in the aftermath of European rationalism and its Utilitarian and Positivistic offspring. It is one thing for early Chilean presidents to have been influenced by carriers of the thought of Rousseau, Bentham, and James and John Stuart Mill, and quite another for contemporary political leaders to be surrounded by men who reflect the ideas of Marshall, Keynes, Tinbergen, Prebisch, and Samuelson.

The questions posed by moral philosophers are of a different order from those raised by social scientists who take extant power orders as a given. For the former, for example, the place of education in the achievement of a good order is the problem. For the latter, it is the function of education in the achievement of a soundly developing economy. Both are, of course, respectable endeavors. But the moral philosopher is overtly political in his public purposes, in the sense that he states his ethical position and attempts to pursue it through prescription. The applied social scientist is ostensibly apolitical; he accepts the ethical implications of any political system in which he chooses to offer diagnoses and prescriptions. It is not that the one is "good" and the other "bad." Rather, the ethicist becomes immediately consumable only when questions of total social organization arise. In less intense periods, he becomes an "egghead" or a "consultant," but only very rarely a designer of basic policy, and even less often its implementer. In "normal" times, the "technician" designs the means intended to consolidate or elaborate, but not to innovate grandly. A country that comes upon its moment of structural truth when intellectual fashion touts the virtues of technique and technicians cannot fill its intellectual vessels with the stuff of ultimate social decision; it is prone to confuse technics with purposes. Chileans of the last century could drink of the thoughts of Europeans and North Americans who themselves had just passed through their crises of national being. Venezuela, however, delayed its emergence from its time of troubles until this century. As it addresses the fundamental questions of how and what to be, it has been nourished only by generations of thought on how to consolidate what already is.

Even though hampered by the lateness of its national consolidation, Venezuela still followed the classical pattern to some extent, honoring at least two political leaders in the *pensador* tradition. One was Rómulo Gallegos, teacher and novelist, who by precept and action created Venezuela's first victorious generation of civilian, reformist political men— the social-democratic counterparts of the middle class, secularist Radicals who had emerged so much earlier in Chile, Argentina, and Uruguay. Gallegos was returned to the presidency in 1947 in Venezuela's first democratic election, only to be ousted nine months later by a military coup. The other Venezuelan leader of the same stripe is Rómulo Betancourt, party heir and colleague of Gallegos, although held in lower intellectual esteem.[1] Between these men and some of their contemporaries, and Venezuela's distinguished men of the independence period—Bolívar, Miranda, and their colleagues—the country offers little by way of politically informed intellectuality. A pathetic book, *The Educational Ideas of Eminent Venezuelans*[2], serves only to underscore the century-long poverty of Venezuelan social thought. It lays claim to Andrés Bello because of his Venezuelan birth, even though Bello had no direct connection with Venezuelan politics or educational development. Otherwise, a series of respectable but minor and ineffectual figures are mentioned to further the author's purpose of spreading national values by expounding the grandeur of Venezuela's past. A more accurate interpretation is exemplified by the following quotation:

The Venezuelan political situation between 1830 and the end of the century may be summarized by the famous sentence of one of its presidents, Guzmán Blanco: "The country is like a dry hide, you step on it on one end and it pops up on the other." It is true that between 1830 and 1845 there was a period of relative peace; however, one Venezuelan historian points out that "between 1830 and 1900 there were 39 significant revolutions and 127 minor revolts; in total, 166 revolts, which together lasted 8,847 days." Between the years 1858 and 1899 alone there were 418 battles in the country, that is, an average of 10 per year. The characterization that Gil Fortoul [a Venezuelan historian whose most important work is *Historia constitucional de Venezuela*] gives the forms of government during this period helps to clarify this panorama of political instability: "From 1830 to 1861 the government was an oligarchy; it was both dictatorial and anarchic from 1861 to 1862; during the Federation, a military anarchy, and after that alternatively autocratic and eclectic."[3]

Venezuela's long period of *caudillismo* was but an extension of the social fragmentation of the even longer period of Spanish colonial rule. Like Chile a backwater of empire, Venezuela did not have the advantage of the neat geographical coherence of Chile's long central valley. Decentralization was invited by the difficulties of communications among plains areas along the Orinoco River, the Caribbean coastal area, the eastern region, and the politically critical Andean zone. Accentuating these geographical elements was the ethnic mix of the population, made up of Indians, Negroes, *pardos* ("mixed bloods"), and *criollos* (Europeans born in the New World) and *peninsulares* (Europeans born in Spain). Under such conditions, political order was fragile.

[T]he permanent restiveness of Indians, Negroes, and pardos . . . was a chronic source of turbulence, keeping the menace of public violence ever-present and making it impossible to mask the harshly repressive features of the colonial regime. Official importation of slaves is first recorded in 1525, but the first sizeable concentration of Negro workers came to the gold mines at Buria in mid-century. The first uprising followed almost immediately. Fugitives from the mining camp organized mass desertions of both Negroes and Indians, mounted a small army, and marched on Barquisimeto.

As the slave traffic and miscegenation flourished the class composed of mixed-bloods, as well as Negroes and Indians who were technically free men but bound in various forms of servitude and legally prescribed social inferiority, became the largest group in the society . . . . Countermeasures against the rebellious rose in severity as the climate of dissidence and conspiracy made itself felt.[4]

The colonial educational system, such as it was, denied entrance to persons other than whites. The prohibition was easily effected, because schools were very few in number. The first primary schools were opened half a century after the founding of the colony—the first in the state of Coro in 1560, and the first in Caracas in 1591. Secondary schools were instituted in the middle of the following century; some were religious seminaries, others academies standard for the time. One of the latter, the Seminario de Santa Rosa de Lima, established in Caracas, was the forerunner of Venezuela's first university. After almost 75 years of petitions, the Spanish crown finally chartered an institution of higher education in 1721 to provide for meritorious but impoverished white students, and to develop a better-trained clergy.[5] The university granted a total of 2,270 degrees between 1725 and 1810, the year the wars of independence broke out. Of these, 1,625 were *lycée* degrees—*bachilleres*. Some 1,028 of them were granted in philosophy, 170 in law, and a mere 33 in medicine. Another 328 were the first true university degree, the *licenciatura*.[6] Gil Fourtoul, president of Congress in 1911, the historian referred to earlier, has commented harshly on the rigid intolerance and medievalism of this institution:

The "royal and pontifical" University of Caracas was a focal point of the most conservative ideas of the Colony, and even into the nineteenth century, on the eve of the declaration of independence, a spirit predominated in it totally opposed to that of the entire civilized world. One example among many: *The Gazette of Caracas* of February 19, 1811, inserts an article by Guillermo Burke on religious tolerance, and in the following number publishes three attacks on it, one by the Franciscans of Valencia, another by Dr. Antonio Gómez of Caracas, and another by the University, the last entitled *Politico-religious intolerance vindicated* . . . . The full council unanimously approved [the article] and ordered its publication after obtaining permission of the archbishop. In the University's article one reads, "The authority of kings is derived from heaven; the persons of kings, even though they be tyrants, are inviolable, and although their will is not always to be confused with that of God himself, they should always be respected and obeyed. The Inquisition is a necessary and legitimate tribunal; there is no recourse against the general corruption other than politico-intolerance." That is what the University was saying while some of the most radical laws ever passed in America[7] were already being prepared.

142

Even at that late date, with independence but a few years away, racial exclusions were legally imposed. Eligibility for degree examinations in the university depended in part on the rector's determination that the aspirant was "legitimate" and "clean of all bad races."[8] By this time, however, it had become possible for more affluent *pardos* to buy certificates testifying to their whiteness. The chance to learn required money plus the right color, demonstrating that education was the exclusive domain of the privileged in both senses. At the turn of the century, Caracas had slowly become the country's administrative and economic center, with a population of around 30,000. Venezuela itself is estimated to have included at that time some 900,000 persons, broken down ethnically as follows:[9]

Ethnic and Social Categories	Population No.	Per Cent	Per Cent by Major Ethnic Categories
Whites, Iberians & Canary Is.	12,000	1.3	
Whites, Creoles	172,727	19.0	20.3 Whites
Pardos	407,000	45.0	
Negroes, free	33,362	4.0	
Negroes, slaves	87,800	9.7	61.3 Blacks and *pardos*
Negroes, runaway	24,000	2.6	
Indians, tributary	75,564	8.4	
Indians, nontributary	25,590	3.3	
Marginal indigenous population	60,000	6.7	18.4 Indians
Total	898,043	100.00	

Venezuela's short-lived moment of national glory was bought by the actions of Simón Bolívar, the major liberating leader of Latin America, and some of his associates. Their roots, however, were not sunk only in Venezuela. Trained in Europe and associated with European and North American ideas, they were able to relate themselves to lieutenants and followers in Venezuela, but not to consolidate domestic power after gaining freedom from Spain. A famous letter from Bolívar to an associate makes this point immediately before the culminating battle of the revolution at Carabobo:

These are not the kind of men you are familiar with there; they are the ones you do not know: men who have fought a long time and regard themselves as highly deserving but humbled and miserable and without hope of winning the full fruit of the conquests of their lances. They are determined *llaneros* [plainsmen] who never believe themselves the equals of men who know more or seem better. I, myself, who have always been at their head do not yet know of what they may be capable. I treat them with utmost consideration but even this consideration is not enough to inspire in them the confidence and frankness that should reign among comrades and fellow citizens. Persuade yourself . . . that we are suspended over an abyss or better on a volcano about to explode. I fear the peace more than the war . . . .[10]

Bolívar was correct. His political power in Venezuela having evaporated after the expulsion of the Spaniards, he was left without a political future. Indeed, there was no *national* ruling group to assume power. Potential leadership groups were reduced by divisions on independence, the withdrawal of the colonial leaders, and the attritions of warfare; they were not strengthened by education and an attachment to a firmly defined national area. The embryonic nation had not even a fragment of a coherent upper class. The decay into *caciquismo* occurred, justifying Bolívar's fears. *Caciques* ruled regions, and regionalism limited the power of the *caudillos* who wore the sashes of the national presidency. José Antonio Páez, one of the irregular guerrilla leaders feared by Bolívar, but one on whom he had to rely, became the first in the string of *caudillos* to be Venezuela's "presidents" for a century. Bonilla neatly sums up Páez and the era he introduced:

> The term *caudillismo* brings to the forefront the central role of "individualized, entrepreneurial political violence" as well as the social disorganization, arbitrariness, and turbulence that marks the next hundred years in Venezuela. Though these features of the emergent political system unquestionably marked later political events, from the perspective taken here it is important not to lose sight of the more intricate connections among the several power sectors that were in a position to abet or challenge the caudillo. In this connection two vital points should be noted about the 1830 fusion of caudillism and criollo conservatism: (1) the presence of caudillos in this coalition did not mean a primacy of strengthening of military institutions, and (2) the dominance of conservative values and interests did not lead to a reimposition of Church power or privilege. Precisely this—its emphasis on civilism, secularism, and legal equalitarianism (constitutionalism)—gave the first Páez regime its reputation as a golden period of Venezuelan democracy.

> Páez and his oligarchic following were led into their opposition to army and Church by their animosity toward Bolívar as well as by broader considerations of policy and political strategy . . . .[11]

Venezuela, then, is unlike Chile not only in the duration of *caudillismo* and the times of troubles, but also in the fact that Church-state

144

discord was not permitted to play itself out in the nineteenth century. Not only did the Church remain a weak institution far into this century, but in the absence of overt competition between the two leading contenders for man's public affections, debates about secularism were damped.

The history of Venezuelan education in the last century is by and large the story of good intentions, the pallid reflection of ideological debates taking place elsewhere, and of inaction. All the constitutions of the last century stressed the importance of an educated citizenry, placed in the hands of Congress the power to act on public educational matters, and recognized the role of private schools. But governments did little, especially because regionalism permitted national governments to let the states handle educational matters. And the states, needless to say, were in no economic or normative position to move. The weaknesses were, of course, recognized. A minister of Interior and Justice, in a report to Congress in 1849, said what was to become a refrain and, as a matter of fact, still is:

> It is inexplicable that in the midst of these forests and in the center of the tropical zone, with agriculture and livestock as the bases of wealth, with immense plains . . . there is not a class in botany in the whole country, nor of physics and chemistry applied to agriculture, nor of agriculture itself, nor of that portion of natural history related to our lands and our interests, nor of veterinary medicine, nor of any natural science related to our temperatures, territory, and products.[12]

Only the year before, the head of the office of public education, José María Vargas, had pointed out that only 121 of the country's 537 parishes had a primary school. As for those that did exist, almost all were "poorly equipped . . . with teachers who, usually lacking the qualities needed for this delicate task, miserably make their unhappy pupils lose the most precious time of their lives."[13] Secondary schools had been established in only 12 localities. Needless to say, only one of them, in Caracas, was for girls. Vargas also provided some comparative statistics, starting with the statement that in the United States, all children are educated! He continued that at the primary level 1 of every 12 is educated in Holland, 1 of every 13 in Austria, and so on down the line to the figure of 1 for every 114 in Venezuela.[14] As a solution to the educational deficit, Vargas proposed the establishment of universal free and obligatory primary schooling, supported by revenues earmarked in accord with population changes, and with instruction provided by teachers trained in normal schools.

Twenty-two years later, the most important educational legislation of the last century mandated obligatory elementary education. This statute of June 27, 1870, was one of the first governmental acts of the newly established dictatorship of Antonio Guzmán Blanco. Guzmán was a Liberal *caudillo* who today has few defenders. His admirers have called him the "civilizing autocrat, the tyrant, a new type of chief created by our America to defend a certain libertarian ideology, somewhat anticlerical and antiaristocratic."[15] Other judgments are harsher:

> Guzmán Blanco, a man of legendary egomania in a nation whose politicians have not been given to self-effacement, was the first to elicit and systematize the unbridled sycophancy that every strong man to follow was to claim as his due and that was at the same time the most definitive mark of the intellectual and moral capitulation of his bourgeois adulators . . . . The number of his decorations, the acclamations and oratorical tourneys in his praise, the commemorative volumes in his honor are beyond reckoning. One such volume, entitled *Sketches of the Illustrious American, General Guzmán Blanco, in the Multiple Facets of his Privileged Nature for the Album of his Children*, celebrates in high-flown verse the dictator's unmatched qualities of personal beauty and physique as well as his accomplishments as soldier, diplomat, administrator, orator, man of letters, and director of national progress.[16]

The legislation of 1870 provided for "obligatory and required public instruction" and for "free and voluntary education."[17] The former, which it is the obligation of the "public authority" to provide gratis and "preferentially," or with priority, must indicate the "general principles of Morality, Reading and Writing of the Mother Tongue, Practical Arithmetic, the Metric System, and the Compendium of the Federal Constitution." As for "free instruction," it comprehended "all other knowledge which Venezuelans may wish to acquire in the various fields of human knowledge. This type of instruction will be offered free by the Public Powers to the degree to which it is possible for them to do so." Four years after the legislation was put into effect, 135 of the 332 primary schools it had set out to establish were still nonexistent. Within the Federal District—that is, federally ruled Caracas—there were only 1,622 students in primary schools in 1875, all in upgraded classes under the supervision of a single teacher, usually indifferently prepared. A total of 22,669 students attended the primary schools of Venezuela in that same year.[18] The national population was around 1,785,000 in 1873, the date of the first national census.[19] The act was not entirely *fachadismo* ("façadism"), for some schools were created, and normative decisions were given some effect. Religious instruction was no longer a part of the required curriculum in public schools, but the obvious insuffficiencies of public education opened opportunities for

Catholic schools which have had well-documented lasting effects. The Guzmán Blanco period also saw the creation of the Ministry of Public Education, the first true attempt at administrative specialization in the field.* The issue of "freedom of instruction" arose in Venezuela during this period, as it had earlier in Chile. *Libertad de enseñanza* was constitutionally guaranteed, but its bounds were spelled out in a decree of December 20, 1872, fixing as limits on private schools "prior approval from the federal government to the directors of private colleges for their establishment, prior approval by the federal government of the appointment of professors, the annual despatch to the government of a certified copy of the examination procedure [and] use in teaching of the same texts prescribed for official schools . . . ."[20] The decree also required that the principals and teachers in private schools had to hold opinions publicly known to be "republican and liberal." The flurry of concern with education during this time is also revealed in the national budget. The high point was reached in 1887–88, when education received 12.3 per cent of the national budget, a figure not to be equaled until the 1950s.[21] Whatever marginal educational improvements may have been made, Venezuela came into this century an essentially illiterate country, dependent upon uncertain cacao exportations for its foreign exchange, with a divided upper class comprised of uneasy old families and a constant stream of aspirants from the provinces, and with biography as a substitute for national history. Silva Michelena describes *fin-de-siècle* Venezuela as follows:

> At the beginning of this century Venezuela could be described as typically underdeveloped. It was essentially a one-product economy from whose export the country derived the major part of its income. Approximately 85 per cent of the work force was involved in agriculture, and the per capita rate of growth of the economy was almost stationary (0.3 percent), as it had been since the beginning of the republic's life and as it continued to be during the first quarter of the twentieth century.

> Because the economic route was closed, the only remaining road to upward social mobility was through participation in armed bands or political revolts, for education continued to be the privilege of a very small elite. Even though a central government existed nominally, its power was challenged permanently by various regional caudillos who periodically succeeded in overthrowing it. Cultural power . . . was strictly controlled by the central government or

---

*The Ministry was established on May 24, 1881, and was initially divided into an Office of Popular Education and an Office of Higher Education. A later decree of September 24, 1883, logically extended the Ministry's power over higher education by abolishing university autonomy and absorbing revenues formally earmarked for higher education into the general fund for public education.

by caudillos who aspired to power . . . the armed forces were always factional, never national, in character. Finally, the existing political parties, like the government itself, never penetrated the masses and never became more than semiprogrammatic. This was the situation in Venezuela when the Minister of War, General Juan Vicente Gómez, gained control in 1908.[22]

Gómez ruled Venezuela from 1908 until his death in December, 1935. The functional effect of his rule was to collapse into one man and one short period the analogous span of Chilean history from 1830 to 1891—from the integrating dictatorship of Portales to the ill-fated attempt of Balmaceda to establish an activist, economically interventionist free-enterprise middle-class government. But in Venezuela these functions were carried out within a structure and a set of practices quite at variance with the Chilean experience, for Gómez ruled harshly and only most grudgingly accepted any measure of political competition or quasi-autonomous political organization. Functionally, the bases of further change were established in the Gómez period; structurally, the ability to work these changes into existence was weak. Daniel Levine has weighed the Gómez administration as follows:

> Social change is subversive. The firmest dictatorships often unwittingly lay the foundations for subsequent expansion and liberalization of political life. From 1908 to 1935, Venezuela suffered through the bloody dictatorship of Juan Vicente Gómez. His autocratic regime unified the country administratively and politically, effectively eliminating all traces of the nineteenth-century heritage of regional conflict and civil war. The oil revenues that began to flow in the 1920s reinforced the Gómez regime and helped create a national army and national bureaucracy—in short, an effective state machine for the first time in Venezuelan history . . . . .[23]

Oil had come to have an influence in the first years of the Gómez incumbency, permitting an independent source of revenue to the federal government of great aid to Gómez in his task of beating back regional rivals. The most direct result of this new source of funds at the national level was that Gómez was able to professionalize his army, turning it from an uncertain force of irregulars into a reliable arm of his administration and, later in the century, into an independent focus of political power. It is germane to our comparative story that a Chilean army officer and limited support personnel were brought in to carry out this task of professionalization. The Chilean army was one of the first in Latin America to be professionalized. The model for Chile was the Prussian army, at that time riding the crest of its victory in the Franco-Prussian War; in turn, the Chileans imparted the same training and world view to the other Latin armies with whom they worked as advisers. Gómez has been called the last of Venezuela's *caudillos* precisely because of his role in building the armed forces and in implanting the supremacy of the central government. After Gómez, Venezuela was privileged to have true national dictators instead of dukes uneasily balancing among competing peers.

The length of the Gómez rule, its ferocity, and its end on the eve of a period of extraordinarily rapid international military, ideological, economic, and scientific change force a kind of analysis for which the social sciences are ill-equipped. That is to say, the last four decades of Venezuelan history chronologically compress profound change, and the effects of velocity on the quality of occurrences is little understood. And these happenings were played out against a very shallow historical background of a country without history or culture, an appreciation we have already mentioned as being common among Venezuelan intellectuals. Many studies of Venezuela speak of this phenomenon. "Modern political life began for Venezuela in 1936 . . . . The relative youth of most social and political organizations means that the past is present in many aspects of contemporary life—the issues that define its conflicts, the organizations that guide them, and the institutions that contain and channel them are all of recent vintage." [24] Or, to take a more poignant analysis, "What are the consequences for a nation presently committed to democratic, neocapitalist development of having gestated a bourgeoisie in a climate of overwhelming terror, corruption, and individualized favor-seeking? One consequence is to have it perceived retrospectively as 'ornamental and narcissistic,' as pretentious, callow, servile, self-serving, hypocritical, and anti-national." [25] Bonilla answers the question more fully as follows:

> . . . [C]ontemporary Venezuelan elites, except for a fraction of the entrepreneurial class, are the vanguard of rising middle sectors. Only among a select group within the economic elite is any evidence to be found of stability, continuity, and the transmission of status across generations. Major blocs within the political and cultural elites are of modest, provincial, middle-class origins. That background, for early experience of politics, means immersion in the milieu of violence, arbitrariness, and clientelism that permeated political life at all levels in Venezuela from the turn of the century at least until the death of Gómez in 1936 [sic]. In the social context of everyday life, this

---

*The Salvadorean army was also professionalized by the Chileans. The Chilean mission to El Salvador was headed by Carlos Ibáñez del Campo, president of Chile from 1927 to 1931, and again from 1952 to 1958.

background means the continued immersion in a world of limited intellectual perspectives and petty bourgeois sentiments and values . . . .

. . . as a group, elite individuals in their public life are ostensibly dedicated to rationalizing, reforming, and moderning functions whereas in private they remain steeped (apparently quite by choice) in a family- and class-rooted traditionalism heavily freighted with idealized sentimentality in personal relations and preoccupation with external formalism, decorum, and propriety as certification of family status and individual worth . . [26]

During the Gómez period the export economy shifted from cacao and hides to oil. Governmental expenditures increased over five-fold in quite stable *bolívares*. An initially slow drift of the population from the farms to the cities became a flood after 1936. Foreigners began to come to the country, first slowly as in the case of the internal migration, but later in increasing numbers. The small, thin, stable aristocracy became watered down as the sources of power began to multiply. And the hard face of dictatorship also became etched, hints of the cracks that were to appear only after Gómez's death. As the economic institution and its class effects slowly became more complex, the Church also re-emerged, favored by the strong religiosity of the Andean caciques who surrounded their *caudillo* in Caracas. Some of the issues raised by these changes surfaced in the spate of educational legislation that came during the Gómez period; the intensity of the issues was foreshadowed in the first political stirrings of students passing through Venezuela's still puny educational system.

The educational code of 1843 and the 1870 decree establishing obligatory primary schooling are Venezuela's only two landmark pieces of educational legislation until the last decade of the century. Between 1893 and 1935, more than a dozen statements and restatements of the legal norms regulating education were promulgated.[27] The issues concerned the extension of access to schooling as well as the physical size of the total plant, the form to be taken by primary education, the classical question of *libertad de enseñanza*, which was to become more acute as the Church regained power and the public schools languished, and the issue of the proper relation between education for males and females.

A detailed listing of the laws of the period is beyond the scope of this study; instead, some examples from the flow of legislation will be taken in order to reveal the general shape of the perception of problems and of their appropriate resolution. For example, the regulations governing the Federal Schools for Girls, issued in 1899, were the first to make the curricular content for girls the same as for boys, a change made under

150

the guise of preparing the girls to become teachers of the "popular masses," since they were destined to become primary- and secondary-school teachers.[28] In 1903 a decree was passed limiting the number of public schools in the Federal District to 50, and in the entire country to 500. This number was so obviously insufficient—especially since we are still dealing largely with ungraded and single-classroom schools—that in the same year the decree was rescinded, the authorized number for Caracas was doubled, and that for the entire country raised to 600. Budgetary troubles were avoided by cutting teachers' salaries by 40 per cent.[29] In 1905 coeducation was introduced, and finally the Code of Public Instruction issued in 1912 established graded public primary schools.[30]

During these early years of the century, religious instruction was voluntary in public schools, and ostensibly was available for any religious creed professed by the student. In line with this attempt at secular enlightenment, an effort was made to break away from old styles of teaching and to adjust to the new techniques, and attitudes about students, being developed in Europe and the United States. For example, the already mentioned decree of 1899 regarding girls' schools stated: "Teaching will be intuitive and practical, starting with the observation of concrete objects and then to be raised to abstract ideas; therefore, prohibited is all empirical teaching based exclusively on the use of memory, and any procedure which makes teaching mechanical and tiresome."[31]

The civic thinking of the intellectual innovators of the time is revealed in the themes prescribed for the required courses in "moral and civic education." In the first year of primary school, students were to be taught "discipline and obedience to superiors (parents, teachers, and authorities), while the child lacks sufficient wisdom or discernment to compare his rights with his duties." The instruction was to be directed toward showing the difference between "respect for superiors and blind submission to violence or the caprices of others." In the third year of primary school the course material was to include "the duties of man toward family and society," "decorum and personal dignity," and "personal efforts and their advantages."[32]

Rumblings of the chronic Church-state dispute continued throughout the early years of the century, to be resolved in favor of the Church in 1914. Legislation to that date had established a slowly increasing area of state inspection and supervision over Catholic schools, but in 1914 the increasing clericalism of the Gómez regime was institutionalized as a result of a government-instigated court abrogation of the existing supervisory legislation. Complete and unrestricted freedom for private schools became the law. The *Estado docente* was dealt a body blow in the following words:

> The National Constitution in force, in Clause 12 of Article 22, establishes liberty of instruction, without any limitation, as one of the guarantees of Venezuelans. But this guarantee, implanted in our Constitutions from 1864 until today, has had no influence on the organization of education; further, it has been formally violated by our school legislation, which has been maintained and developed on the principle of the monopoly of many subject-areas by the State, and on the strictest and most severe subjection to the Executive Authorities of those subject-fields whose development has been especially left to private authorities.[33]

The law stated that any citizen could establish schools for the teaching of any subject without prior permission from the state, and also without the need to adjust to regulations, programs, methods, or textbooks prescribed by public officials. The law also made schooling obligatory for children between seven and fourteen years of age, antedating similar Chilean legislation by six years. Action matched words in the matter of the weakening of the *Estado docente*, but certainly not in the matter of educational opportunity. In the first decade of the century, an annual average of 4.9 per cent of the national budget was dedicated to education at all levels. Between 1910 and 1920, the average rose to 5.2 per cent, but fell again to 4.3 per cent in the third decade, rounding out at 5.2 per cent in the last five years of the Gómez period. Attendance was pitifully low. There were 17 public secondary schools in 1927, an increase of one over 1920. The total enrollment in all secondary schools, public and private, in that same year was 1,183 students, of whom only 43 were female.[34] Approximately 710 students were registered in the Central University.[35] The federal primary schools listed 76,639 students at the end of 1938, with the further estimate that only some two-thirds of this number regularly attended classes. An additional 9,996 students were enrolled in municipal schools, and 9,958 in state schools, of whom it is also estimated that some two-thirds attended regularly. The private primary schools had 14,827 registered students, with four-fifths estimated in regular attendance.[36] Thus, about 113,000 persons were formally attending school at all levels in a country whose population was estimated in 1926 as 3,026,878.[37] As is immediately evident from these figures, the bottleneck in the educational flow was the secondary school. And it is also evident that even many of the privileged failed to pursue personal educational development very far. The relation between secondary- and

152

primary-school enrollment figures was on the order of 1.2 secondary-school students for every 100 in primary schools. The path onward from secondary school was much easier: there were some 69 university students for every 100 secondary students.

The Gómez period obviously created latent conditions for change, but attempts to manifest change were damped by political terrorism, by self-serving potential innovators, by the dilution of middle and upper groups by international actors accompanying the new oil and related interests, by the persistence of tensions between institutions representing sacred and secular approaches to social life, and by the continuing effects of regionalism. The theme of this book leads us to add another major inhibiting factor: that is, the inaccessibility and short duration of education, which prevented people from experiencing the shared and diversified social life that would have created at least normative predispositions toward a less alienating civic life. Given the political situation, and the provincial nature of social life, we should expect that goads to change could come from only one organized source, the university students and their potentially few allies within the starved group of intellectuals not in imposed or self-exile. In an article written in the 1960s,[38] K. H. Silvert speculated that university students reached the peak of their political potential precisely in such situations as were found in Venezuela in the mid-1930s, simply because of the unavailability of alternative ways of being politically effective. It is in the absence of responsive political institutions that persons intellectually and emotionally prepared for citizenship are most likely to identify their own institutional situs—in this case, the academy—as a substitute, no matter how clumsy or unseemly a one, for instrumental locales that would otherwise be more appropriate. We consider it one of the stronger tests of the concepts advanced in this book that student groups were the only effective and continuous sources of dissidence during the Gómez period, and that from them sprang the full array of political institutions and leaders that dominate contemporary Venezuelan *national* history. Indeed, whatever there is today of the "national" about Venezuela was gestated in the higher reaches of Venezuela's educational system. This interpretation is virtually universal among writers on Venezuelan political history; a typical selection from one reads as follows:

[T]he majority of the children of the petite bourgeoisie attended [public schools]. From this group and especially from those who studied with Rómulo Gallegos—future president of the republic—emerged the leaders who, acting as members of the Student Federation of the Central University of Venezue-

153

la, repeated in 1928 the student demonstrations of 1912, but with more significant political consequences. These student movements brought to the surface the discontent that characterized other sectors of the population; this discontent, in turn, made the students aware of the need to expand their organizations to include the interests of these other groups, who had never found adequate means for expression either in organizations or in the press. Both channels were strictly controlled.

The student movements were also the first political manifestation of the change that had come about in the sources of government power . . . .

By the end of the second decade of this century fundamental changes had been realized in Venezuela's economic and social structure, but it would not be until after the death of Gómez, at the end of 1935, that these transformations were to have any important political consequences.[39]

It is usual that, when an iron dictator leaves the scene, his immediate successor is a lieutenant. The reason, obviously, is that no dictator can be of "iron" unless he is able to stifle opposition. In the simple absence of organized alternatives, succession falls to a designated heir. This syndrome has repeated itself many times in Latin America and, of course, it occurred in Venezuela. Gómez was succeeded by his Minister of War, General López Contreras, who in his turn was succeeded in 1940 by his own Minister of War, General Medina Angarita. Gomecismo came to a definitive end only in 1945, when a military coup ousted President Medina. But we are getting ahead of the story.

It was also usual in Latin America that political oppositions could learn and integrate themselves in exile, preparing for the day of a possible return. Given contemporary international cooperation among police and military agencies, this practice is now under attack. But in the 1930s, when many Latin American countries had fallen under harsh dictatorships, the phenomenon was common and of great significance to post–World War II political events in such countries as Venezuela, Guatemala, and Peru, with variants of the same situation in many others. We have been able to find no exact information on the numbers of exiles who were forced to leave Venezuela in the last years of the Gómez regime, but all important civilian leaders after 1945 underwent the experience, as did many of their closest aides. The temper of the times, and the conventional wisdom thereof, are important to events. The 1930s were the time of the rise of fascisms in Europe, with their attendant ideological explanations, and of a spreading infatuation with socialisms of various stripes. They were, for Latin Americans in particular, also the times of the Spanish Civil War, of a Church that seemed irrevocably on the side of corporatist regimes, of the Cárdenas presidency in Mexico and an apparent "popularization" of the Revolution in that country; and the United States had its New Deal and a TVA that promised structural change within constitutional norms permitting an effective extension of democracy. Persons from the center to the left had nationalist and democratic heroes, and models to follow. At least as importantly, there was a defined enemy—fascism in its several guises. And, finally, there was the war, seen as a clear confrontation between democracy and totalitarianism. When refugees began to trickle back to Venezuela in 1941 at the start of the liberalizing Medina administration, the Communists came with Popular Frontism in their armamentarium, and the much more numerous center and center-left national democratic elements returned in the belief that they were in possession of organizational mechanisms as well as ideological rudders, and that the international climate would be hospitable to their democratizing efforts. In the short run they were wrong on all counts.

The first truly national political party in Venezuela, later to be called Acción Democrática, was granted legal status in 1941. Run by the student dissidents of the 1920s and 1930s, it quickly became a national force, filling a need that could be denied only at the cost of greater repression than President Medina was willing to muster. Levine has said of the AD at this time:

> According to Rómulo Betancourt, from the very beginning "The leadership of AD established for itself the watchword of: 'Not a single district, not a single municipality without its party organization.' "
>
> Every major political party to follow AD has heeded this advice. Today, if one travels in the most remote and isolated areas of Venezuela, almost every collection of houses big and permanent enough to be called a town has several party headquarters. Acción Democrática pioneered the building of a new kind of political party with a permanent organizational base—full-time parties, which operated all year round. . . . Each party built its organization both vertically and horizontally: vertically the parties reach all levels, from neighborhood through region to nation; horizontally, the party is affiliated with and sponsors functional groups like student wings, labor sections, women's fronts, and the like.
>
> For a long time, AD was the only party with a national organization of this scope and depth. . . . A prominent Christian Democrat later acknowledged the unique character of the early years of AD, noting that "Acción Democrática was the meeting place of anti-Gómez Venezuela. The mental state of our country facilitated the growth of AD." [40]

In 1945, a small group of army officers planned a coup against Medina. Seeking popular support because of their small numbers within the military, they turned to AD, which accepted the invitation, suspecting that the electoral path would not be honestly open to all comers. The successful coup introduced a three-year period of AD rule, called the *trienio*. This *golpe* was one of many civilian, progressive regimes established in Latin America after the war: in Guatemala, Cuba, Peru, Colombia, Brazil, and elsewhere. A return to military or other forms of authoritarian rule also occurred in almost every case; in Guatemala, in 1954; in Cuba, in 1952; in Peru, Colombia, and Venezuela, in 1948. The Chileans, too, in 1948, saw the breakup of their long-lived Popular Front, and a return to a Radical-Liberal alliance of center-right cast, a move that was made evident by a cabinet shift, not by armed revolt, of course.

Many reasons are given for the countercoup of 1948. An important one is that AD tried to do too much too fast in a politically unlettered country. Unions were organized; an opposition party (COPEI—a Catholic-oriented party later to assume Christian Democratic characteristics) was legalized in 1946 and coalesced anti-AD sentiment; the Marxist groups unified within a single Communist Party; elections for congress and for the presidency were called in 1947 (Gallegos was elected president); a constituent assembly did its work; municipal elections were held; and so on through a long chain of activities normal to routinized democratic systems, but all new and untried in parochial Venezuela. Obviously, there was also fear of AD's equalitarianism, and the touchy race-class situation, persistent since colonial days, came closer to the surface as AD turned its attention to less privileged (and therefore more "colored") people. The army, too, had learned that it had autonomous interests; thus it broke from a close dependence on given economic and class groups and began to agitate for its own mobility purposes. The first democratically elected president in Venezuela's history was thrown out of office after an incumbency of only nine months:

The new powerful goverment [of Gallegos] became, in the minds of the masses, the new great paterfamilias, not a modern secular state. This feeling obviously also indicated a lack of political efficacy among the political groups that were the sources of support for Acción Democrática. This fact seems to be confirmed by the few protests elicited when it was overthrown—those that were forthcoming reflected a loyalty to the party rather than loyalty toward

156

the democratic system that the party had been trying to establish. Similarly, important members of Venezuela's elite did not maintain loyalties toward the democratic system.[41]

A crude way to sum up AD's defeat was that the party provided leadership, but that the country could not provide followership. National appeals cannot be understood by non-national people; the substitute of charisma was not in Gallegos' power to command. Nations need citizens, and Venezuela's institutions had prepared few of them. Although unprecedented attempts were made between 1935 and 1945 to expand the educational system, the needs were so great that only marginal improvements could be made. In 1935 only 15.5 per cent of the age-eligible children were in primary school, a figure that doubled by 1945. Those in secondary school in the former year represented only 0.4 per cent of the relevant age cohort; in 1945 that percentage was up to 2.9.[42] More importantly, attention began to be given to teacher-training. From the 3 normal schools of 1935 (2 public and 1 private), the number had risen to 11 public and 20 private schools—a ratio emphasizing the increasing importance of the Church in both public and private education, for Catholic normal schools provide many of the teachers in the secular private and public systems. Normal-school student enrollments rose from a meager 141 in 1935 to 2,781 a decade later, a striking and highly significant increase to be reflected later in periods of limited employment opportunities for teachers. University enrollments went up more slowly, of course, dependent as they were upon a stream of prepared students; the figures, however, still doubled in the ten-year period.[43]

Just as the army had called on Chileans for their professionalization, the Ministry of Education in this period called on the Pedagogical Institute of the University of Chile for assistance in establishing a similar university-level school for the training of secondary-school teachers. The heavily positivistic leanings of the Chileans, still in evidence in this period, were thus transferred at second hand to Venezuela. Of a total of 273 secondary teachers in 1944, about a fifth were graduates of the new Institute. Only 76 of these teachers had any university degree at all.[44] (As mentioned previously, the Venezuelan teachers whom we interviewed had greater experience of some university training but fewer completed degrees than their Chilean counterparts.) The educational significance of this transitional decade has been summed up as follows:

. . . [T]he decade after the end of the Gómez dictatorship was one which saw greater attention paid to education, in terms of the development of its resources, including the bettering of financial conditions . . . the number of schools, the quality of the teachers and the general attitude toward education. But education was still limited to a fraction of those who might have participated in it, around 30 per cent of those of primary school age and a mere 2.9 per cent of those of secondary school age. Moreover, the system remained classbound, with secondary and university education available in general only to those who had the financial backing to remain outside the job market. . . . This was true because education, despite the opening of additional opportunities in vocational and normal schooling, remained essentially a single line of march since these alternative routes were available only to a small fraction of those who might have wished to use them.[45]

The decade of 1948–58 was on the surface merely a return to military dictatorship in Venezuela, that of Marcos Pérez Jiménez. But it was as well a test of the nature and depth of the changes that had occurred in the ten-year post-Gómez transition, and the tryout of the *trienio*. Bloody, repressive, profoundly antidemocratic in ideology as well as practice— certainly the Pérez Jiménez regime was all of those, and with grisly elaborations. But the slumber of the Gómez years was not repeated. Venezuela emerged from Pérez Jiménez readier to attempt a politics of national participation than it had been in 1945, a change that had to do not only with the economic developmental activities of the dictatorial administration, but also with the persistence of the plural opposition that grew from the institutional roots that had begun to sprout after 1936. Pérez Jiménez left a different Venezuela in 1958 from the one he had found in 1948 not only because of his policies, but also because many other Venezuelans had found the means to begin to change their own country.

The Pérez Jiménez administration inherited an educational system that had been greatly expanded during the short *trienio*. In the first year of the AD junta, educational expenditures by the state were doubled, and substantial increases were also allocated in the two succeeding years. Primary-school enrollment rose by almost 45 per cent, secondary-school enrollments by more than 92 per cent. In terms of the ratio of students in private and public institutions, the former increased from 10 to 15 per cent of total enrollments at the primary level, but public secondary-school registrations went from 55 to 76 per cent of the totals between 1945 and 1948–49. Clearly, the new administration was attempting to make education more "democratic," to open it to the less privileged to move into the upper reaches of the educational system.

158

They sought this end by encouraging secondary education and pushing for greater attendance. During the three years the fraction of age-eligible children attending primary school rose from 30 per cent in 1945 to 36 per cent three years later; in the secondary schools the fraction rose from 2.9 per cent to 4.6 per cent.

University enrollments, although still pitiably small, also rose. The junta in 1946 reopened the University of Zulia in Maracaibo; the institution had been established at the beginning of the century, and then closed for four decades. The reasoning was that "university education needed sites in regions of the country where the conditions of the environment guarantee that such education can be imparted profitably." [46] The other two universities in the country were the Central University in Caracas (with a student body of 3,548) and the University of the Andes (with 904 enrolled). There were no private universities.

Two policy-changes of great importance were made at this time. The first was contained in a decree issued in 1946, granting autonomy to the universities. Such autonomy not only extended legal personality to the universities, broadening their potential base of financing, but also enhanced the political implications of the universities: they were free to establish their own academic criteria entirely independent of the state in matters of curriculum, hiring and firing, and student selection. The policing of university grounds was also left to academic authorities, a matter that can be of some moment in periods of civil distress. The only limitations on the authority of the universities were that their rectors and secretaries were chosen by the President of the Republic, and were also subject to dismissal at his discretion. [47]

The other policy innovation was in the perennially troublesome field of Church-state relations. Education was declared to be an "essential" function of the state, and the 1948 Organic Law of Education forbade any teaching of "partisan propaganda" or of "doctrines contrary to the democratic principles consecrated in the Political Constitution of the Republic or which favored the development of religious, ethnic, or social antagonisms." [48] Some effectiveness was to be given to these declarations by putting private education under governmental control in the awarding of diplomas. As we have seen in the case of Chile, this requirement was viewed by proponents of private education as the weapon that imposed state-controlled curricula and removed some of the reason for the existence of private schools. And it was seen by anticlerical supporters of public education as necessary to equalize standards and prevent "antinational" and anachronistic instruction. As the Minister of Education in 1948 put it:

The Venezuelan school must adopt a position of frank belligerency against those doctrines which, transgressing against culture, annul human value, liberty, and social justice, and the Venezuelan teacher must fight for the triumph of democracy so that it can continue to be a regimen of human perfection and the harmonious mingling of people.[49]

These postures of the *trienio* could not be translated into action. They were discarded by the Pérez Jiménez regime, although the quantitative expansion begun between 1945 and 1948 was continued, but at lowered rates. Despite an immediate decline in the budgetary percentage given to education, absolute budgetary increases saw the share of educational funds go from 119 million bolívares in 1948–49 to 178.3 millions in 1957–58.[50] Even in 1958, however, some 52 per cent of Venezuela's population was still illiterate, a problem which was to be attacked strenuously only after the overthrow of Pérez Jiménez. The number of primary-school students rose from 442,112 to 751,561 in the ten-year period, an increase of 67.7 per cent, while academic secondary-school enrollments rose from 22,299 to 55,194, an increase of 147.5 per cent.[51] These changes were in one sense a reversal of the *trienio* trend, for the general increase hid a loss in the percentage share of students attending public schools. At the end of the ten years, the public portion of primary-school enrollments had dropped from 85 to 81 per cent, while at secondary levels the decline was much steeper, from 76 to 55 per cent. This trend was part of a general lowering of concern with problems of the poor, for the Pérez Jiménez government was dedicated to the notion that rapid economic growth would take care of poverty through market mechanisms. However, the manpower demands of economic growth prompted the government to expand vocational and normal-school education considerably, the former's enrollment growing 290 per cent, to 19,357 students, and the latter 94.6 per cent, to 8,260 students. Of the vocational schools, 89 per cent were public—the only sector of education losing in its percentage of private underwriting.

The universities most clearly show the government's trend toward private schools. For the first time in Venezuela's modern history, private universities were permitted to function: the Andrés Bello Catholic University and the Santa María University were both established in 1954–55. The former is Jesuit-sponsored, the latter organized through secular private initiative. By 1957–58, these universities counted 2,082 students, about a fifth of the 10,270 university students listed for that year.[52] Most significantly—and most obviously to be expected in a dictatorship—

160

university autonomy suffered,[53] and access to the public universities was economically circumscribed in a vain attempt to contain the political beliefs of the students. The Central University was closed in 1951 after an extended dispute involving the creation of the private universities as well as other matters, and reopened with the imposition of tuition fees, breaking a tradition of free university education that dated back to the time of Guzmán Blanco. The impact of the measure has been described by Rómulo Betancourt, a leading figure in AD and the man who succeeded Pérez in the presidency, as follows:

After the closing of the Central University for almost two years, the institution was reopened in September of 1952. And on the university bulletin board appeared the sums to be paid: registration fees, Bs. 115; and tuition for the academic year on a scale like this—Engineering, Bs. 810; Medicine, Bs. 780; Dentistry, Bs. 1,050; Law, Bs. 650; Agriculture, Bs. 600; Architecture, Bs. 510; Laboratory, Bs. 300. To this had to be added the required payment for examinations, at Bs. 24 per test.

Nowadays, to obtain a doctorate in Venezuela a nation with . . . [U.S. $900,000,000] of public expenditures for a population of five million, is a situation so expensive that it is only within the reach of a minority . . . in the population. . . .

The regressive novelty of paid university education aims at two objectives easy to see. The first, to impede the access to professional training of youth of lower extraction, reserving it for the privileged strata of the population, and with this, eliminating the most revolutionary elements from within the classrooms. The second, to create for the future professional elites without a reformist impulse, capable of being won over by the thesis so generally held among some capitalist sectors of Venezuela that "order," no matter whether despotic and imposed by blows, better assures the peaceful enjoyment of material wealth than democratic systems of government with guarantees for the free play of social forces.[54]

The Pérez Jiménez regime did not supplant the policies of the government it replaced with other than rude and untested ideas that combined suspicion of "intellectuals" and liberal education with a bias toward low educational budgets and private—and, therefore, presumably conservative—educational institutions. And, as is common in such governments, teachers and university students were prime targets of political persecution. Some were killed, many imprisoned and tortured, some exiled, and others dismissed from their positions and barred from taking any further active role in education. Strenuous efforts were also made to

161

render ineffective the Venezuelan Federation and the Venezuelan College of Professors, the unions for primary-and secondary-school teachers.*

The Pérez Jiménez regime left Venezuela with the usual heritage of piratical developmental practices: extreme inequalities of income distribution, a bloated public bureaucracy, an unplanned mixture of private and nationally owned enterprise, an insufficient educational plant and archaic scholasticism mixed with crudely technological education, under- and unemployment, stunted parties, weakened organs of local government, and a military force that had learned to justify its "mission" as being the ultimate guardian of the nation's integrity as they themselves defined it.[55] The encompassing concept of regimes of this type is that they are above politics, apolitical—that politics is an evil, parties a luxury, legislatures a bother, and judiciaries to be employed to lend an aura of legality to government by decree. As is also usual with regimes of this kind, they enter into economic difficulties. The persistent opposition of the remaining party structures, the unions, the student groups, and other organizations given life in the 1940s coincided with emerging interests of certain national business groups and with a small dissident section of the military, leading to a three-day general strike in January, 1958. On the 23rd day of that month, Pérez Jiménez fled the country, and Venezuela returned to constitutional, civilian, elected government, a situation in which it still finds itself.

The events of the subsequent years cannot be well understood in isolation from more general hemispheric currents. As we have seen throughout these two historical surveys, Latin American countries react to ideas from abroad, making them their own, sometimes bowdlerizing them, sometimes enriching them. Foreign companies and governments take active roles in the politics of Latin American countries; individuals leave Latin America and spend time either in political exile or in pursuit of education, imbibing other aspects of foreign culture. At the same time, general diagnoses and a sense of purpose spread, changing the meaning and the conceptual rhythms of the times.

The late 1950s and the early years of the succeeding decade were perhaps the last period of democratic romanticism in Latin America.

---

*These occurrences were so notorious that they need no citational support. Legal proceedings after the overthrow of Pérez Jiménez judicially established these charges in specific cases, and the dictator himself, who sought exile in the U.S., was, in a highly unusual action, extradited to Venezuela, where he was tried and imprisoned for fraud. After his release from prison, he made his home in Spain, from whence he has campaigned for public office, winning a senate seat in the elections of 1970. He was later disqualified.

Military dictatorships fell one after another, and party politics and free speech and electoral mechanics began to function in a hemispheric atmosphere warmed by the tone and style if not by the content of the Alliance for Progress. Argentina's Perón had been overthrown in the mid-1950s, and in 1958 the first legally elected civilian since 1927 took office in that major country. Brazil was in a process of civilian-led development in which national parties were for the first time beginning to supplant the regional structures, and a sense of Brazilian nationhood was beginning to assert itself. In Cuba in 1959, Batista was supplanted by Castro, initially to the plaudits of the Caribbean's social democrats, and then to their increasing dismay. Rojas Pinilla, Colombia's counterpart of Pérez Jiménez, was overthrown in 1958, and a coalition of Liberals and Conservatives promised electoral politics. Peru, too, seemed to be embarked on formal democracy; Bolivia attempted reformist governments; and the early 1960s saw the assassination of Trujillo in the Dominican Republic. On the left, socialism began to be cut loose from Russian sovietism. The domestic political sense of Stalinism had been made clear by Khrushchev, and the distinction between economic collectivism and democratic socialism was beginning to be widely understood. Thus, Marxist movements in Latin America, although highly fragmented, could begin to move in national and culturally specific terms.

The few Kennedy years contributed significantly to this sense of democratic derring-do. The establishment of the Inter-American Development Bank, the attempt at a multilateral approach to development through the Alliance for Progress, and the acceptance in the United States of the utility of national developmental planning combined with a pledge of nonintervention in all matters except those immediately affecting the Cold War, giving center-left governments in Latin America a sense of affinity with the U.S. which they had not before felt. The development ideas of the time also fit comfortably with reformist minds of social democratic cast. The raw economic developmentalism of the early 1950s had given way to more complex, although still little understood, ideas of social development. Technicians, education, literacy, planning, participation, civilian rule, moderation, and effective reformism—these were the words of the day. The Bay of Pigs, the Missile Crisis, the landings of American troops in the Dominican Republic, Project Camelot, and the effects of Vietnam combined to kill this spirit of international comity in the task of national development. By the close of the 1960s and the first years of the 1970s, formal democracy in South America was in shambles except for Venezuela, the very country which for so many years seemed so politically benighted, so fated to primitive and sometimes savage governance. By 1973 Uruguay had lost its last vestiges of substantive democracy; Brazil was rounding out a decade of military dictatorship in alliance with international sources of capital; and Chile had become a corporate state under military rule, Peru a developmental military authoritarianism, Bolivia a right-wing military dictatorship, Paraguay remained the personalistic autocracy it had been for so many years, Colombia lost in its feckless attempts to make formal democracy work within a pattern of rigid class-related politics, and Ecuador was unable to develop sufficient institutional maturity to handle its problems with continuity and effectiveness.

The possibility of so bleak a hemispheric future was not reckoned with by the Venezuelans who took power in 1958. The three major parties (AD, COPEI, and the URD—Unión Republicana Democrática, a secularist, center-left grouping) joined in an accord to govern by coalition, no matter which party won in the elections of late 1958. But AD, still the major party, was ideologically torn in a way that was to reflect on relations among the parties to the coalition. AD had been the subject of the harshest repressions of the Pérez Jiménez years. Therefore, many of its leaders had to flee into exile, while their juniors braved the possibilities of torture and imprisonment to keep together what party organization was possible. The older leaders abroad took on ideas of effective reformism; the younger leaders at home often assumed the need for a more radical and even violent politics. Determined not to repeat their mistakes of the mid-1940s, the seasoned leaders decided that reformism and effective nation-building were possible within a context of political friendship with the United States, cooperative interaction with foreign companies, especially oil companies, and of putting aside their traditional anticlericalism for a policy of accommodation with the Church in the assumption that agreement could be reached on a legitimate area of entirely secular concerns. They were buttressed in these views by a gradual decline of McCarthyism in the United States and the emergence of more sophisticated notions of the real relations between governments and businessmen. They felt supported, too, by the growth of Christian Democracy in Chile, and the emergence of a greater tolerance of diversity within the Vatican. These views were strengthened by the activities of the Kennedy administration and of Pope John XXIII; they were also reinforced by what the older AD leaders thought to be the unnecessary hardships suffered by the Cubans in the early years of the Castro government, and by the increasing dependence of Cuba on the Soviet Union.

The younger leaders who had stayed at home did not, by and large, share these views. More sympathetic with Castro, less trusting of the United States and of foreign companies, in strong opposition to the Church they could see at home and mistrustful of the Church in Rome, they saw no reason to exchange tried antipathy for untested sympathy.

These internal controversies led to a schism within Acción Democrática and to the formation of a new party, the Movement of the Revolutionary Left (MIR). This incorporation of young activists into the leftist opposition soon was reflected in more virulent opposition and in the increased political participation of the marginal inhabitants of the cities. The young leaders had worked among these people to overthrow Pérez Jiménez and therefore enjoyed great prestige among them. The growing virulence also stemmed from the miserable conditions created by the high rates of unemployment caused by the economic crisis and distortions in the occupational structure. In 1962 the unemployment rate was over 14 percent; it is estimated that the average rate in the cities was over 17 percent, and it is probably true that it was as high as 25 percent in the "marginal" neighborhoods of the cities.[56]

The result was an outbreak of armed violence in 1961 that transformed itself into organized urban guerrilla campaigns, the first and most prolonged movement of its kind in any Latin American country. Put down by an effective integration between the political organization and police and military activities, the violence seriously disrupted urban life until 1965, and then—after clear defeat—was transferred into a weakened guerrilla movement in rural areas, where sparks were still occasionally seen in the early 1970s. The Communists, who had been uncertainly allied with the guerrilla movement from its inception, withdrew from such activities completely and formally in 1967.

Complete withdrawal from armed struggle was authorized for the Communists in the Eighth Plenum of the Central Committee, held in April 1967, which concluded that the guerrilla movement had become isolated and had turned into a blind alley. . . . The consensus among Communist leaders was that the guerrilla movement had been defeated not so much militarily as politically: never able to generate mass support or get off home base in its operations against the government. Pedro Ortega Díaz, a Communist Deputy in the 1959–63 congress, has provided the key to the Communist analysis of their defeat. His comments provide the clearest possible example of the full significance of that defeat for the strength and long/term viability of Venezuela's political institutions:

"We must never tire of repeating the distinction that must be made in fighting a government based on open military dictatorship and combatting a class dictatorship based on representative democracy, and respectful of certain forms. Our own case is all too expressive. The dominant classes were able to isolate the revolutionary vanguards in Venezuela, because we did not know how to adjust our struggle to the fact that there existed a form of domination based on representative democracy . . . . I repeat this because it is always easier to continue in the same simplistic vein:

'They are the same, both try to maintain Yankee rule.'

'Both serve the same boss.'

'Both use the army and police when their rule is threatened.'

'And though all this be true, *nevertheless we must learn to fight the two forms of domination in different ways.'* "[57]

The turbulence did not prevent the first AD President, Rómulo Betancourt, from being routinely succeeded by the second, Raúl Leoni, President of Venezuela at the time the survey materials in this study were taken. In 1969 a COPEI administration took office, and in turn COPEI was succeeded normally in 1974 by a return to AD leadership. The regularity and normality of these electoral procedures are unequaled in contemporary Latin America, and their importance is not gainsaid, as the quotation above demonstrates.

The AD administration immediately set out to overcome the losses in educational development during the Pérez Jiménez years. The quantitative increases were dramatic, but the "sense" and the "spirit" of educational reform were without shape, although informed by democratic good will. As the Four Year Plan for 1960–64 put it:

. . . [T]he school system is . . . the principal vehicle for transmitting to younger generations the major part of the cultural baggage of peoples, as well as for inculcating the general principles that the society has outlined as norms. . . . If despotism advocates submission and flattery, we must educate for liberty and pride. If despotism acts to separate and to oppose one Venezuelan to another, democracy can only educate for union and mutual respect. If tyranny seeks submission to a discipline of fear, maintained by persecution, democracy can teach only a discipline that results from the enthusiastic attachment to the idea of dignity and respect for man.

In Venezuela one must educate for the democratic order, for the spiritual superiority that the life of that order requires as a fundamental condition, and for the economic organization and productivity that permits us our own control over our natural resources and our heritage. What is important, then, is

166

not only to establish schools, make adults literate, open establishments of technical and industrial learning, facilitate access to middle-level schooling for more Venezuelans, or to create universities, since all this is not sufficient for an educational policy. What is really important is the sense or the spirit in which it is done.[58]

This quotation is typical of the times, and not only of the era in Venezuela. Strikingly different from the expressions of the nineteenth century in Chile, it says nothing about reason, nothing about developing the internal resources of individuals in the belief that "right" thinking can lead in only one general social direction, and that from this commonality of "rightness" will come beneficial social interaction. Instead, the Venezuelan expression of the matter suggests that schools imbued with the proper "sense" and "spirit" will mold students in democratic ways, just as schools established in other frames can turn human clay into undesirable patterns. The purpose, as has been said, is of democratic good will; the premise is that the manipulation of situations and externals is sufficient to work the social transformation being sought. The problem, then, becomes a technical one, simply administering into being the democratic ethic mandated by the political course of events. The relation between an ethical political determination and the very nature of man and social organization is not at issue, for the tacit assumption is that the qualities of man and society are infinitely malleable.

Impelled by this sense of great freedom of effective opportunity, the AD set out to create an educated citizenry. The field work for this study began in 1967. From the end of the dictatorship to just prior to the initiation of our interviews (that is, from 1958 to 1966), enrollment in primary schools jumped 97 per cent, from 751,561 students to 1,482,333. The annual rate of growth was about 12 per cent. Students enrolled in secondary education rose by 244 per cent, at an annual rate of 30 per cent, going from 55,194 to 189,583 in numbers. And, contrary to the increasing practice of the dictatorial governments, the expansion was largely in the public schools, signaling a growth in educational opportunity for the less privileged. In 1965–66, some 86 per cent of the primary-school enrollments were in public schools, as were 69 per cent of secondary-school enrollments. Vocational education, traditionally the domain of lower-class students, also showed an extremely high percentage increase for the period—up 380 per cent to 93,120 students, an annual growth of 48 per cent. But university enrollments topped all in rate of growth: in 1965–66, there were 43,977 university students, up 328 per cent from 1967, the average annual increase being 41 per cent.

Teacher-training did not expand nearly so rapidly in the public sector, increasing only 55 per cent. Private normal schools held their relative strength better than any other sector, having 56 per cent of all students in this sector. A tightening job market, and the higher dedication and professionalism of the Catholic normal schools, contributed to the drop in public enrollments and the converse maintenance of the private endeavors. The Pedagogical Institute, however, grew enormously, after having been arrested in its development during the years of the dictatorship. Its registrations increased to 2,848 in 1965–66, 723 per cent more than in 1957–58, assuring the importance of the public sector in preparing teachers for secondary schools.

The educational deficit remained high, however, for even in the last years of the second AD presidential period, only 61 per cent of the relevant age group was in primary schools, 34 per cent in secondary schools. (The figures were only 44 and 11 per cent, respectively, in 1955.)[59] The ratio of primary- to secondary-school students was eight to one and, as measured against students in all kinds of secondary education, it was five to one. As for the relation between secondary and university students, the ratio had fallen to four to one. The educational flow was beginning to even out through the pipeline, and diversity was setting in, for 39 per cent of all secondary-level students were in vocational- and normal-school training.

Social troubles still beset the systems and the students, of course. The effects of poverty contributed importantly to keeping a national average of 15 per cent of primary-school students from regular attendance. Regional differences made this rate vary widely. In the capital, for example, average attendance was up to 88 per cent, but in the rural states of Apure and Barinas, attendance was around 76 per cent. About 15 per cent of all primary-school students were repeating grades, as were almost 10 per cent of secondary-school students. The rate of successful completion of schooling is another important indicator of efficacy of the system and of ability of students to attend. Only a third of entering primary-school students completed the required six years at that level, and the same percentage of entering students managed to complete secondary school. Over-all, the chance that a first-year primary-school student would be graduated from any kind of secondary school was but one in nine.[60]

The regional differences in the quantitative and qualitative availability of schools underscore the probability that even the newly expanded educational system was hobbled by class differences and was not as yet overcoming them on any massive scale. At the secondary level, for example—and this study makes clear how important such schooling is to social maturity—there were 571 academic high schools in Venezuela in 1966. But more than a third of them were in the Federal District and the adjacent state of Miranda, although they contained only a little over a fifth of the national population. The capital has only a fifth of the vocational schools, but they are the highest-prestige schools providing the best economic opportunities. For instance, Caracas had the only secondary-level school of social work, half of the nursing schools, and almost a third of the industrial high schools. Three of the seven universities are in Caracas, and they enroll two-thirds of all university students.[61]

Aside from these distributional characteristics of Venezuelan education, the difference between the public and Catholic sectors of private schooling reinforces social difference. We have already pointed out the many status distinctions between students in the two kinds of systems, a fact commonly noted in the relevant literature. For example:

> . . . [I]t is clear that those students who are enrolled in private schools tend to do better academically—and thus presumably to attain greater status—than do those enrolled in public schools.

> Differential prestige for public and private schooling would seem to result not only because those from high socio-economic background tend to congregate in private schools but also because private schooling in Venezuela has largely confined itself to types and levels of education which are relatively easily established and maintained. In particular, private education, because it is free to reject students to a much greater extent than is public education, has relegated the education of children to a secondary position in its efforts 'to maintain standards' and thus to maintain prestige. . . .

> . . . if private education offers special advantages and benefits to its students, as private school proponents allege, it has denied these advantages and benefits to large groups of students because of its distorted representation within the educational system.[62]

Partisan politics also has much to do with the identification of private schools with privileged groups. The guerrilla activities of the 1960s had as one of their most important centers the Central University in Caracas, and students have taken a highly visible and active part in opposition to governments since the 1930s. We have seen the origins of AD and URP and, indirectly, even of COPEI in the universities. The Venezuelan Church has generally eschewed identification with either the more reformist elements of Christian Democratic movements or with the much more radical Church-centered groups in Brazil. Opus

Dei, the semisecret Catholic lay organization so deeply involved in the governance of Spain, reputedly has great influence in Venezuela. Whatever the facts may be, the image clearly is that the Church as an institution is conservative. Therefore, the children of the well-to-do are considered ideologically safer in Catholic schools and universities than in public institutions.

> The focus on education and anticommunism has produced an extraordinary accommodation between the largely Protestant American community [in Venezuela] and numerous programs administered by Catholics that have in fact been mounted by a combination of resources and leadership representing both the U.S. business sector and a small but influential Venezuelan group. Many North American contacts with Venezuelans are limited almost exclusively to this small circle, who are the single source of interpretation of Venezuela; it is one that is both readily available and persuasive, for it largely echoes their own propaganda. Because in practical terms the Church is considered the only ideologically trustworthy educator in sight, the marriage of free enterprise and social concern is made effective in Venezuela almost exclusively through the agency of Church-centered groups.[63]

At the time our survey was conducted in Venezuela, 605 schools were associated with the Venezuelan Association of Catholic Education (AVEC— Asociación Venezolana de Educación Católica), of which 558 were registered with the Ministry of Education and thus eligible to extend valid certificates to their students, but in turn were required to employ governmentally prescribed study programs. Of these, 120 were for boys, 202 for girls, and 283 coeducational. Most of these schools covered the primary grades through academic preparation at the secondary level and were situated in the major cities. Greater Caracas had 186 of them, 42 were in Zulia (which includes the oil city of Maracaibo with its heavy concentration of foreign residents), 40 were in Táchira, 35 in Lara-Yaracuy (centered in the city of Barquisimeto), and the remainder were scattered in smaller cities, with very few in rural areas.[64] Student enrollment totaled 182,092, of whom 81,194 paid no tuition. About 46 per cent of these students (83,872) attended schools in Caracas. Most of the scholarship students attended mission and vocational schools, and very few were received into the secondary levels. The total enrollment at all preuniversity levels comprises about 10 per cent of the schoolgoing population of the country.

The ideological confusions and the historical events of the 1960s and 1970s have left perceptions of the role of education in development indeterminate everywhere. Indeed, the very definition of development

170

itself has become amorphous. Venezuela's rates of economic growth have been impressive for the past 25 years. Averaging some 8 per cent in the 1950s, and then becoming sporadic in the early 1960s only to start up again at relatively high rates, the Venezuelan economy, accompanied by rapid urbanization, has been healthy by standard indicators. Obviously, much remains to be done in the simple construction of the machinery of the educational as well as the economic systems. By the mid-1970s, for example, it was still being estimated that some 400,000 children of school age were not receiving instruction, either because they had dropped out or never had begun. Appraisals of the Venezuelan scene can be confusing: is the tank half-empty or half-full? The closing comments of two books cited earlier give poignant evidence of wrenching scholarly disagreement in judging contemporary Venezuela. Frank Bonilla begins his final paragraphs by stating that "The exhaustion of the development paradigm as a design for the emancipation of nations like Venezuela becomes more and more evident as the decade of the sixties closes." He then concludes:

As the realization grows that the battle as earlier defined has been lost on other institutional fronts, pressures and hopes shift to new areas. National armies, national parties, national bourgeoisies all have fallen short of the immediate challenge. The present crisis of the universities signals the transfer of expectations to the cultural sphere as well as the apprehension of new dangers within it. In none of these areas did Venezuelan middle-sector elites, speaking in the mid-1960s, display any manifest sensibility. The most articulate among them were still beginning to assimilate and manipulate the rudimentary ideas of development, planning, and social reform. Enlightened leadership and the long-term effects of education and increasing participation continued to be viewed as main levers of long-term change. From this perspective the mesocratic vanguard hardly seems relevant to the Venezuela that would be.[65]

Daniel Levine takes the opposite view:

Venezuela seems to have solved some of the deepest riddles of political development: mobilization with legitimate authority, containing the military, and combining conflict and competition with institutional and procedural consensus. In reaching these solutions, Venezuelans have built a powerful and complex political infrastructure, a solid foundation for future development and change with institutional continuity. But authority and legitimacy are delicate creatures, and bargains can be broken. In Venezuela, the future lies with cautious men.[66]

One of the points that Bonilla makes is that today the formation of national community in the contemporary world faces not only the customary foe of internal traditionalism, but also the external forces of the international world. Levine, who has directed his gaze to the elaboration of domestic political organization, sees complexity and power which had never before existed. The history we have abstracted concerns the creation of power, the role of politics in producing the ability to act out of the will to do so, and the mustering of support not merely from an economic order, but also out of the mists of world views and the concreteness of organization. The time in which these events have occurred has been short, however, and the ideas at large in the world simplistic. Venezuela still lacks a coherent national culture, which is its greatest educational deficit, far transcending in importance the realities of its school systems. And its leaders lack a sufficiently profound intellectual-ethical sense of self-interest to ensure a relatively safe passage for Venezuela through the conflicts between democratic and authoritarian organization that beset so many Western countries.

The coherence between this historical treatment and the foregoing survey data should be clear. We have seen confirmation of such details as the relative prestige distinguishing Catholic and public schools, of the reasons that Venezuelans distinguish much more crudely among social classes than do Chileans, of the fragility of family structure among the poor that has caused parents to refuse to answer occupational questions, and of the reasons that the persons we have studied outpaced their parents so greatly in educational attainment. These descriptive confirmations of our survey should embolden us to employ the most significant difference that appeared between Chileans and Venezuelans: the much greater ideological constraint of the latter, their much higher propensity toward ideational differences reinforced by appropriate situational differences. Clearly, Venezeulans are not so mentally trapped by their circumstances as would be less developed persons. Their history reveals that some, at least, have been able to remove—though not divorce—their personal social circumstances both from their ideals and their behavior. But the transition from situation-ideas to ideas-situation is far from complete. The world's conditions will not make easier the task of enlarging the effective use of reason for national change in to-day's Venezuela. Unlike her continental sisters, however, Venezuela still retains the option of pursuing change with the head rather than the strong arm.

seven / Conclusions: On Freedom and Lesser Matters

Freedom is the master theme of this study. Although both authors yearn unabashedly for a civic life of utopian freedom, we had not planned this study to delve so deeply into the subject. Instead, we had intended to remain at a more formal level, dealing with educational and political systems as manifestations of given kinds of societies and leaving the matter of freedom to ideological taste. To our combined dismay and gratification, however, the matter of freedom intruded itself willynilly, forced into consideration by the nature of our findings and the evolution of our theoretical understanding. Indeed, waiting behind every turn of our data and twist of our reasoning, we found the classical questions of freedom and constraint, liberty and order, man as doer and God as determiner. The idea that wishful thinking may have seduced our intellects has naturally occurred to us. Also tempering our enthusiasm with the essentially optimistic conclusions at which we have arrived has been the pervasive pall of pessimism emanating from most contemporary social commentary, both lay and professional. But our findings, our thinking, and our affective sets drove us to resist the conventional emotionality, even at the risk of courting misunderstanding of our personal political convictions and professional approaches. For instance, we are very well aware that our insistence on employing such passé terms as "modern" and "traditional" may invite our being labeled as hopelessly anachronistic or even foolish. However, we find them useful; they respond both to our common sense and our theoretical schema. If the social sciences are indeed in a state of intellectual crisis within a disarrayed world, we prefer to confront challenges to understanding by shattering only false idols; some of the traditional gods we find still useful guides to comprehension.

Our evolving ideas about the meaning of developmental change and the normative shifts in Chileans and Venezuelans as they proceed through formal education combined to force us to think directly about social causality. When one seeks to juxtapose changes in individuals with changes in social orders, there can be no evasion of a consideration of cause. And to think about cause is quite necessarily to be forced into a preoccupation with the relation between determinism and the limits of freedom. There is nothing esoteric or mysterious about this concern. It is as quotidian a problem as where to shop or what morning newspaper to buy, as mundane a daily political subject as disagreement between a fascist and a democrat—or a modern man and a traditional one. The present-day generality of disarray, crisis, and failures of everyday routine are leading many social scientists to a crowning obfuscation, the collapsing together of categories of difference by assuming that the omnipresence of disturbance is the reflection of a single crisis. Perhaps, at some uselessly general level, the "global" crisis is the same for us all because it is merely a reflection of the "human condition." But what the individual peoples of the world within their societies can do about their part of whatever universal crisis there is, and also about their specific troubles, obviously varies widely. No service is done to our thinking by erasing the patent differences between modernity and tradition, democracy and the many forms of authoritarianism, or the "advanced" and the "primitive." We wholeheartedly agree that many of the characteristics commonly ascribed to those contrasting states have been puerile, ethnocentric, self-serving—just wrong. But we certainly do not agree that the *situations* those often weak and misleading defining characteristics have distorted for us do not exist "out there."

For all too many persons the failure of most paradigms of development has suggested that the notion of development is itself a sham. Thus, if the kind of reasoning we have employed does not work, let us secure the coffers and hold on to as much as we can of what we have.

. . . We have become aware that rationality has its limits for engineering social change [writes Robert L. Heilbroner][1] and that those limits are much narrower than we had thought; that many economic and social problems lie outside the scope of our accustomed instruments of policy-making; that growth does not bring about certain desired ends or arrest certain undesired trends.

Hence in place of the brave talk of the Kennedy generation of managerialists—not to mention the prophets of progress or of a benign dialectical logic of events—there is now a recrudescence of an intellectual conservatism that looks askance at the possibilities for large-scale social engineering, stressing the innumerable cases—for example, the institutionalization of poverty through the welfare system, or the exacerbation of racial friction through the efforts to promote racial equality—in which the consequences of well-intentioned acts have only given rise to other, sometimes more formidable problems than those which they had set out to cure.

We, too, are fearful of a further decline in social decency and public freedom. But we do not share a sense of fated pessimism. On the contrary, we have a reservoir of guarded optimism, stemming from our belief that even though, obviously, "rationality has its limits for engineering social change," we are far from exhausting those limits. If anything, far too little reason has been used, and far too much rationalization and engineering. Indeed, we directly challenge the idea that rational men would seek to "engineer" change, in the sense of directly manipulating it into being for the forced consumption of the "objects" of the engineers' ministrations. Establishing effective freedom so that objects can become subjects, bringing about their own self-reinforcing change, would be more desirable, more effective, and thus, more "rational." The fact that, at international levels, this approach to development has rarely been taken is itself a backhanded cause for optimism, even if we know that building the sovereign effectiveness of a foreign people is not a common procedure in international relations.

The stock of reason is not the only resource in the solution of social problems that is far from exhausted. The latent intellectual ability and affective willingness of people to participate in social efforts is also far in excess of what they are usually called upon to deliver. The factual core of this book fully supports those statements in the cases of Chile and Venezuela. The theoretical core strongly suggests that those conclusions are applicable to many more countries. Specifically, the central findings and concepts of this study are as follows:

The Factual Core. In Chile and Venezuela persons who manage to achieve secondary or higher education tend to be able to free their social attitudes from the narrow limits of their situations of origin and to think broadly about their total social settings and their own parts therein. They develop the skill to reason differently about different social activities, and to segregate a set of secular activities that they see as fittingly subject to voluntary, willful change. They learn, thus, to tolerate ambiguity, and to create contradictions—not the least of which are the ability to see the difference between the real and the ideal, and between education as class-reinforcing and education as inculcating universalizing ideals. They tend to become latently free to exercise a broader range of social choice than would have been possible for them without the educational experience. They develop, in other words, the talent of intellectuality, which involves the practice of some measure of intellectual autonomy within the bounds of a specific social and historical setting. Intellectuality is a prime element in change, for it involves thinking about change, being the ability to think simultaneously about oneself,

175

and about one's *persona* in relation to an idealized vision of self and society. Our findings in this regard are statistically strong and clearly patterned. They reveal unmistakably that political and educational differences are tightly intertwined, both among the groups, as well as between the two countries we have studied. In this respect we consider the study unequivocal. We also consider the more advanced educational systems we have examined an unmistakable success in this dimension, whatever other faults those systems may have.

The Conceptual Core. Sufficient exposure to education tends to teach people to loosen their attitudes from a narrow, apparently determined relation to social station. This skill lies at the very heart of modernity, the reflection within individual psyches and intellects of the capacity of modern societies to encapsulate the effects of change. The modernity of a society in the last analysis is measured by its ability to control the effects of action; the fewer the necessary—and therefore, uncontrollable—effects of action, the more modern the society. The limitation of necessary effects is, in other words, the measure of efficacy and efficiency of control over the physical and social environments. An absolute increase in such control is a superficial way of defining development; however, it is the *way* in which the control is increased, the *discipline* of the control, that provides the more substantive measure, and tells us why so much "engineering" has been misplaced, and so much ostensible rationality mere rationalization—a refinement in ordering without attention to the articulations among the elements being ordered. To take two common examples, industrialization is not automatically modernizing per se, but only to the extent to which it permits greater refinement in the working and the containment of the effects of change. Similarly, urbanization is modernizing only to the extent to which it enhances the ability of people to control—to permit a community consciously, willfully, and rationally to enter into the causal nexus of relations. Under some conditions, industrial urbanization can have antimodernizing effects. The experience in the United States is that urbanization was in its inception modernizing in effect, but now has become partially antimodernizing.

This approach to development has permitted us to reconcile individual and social characteristics, speaking of both within the same conceptual frame. Specifically, it has permitted us here to write about individuals and about political change, employing common concepts for both, despite their differing levels of generalization. This common conceptual underpinning has also allowed us to employ social survey data and historical data to speak to the same set of problematic relations.

176

What we have learned about education and political attitudes in Venezuela and Chile will not surprise the specialist. The factual findings are not in dispute, at least not yet. The reason for the lack of disagreement is all too obvious: most contemporary social scientists, North American, Latin American, and European, ascribe little importance to what education does directly for individual students, but rather they search out its accomplishments in creating instrumental values, skills to be used in economic endeavors, or to promote the common weal or satisfy the mobility urges of individuals. In the Americas, we have wanted schooling (as distinct from education) to accomplish all things, to be the wellspring of all curative waters for the ills of the society. In the first important post–World War II, North American book to spell out these goals of schooling, we read that the social functions of the American educational system are to provide a basis of communication and a common core of traditions and values, to teach children to work and live together, to help people find ways of realizing their social ideals, to teach the skills for carrying on the economic life of society, and to select and train children for social mobility.[2] The authors of this work, all sophisticated men, were well aware of the burden they and, in their estimation, society at large were placing on the schools. Their opening words are:

> The American public schools are, in the opinion of the people of the United States, basic and necessary parts of our democracy. We are convinced that they must, and we hope that they do, provide equal opportunity for every child. This means that those at the bottom can compete through education for life's prizes with those at the top. All that is needed are brains, a will to do, hard work, and plenty of ambition. In our faith every aspiring student may not have a marshall's baton in his knapsack, but in his public schooling he does have an equal chance with everyone else for the White House.

> This basic belief in the democratic functioning of our public schools is only partly true. This book describes how our schools, functioning in a society with basic inequalities, facilitate the rise of a few from lower to higher levels, but continue to serve the social system by keeping down many people who try for higher places. The teacher, the school administrator, the school baord, as well as the students themselves, play their roles to hold people in their places in our social structure.

> If the American faith in the public schools as a democratic force is to become less fictional, we must examine the relevant facts and determine what distorts this picture. From such information we can gather the necessary knowledge to act intelligently on the problem of who should be educated . . . [p. ix].

The causal implications of this statement, and of evolving educational policy and relevant law during the next twenty years, run as follows:

education improves cognitive skills, which lead to better occupations and higher incomes, resulting in a greater measure of social equality. But by the mid-1960s, researchers were finding that cognitive skills are little affected by the type of school attended by students, and that instead, such skills seem almost totally determined by a combination of family-home-class-ethnic-racial factors. Because education was thought to be the primary route for redressing the social disadvantages especially of black children, these findings caused dismay; the schools could not function to bring us closer to the American ideal of equality, with or without desegregation, busing, improved facilities, or more highly trained teachers. The quality of schooling seemed not to matter:

> . . . During the late nineteen-fifties and early 'sixties almost all American social scientists assumed that schools and colleges played a pivotal role in creating and solving social problems. . . .
>
> The first major challenge to the old consensus was "Equality of Educational Opportunity," a report issued in 1966 by Dr. James S. Coleman and six colleagues. The Coleman Report showed that students' test scores varied dramatically when they finished elementary school. These variations were partly explained by variations in individual students' family backgrounds. They were also related, though not so strongly, to the socio-economic level of a students' classmates.
>
> Once these two factors were taken into account, variations in the resources of the school a student had attended did not seem to have any independent effect on his test score. . . .[3]

The Coleman Report has, naturally, elicited widespread reaction. An anthology of commentary on the work calls it a "formidable achievement,"[4] and sums up the major finding in these blunt words, "The pathbreaking quality of the EEOR [the Report itself; the survey for the Report is usually referred to as the EEOS] had to do with its analysis of the relation of variation in school facilities to variation in levels of academic achievement. It reported so little relation as to make it almost possible to say there was none" (p. 15). These statements should be read very precisely. They do *not* say that schooling matters not at all; obviously, much is learned in school. They do *not* deal in questions of values, but only in a narrow definition of "cognitive skills," having to do with the three Rs and related abilities. The disappointment of Coleman, Jencks, and others is that schools did not equalize cognitive difference *in function of the kind of school facilities available;* therefore, their

178

further disappointment is that equalization of social status could not result from a school-induced equalization of cognitive skills. Thus, schools cannot effectively promote individual occupational mobility, and therefore cannot help overcome the effects of class and race in limiting the opportunities of Americans.

As we have said explicitly in Chapters V and VI, and implicitly throughout much of this study, we have no quarrel at all with these *findings*. Insofar as there is a congruence of concerns, we have found exactly the same: the attitudes we studied are somewhat affected by the type of school attended by a student, but only marginally, and certainly not to the same extent as other effects which are clearly working. For example, children attending Catholic secondary schools lag in picking up the secularist attitudes one finds so widespread in public secondary schools, but the differences are not overwhelming and smooth out somewhat in the course of time. Also, some differences appear between students in rural and urban settings, but they are not striking, a fact we attribute to the overriding effects of national culture. And so on. We found, too, that family and class affect the development of social attitudes, as these two factors operate to create the simple ability to attend school long enough to advance to secondary levels, and as they affect the type of school system and the prestige level of the school being attended. If the kind of school seems to matter a bit more for us than for Coleman and his replicators, then we can attribute the difference to the lower degree of development in Chile and Venezuela, implying that school facilities are neither so fundamentally equal nor so widespread as in the United States.

This area of confirmation is, however, of little significance. We depart fundamentally from the train of research so briefly sketched, in assuming an entirely different relation between education and political and economic life. We see no reason to be disappointed in the educational institution because it does not produce equality or, even more important, equity in social life. To expect such a result is to overlook the structuring of privilege and pattern from which students emerge to go to school, and to which they return every afternoon and permanently after graduation. It is not that the weavers of the American dream do not know this fact. Their problem is in misunderstanding its nature and thus what must be done to change it, if changing it is what they desire. Their expectation was that a cognitively equipped person could, *as individual*, proceed to the job market, which would receive and weigh and advance him on the basis of merit alone, without regard to other factors. This presumption proved to be impossible to submit to a full test, given the

179

solidity of the total structure of inequality. They learned that deprived persons do not attain cognitive skills as well or as rapidly in school as do the scions of the better-off, and therefore the causal chain cannot be begun. And here stands their argument. The thesis exonerates the schools of blame for failing effectively to teach the less advantaged, for socially underprivileged children seem to find it difficult to learn no matter what school they attend, even though learning improves with the help of more favored fellow students. Therefore, we are driven back to "explaining" the failure to achieve equality by citing the inhibiting influences of familistic and class factors. In other words, we "explain" continuing inequality by saying it is the result of present inequality. Even so, the implication remains that it is the inequality of the under-privileged that is to blame, not the inequality of the better placed. That is, the problem remains defined as one of underprivilege, not as one of privilege. In fact, of course, it is the nexus between privilege and its relative absence which begins to outline the problem meaningfully.

Because our theoretical assumptions were different from those of Warner, Havighurst, Coleman, Jencks *et al.,* we have produced not only different "facts" and conclusions, but also a very different feeling. We started, it will be remembered, with the supposition that disjunctive social relations are normal. Thus, straight-line causality was discarded, and we wove a causal concept into our attitude-survey and into the definition of modernity whose full relation was expressed in this chapter. What we examined were not "cognitive skills" in the usual sense; but the social and political attitudes we plumbed are certainly indicative of cognitive skills of another kind—the ability, given an appropriate soci-ety, to live a modern life, to help to cause events. We looked at education institutionally, and found that enough participation in that institution did, unmistakably, help students create secular, relativistic, changeful, and autonomous views. But we make absolutely no presumption that to hold such ideas and have such skills will in itself produce desired social change. Schools, important as they are, remain but schools. They are not armies, international power groupings, social classes, congresses, or social-work agencies. The student rebels of the 1960s, roundly con-demned by many of the same persons who pursued their feckless quest for equality through schooling, were involved in the same problem—how to have national impact in the absence of an effective voice in the national political economy. The social-reform-through-schooling advo-cates and the revolution-through-the-university advocates were doing the same thing: using the educational institution as a lever to what they otherwise would not or could not affect. We do not mean that activities

180

in pursuit of such ends are without meaning or significance. They are, of course. But they cannot *in themselves* bring into being their objectives unless the remainder of the institutional structure is so weak as to permit, in effect, an internal conquest from schools employed as a power base. In Latin America's thinner social situations, that result has, indeed, occurred. It is now no longer imaginable either in Chile or Venezuela, as we explicitly pointed out in the relevant historical chapters. It is also unimaginable in the United States. Nevertheless, in all these countries the role of intellectuals, the schooled, and the educated is of great day-to-day significance.

Our evocation of studies of North American education to further understanding of research carried out in Latin America is, of course, not accidental. It appears to us clear that there are important theoretical points of concordance between certain Latin American and North American social occurrences. Chile, Venezuela, and the United States share the same general type of economic system, related in the same general ways to a class order, and have the same troubles equating generally similar ideals with rapidly evolving economic and technological situations. In this sense of sharing similar dynamics and problems, all three countries are in the same broad category of development. From this point of view, it may be commented that Chile may be even more "mature" than the United States, for its military coup of 1973 confronted the tension between national community and class directly; its contradiction between equality and privilege ripened completely, a crisis not yet apparently at hand in the United States or Venezuela. But in terms of what each nation can do about its troubles, differing levels of development take on great significance, of course. Needless to say, the objective educational, human, material, and technological resources of the United States are far in advance of any Latin country, although their organization for effective employment in the solution of social issues is at this time problematical.

Because the universality of technology is flowing together with the essentially similar social and political systems in the more modern countries of the hemisphere, we can see skeletal outlines of future educational-political relations also in essentially similar comparative light. We think the separation of education and occupational success in the United States to be a reflection of increasing institutional differentiation, another collapse of a deterministic link that we see as potentially extremely positive, although also dramatically dangerous. Latin America, as we have pointed out, is moving in essentially the same direction: the mobilization of masses of people is no longer needed for the tasks of industrial production. Unlike many of our colleagues, we see that trend as inherent to development, and we applaud it. We do not view industrial irrelevancy as productive of "functionally useless" people—unless the only function of man is to work in a factory. And we do not think that educational "success" is to be measured by occupational "success." Thus, for us, the schools of Venezuela and Chile are successful in an appropriately basic way: they are changing the world views of students toward an appreciation of greater autonomous effectiveness. An insistence on measuring education by what it does for an economy instead of what it does for its students can lead to the destruction of national endeavors.

The policy that a modern authoritarianism should follow with respect to education is clear. If our findings are correct in terms of what they reveal concerning the learning of political and social attitudes, then dictatorial regimes can increase their security by preventing most people from moving beyond primary school. Thereafter, careful selection of students on the basis of their attitudinal rigidity, reinforced by technological training admitting only of deterministic social understandings, can provide the stock of engineers and technicians needed to run the producing and policing mechanisms. The critical task of the authoritarian is to prevent the experience of schooling from helping students to develop the attitudes of intellectual questioning and relativism antithetical to governments dedicated to the idea that subjects are children, unable to sustain the ideas of change and autonomous self-direction. As we have found in this study, the politics of dictatorship are the politics of children. Truly democratic politics is the public life of educated persons—not of those who have succeeded only in growing older. The conclusion is inescapable from this study that, empirically, a prolonged educational experience in Chile and Venezuela—and, by implication, everywhere—helps individuals to a potential for self-enrichment. This potential can become social and political reality only if social particularism is reconciled with community universalism. Specifically:

•Class position certainly beclouds vision and judgment. But it is not the deprived who, by their very isolation from class-based power will be able to overcome class-inspired purblindness and become the "universal class." The "inner reality" of total social relations can appear only in the minds of men educated to perceive. The final result of the proper cultivation of personal autonomy, relativism, the tolerance of ambiguities, and the intellectual creation of and action upon the perception of contradictions is the creation of a *truly* universal class, the anticlass—the educated capable of intellectuality.

•The politics of total communities is the giving of patterns, the conceptual ways in which disjunctive relations are synthesized into meaningful patterns and sanctioned by publicly legitimatized coercion. Political institutions perform a mediating role among competing particular interests, of course, but the principal secular function of universalizing politics is the integration, propagation, and imposition of ordered ethical views. The emergence of the state and of national community is a step toward submitting social events to reason, removing the mundane at least partially from religious and theological absolutism. The hardening of state and nation into dogmatic rigidity is destructive of this developmental political role, substituting the state for other faith-based institutions. A democratic politics of total communities is the only politics consonant with the mind of the educated person.

As we said at the beginning of this work, politics in national societies integrates the institutional order. Formal education in national societies is the institution fundamental to preparing persons for autonomous participation in secular and relativistic politics. This effect of education makes possible individual democratic activity in societies. In *incompletely* national societies discord develops around the ability of some individuals and groups to live democratically, and the inability of others to act in effectively democratic ways. In such societies, formal education is a crucial element in creating both the grounds of the conflict and the ability to perceive it. In developing capitalistic societies, the principal brake to continued development has been a stress between the opposing pulls of class and nation. The intellectuality promoted by prolonged participation in formal education, however, tends to lead educated persons to value universal national over particular class interests. Therefore, while education as an institution makes possible partially democratic as well as dictatorial national integration, through time it is inherently in contradiction with class-supportive authoritarianism.

Appendix

BACKGROUND

The initial intellectual impetus for this research was provided by Kalman H. Silvert, who had previously completed a study of education and social development in Latin America with Frank Bonilla.* The results of this undertaking generated a number of ideas, which Silvert believed ought to be pursued. When officials of The Brookings Institution evinced an interest in sponsoring a study of education and politics, he suggested his interest in further research into these themes. The Carnegie Corporation funded the present study through The Brookings Institution, beginning in the fall of 1965. In order to appreciate some of the initiating ideas, we wish to quote from Silvert's letter to the Carnegie Corporation.

One of the most difficult problems both of theory and method in the social sciences is how to lace a knowledge of individual attitudes to the prognosis of group behavior. . . .

An understanding of the "play" possible between avowed attitudes and overt behavior is of more than a little moment. It is not only that most attitude surveys neglect the specific and articulated analysis of the relation between individual attitudes and group behavior—therefore losing some predictive power—but also that many persons concerned with early socialization suggest that comparatively little learning of basic values is possible once formal schooling is begun. Even if we assume that conclusion to be valid, does it then follow that the nature of instruction cannot be so adjusted as to inculcate certain behavior patterns that can make of the individual a functionally developed person in many aspects of his public life?

The matter of "civic culture" also needs some specification. Gabriel Almond, the person most responsible for the contemporary use of the term, has

---

*Dr. Bonilla subsequently withdrew from the study. The materials have been completely reanalyzed and are being published by Silvert in collaboration with Frieda M. Silvert, under its original title, *Education and the Social Meaning of Development*.

often been accused of a "Liberal bias" in this and other constructions. We assume that such a bias is inevitable in political modernization analysis, for a historical baseline necessarily must be sought in countries which ideologically have been classically Liberal at least in the past, and which now are also more or less democratic in political organization. The concept of what a "civically cultured" person is, however, can be elaborated in perhaps a less culture-bound fashion than has so far been done. In some of his previous work Silvert has argued the case for the use of the concept of national integration as the reigning characteristic of modern polities. A person who accepts the state as "the ultimate and impersonal arbiter of secular dispute" also—as part of his system of public values—usually assumes relativistic stances in public affairs, is secularistic in politics, and supports the existence of stylized marketplace arrangements to permit merit instead of ascription to be used as measuring rods for certain purposes (equality before the laws, a certain amount of equality before the economic structure, the existence of compulsory public education to reduce the rigidifying effects of birth-determined status, and so forth). One of the major findings from the Silvert-Bonilla study was that the ability to see society as open and accessible and to empathize broadly across class lines is also a primary characteristic of the modern man as we sought to define him. We intend using an elaboration of these concepts in the present study, as well as the greater sophistication concerning the definition of various levels of non-modern persons suggested to us by our available data.

Silvert, in this same letter, went on to explain the rationale for a comparative study comprising several countries and to sketch the broad outlines of the type of groups to be studied.

Encouraged by the response of the Carnegie Corporation, Silvert discussed the matter with Reissman, and the two began planning the study. During the latter half of 1965 and early 1966, the questionnaire was constructed, the sampling design planned, and contacts established in Chile and Venezuela. In the former country, sponsorship for the study was obtained from the Instituto de Planificación of the Universidad de Chile conjointly with the Ministerio de Educación. In Venezuela, sponsorship was obtained from EDUPLAN, the Ministerio de Educación,* and CENDES—The Center for Economic and Social Studies.

The questionnaire was pretested in Santiago, Chile, in the spring of 1966, and consequently modified in part. At the same time, a number of Chileans who were knowledgeable about the schools helped us select the primary and secondary schools we were to study. The primary feature of this selection was to rank the available schools in Santiago, Chillán, Antofagasta, and Molina according to their social class charac-

---

*Complete copies of the raw data for both countries, on computer tapes and with accompanying code books, were sent to the agencies in each country.

teristics, which when added to a classification of schools according to type (public, private, or Catholic), formed the basis for our sampling framework. Although the samples were not drawn according to national proportions on these characteristics, we sought to insure ourselves that we would have a sufficiently broad distribution of students by class and by school types. The same procedure was followed in Venezuela for classifying schools in Caracas, Maracaibo, Barquisimeto, and Ocumare.

The field work in Santiago was to have begun in the fall of 1966, but as we have noted in the report, it was delayed by the explosion of events called project Camelot. Aside from the loss of most interviews with university students, Project Camelot did not seriously affect the conduct of our Chilean research, which was completed by the end of 1966. In the following year, we completed our field work in Venezuela, again losing interviews with university students because of some aftereffects of Project Camelot and the political climate in the university.

It should be quite obvious that with the field work effectively completed by the end of 1967, we cannot be charged with having rushed into the analysis and print. The "delay" of some seven years was the result of several factors. Silvert was pressed to complete the earlier Silvert-Bonilla project, rightly looking for theoretical continuity between that study and the present one. Also during this period, both Silvert and Reissman completed other writing commitments: *Man's Power* and *Inequality in American Society*, respectively. But much more important than these manifest reasons for delay were the latent ones having to do with the dialectic maturation of the central ideas that form the reason and substance of this study.

We say "dialectic" because throughout the seven-year period Silvert and Reissman continued to argue and explore the central ideas, to spend thousands of dollars for computer analysis of the data, to reassess their arguments in the light of this analysis, and then to go back and analyze the data again. At one point, in 1970, feeling guilty because of the seemingly long delay in writing our report, we ventured a start that would have looked like almost any other research monograph: a straightforward exposition of what we had done, punctuated by many statistical tables showing what results we had obtained. Some 500 pages of manuscript were written in this fashion, but we chose to lay them aside and wait some more because, by then, we had become sharply aware of the gulf between what we had written and the subtle and complex quality of the ideas that we were reaching for. Why, we asked ourselves at the time, could we not follow the style of Weber's *Protestant Ethic and the Spirit of Capitalism* rather than that of the usual research monograph?

In other words, why not write a theoretical book firmly based upon research findings rather than a confined research report? Obviously, we chose the first approach.

THE SAMPLES

Our sampling design was based on our research purposes rather than upon obtaining a representative sample of students, parents, and teachers in Chile and Venezuela. We deemed it more important, therefore, to get enough cases for our class/school-type classification so as to permit us a complex statistical analysis, rather than to sample representatively so we could generalize about each country. Our conclusions and interpretations, therefore, as we have made abundantly clear, are not meant to be generalized to the Chilean and Venezuelan educational systems as such. Furthermore, we were dissuaded from designing such a representative sample because we could not expect to find accurate and recent figures about enrollments in all cases.

The sampling design was based on classifying primary and secondary schools in each locale into (1) public, private, and Catholic, and (2) three class-levels of upper, middle, and lower class. We then sampled specific schools within this cross-classification, seeking to interview all students in the sixth and twelfth grade of each specific school chosen. We had in mind the following approximate number of cases, using Chile as the example here but also applied to Venezuela in the same form:

	Santiago	Antofagasta	Chillán	Molina
6th GRADE PRIMARY N = 1200+				
Public & Private				
Upper class	100	50	50	
Middle class	100	50	50	All
Lower class	100	50	50	
Catholic				
Upper class	100	50	50	
Middle class	100	50	50	All
Lower class	100	50	50	
12th GRADE SECONDARY N = 1200+	SAME AS ABOVE			
UNIVERSITY N = 700				
State	200	150		
Catholic	200	150		

(Select classes to cover year in school and type of curriculum)

188

	Santiago	Antofagasta	Chillán	Molina
PARENTS N = 600+ Selected randomly by primary and secondary children interviewed	300	150	150	All
TEACHERS N = 400+	All teachers in primary and secondary schools interviewed.			

Two unforeseen errors developed about which we could do nothing, although we do not consider them to be serious. First, the record of refusals to be interviewed was lost, so we have no way of knowing how many were initially attempted. Had we been interested in representative samples, this error would have been serious, but in the light of our sampling objectives its seriousness is very much reduced. Second, the coding categories of the class-level of the schools chosen were lost, so that we had no way of knowing which schools were chosen. Fortunately, the school-type (public, private, or Catholic) was built into another coding category so that this information was retained. The major gap caused by the loss of this information was to prevent our comparing the actual class levels of respondents with the class level of the school established by our country experts. As in the first instance above, this error was not damaging because we had sought to obtain a class spread of respondents rather than a representative sample.

The inevitable loss of cases from improper coding and from similar causes was kept satisfactorily low. In Chile, out of 4,584 initial cases we lost 83, for a final, completed total of 4,501. In Venezuela, out of 4,829 initial cases, we lost 7, for a final total of 4,822. In a study of this size, such losses are imperceptible and do not affect the findings. The distribution of final, completed interviews is presented in Tables A-1 and A-2.

THE QUESTIONNAIRE

The object of the first 29 questions asked was (1) to obtain the customary background and identifying information about respondents, (2) to determine information about certain aspects of behavior (as in the questions about political activity), and (3) to obtain information requested by cooperating educational agencies in Chile and Venezuela. Aside from separate Spanish translations of the questionnaire for each

189

Table A-1 DISTRIBUTION OF COMPLETED INTERVIEWS: CHILE

| City & School Type | SAMPLES | | | | | |
	Primary Students	Secondary Students	University Students	Teachers	Parents	TOTALS
SANTIAGO	624	499	155	173	105	1596
Public	228	309		133	55	725
Private	63			24	14	101
Catholic	333	190		16	36	575
Other			155			155
CHILLAN	297	300		213	154	964
Public	148	150		153	80	531
Catholic	149	150		60	74	433
ANTOFAGASTA	372	373	359	162	166	1432
Public	183	188		126	85	582
Private	1	1				2
Catholic	188	184		36	81	489
Other			359			359
MOLINA	233	30		89	197	549
Public	154	30		75	136	395
Private	12			2	14	28
Catholic	67			12	47	126
TOTALS	1526	1202	514	637	622	4501

country, five versions of this first part of the questionnaire were written since different questions were applicable to primary, secondary, and university students, and to teachers and parents.

Part II of the questionnaire, the meat of the study, was administered to all persons without any variation in the phrasing of the questions. The doubts we initially held about the ability of sixth grade students to answer the questions in Part II were dispelled when we completed the pretest, and permanently laid to rest as we analyzed and reanalyzed those responses in comparison with older persons.

A word is necessary here about our decision to use forced-choice rather than open-ended answers to our questions in Part II. On methodological grounds we picked the first alternative because we were administering the questionnaire to an entire class of students in a given school, and the forced-choice is most efficient under such circumstances. Since we were seeking comparisons between the various samples of persons, we did not change the format when interviewing teachers and parents individually. On theoretical grounds we picked the

190

Table A-2   DISTRIBUTION OF COMPLETED INTERVIEWS: VENEZUELA

City & School Type	SAMPLES				
	Primary Students	Secondary Students	Teachers	Parents	TOTALS
CARACAS	*707*	*697*	*215*	*237*	*1858*
Public	408	315	114	135	972
Private		138	54	35	227
Catholic	299	244	47	67	657
BARQUISIMETO	*429*	*334*	*126*	*327*	*1216*
Public	285	180	85	216	766
Private	1	42	3	13	59
Catholic	143	112	38	98	391
MARACAIBO	*381*	*364*	*138*	*114*	*997*
Public	144	164	72	54	434
Private	37	46	9		92
Catholic	200	154	57	60	471
OCUMARE	*387*	*57*	*99*	*210*	*753*
Public	310	57	95	182	644
Private	33		3	17	53
Catholic	44		1	11	56
TOTALS	1904	1452	578	888	4822

first alternative because we were seeking information about rather specific aspects of attitudes towards social institutions, change, and the like. The open-ended type of answer, we believed, would raise severe problems of interpretation and, perhaps, increase the possible categories for analysis as those answers were differentiated and coded.

191

QUESTIONNAIRE*

DO NOT WRITE IN THIS SPACE

Schedule number: _____

City: _____ School: _____ School type: _____ Class: _____

1. Age: (At your last birthday): _____

2. Sex: _____ Male _____ Female

3. Where were you born? (Enter the name of the province and the municipality or city. If born in a foreign country, enter the name of that country.)

Province city	Municipality or city	Foreign country

3a. (If you were not born in [place of study]): Was the place you were born in urban or rural?

_____ Urban _____ Rural

4. Have you always lived in the same municipality or city that you live in now?

_____ Yes, I have always lived in the same place.

_____ No

4a. (If your answer to the preceding question is "No"): How many years have you lived in the municipality or city in which you now reside? _____ Years

5. Where do your parents live? (If deceased, where did they live?)

Province city	Municipality or city	Foreign country

6. What is the nationality of your father? (Indicate the country in which he was born, not his adopted country.)

1) ___ Chile (Venezuela)
2) ___ Another Latin American country
3) ___ Spain
4) ___ Italy
5) ___ Germany
6) ___ Another European country

Separate Spanish-language versions were written for Venezuela and Chile, but the questions were parallel. Separate versions were also written for the different groups of persons who were interviewed. An "" indicates the question was asked of primary- and secondary-school students only; "**" indicates the question was asked of university students, teachers, and parents only.

7) __ Middle East

8) __ North America

9) __ Other. Which? _____

7. Indicate what was the *highest* grade in school reached by your father:

    1) __ None

    2) __ Some primary school

    3) __ Completed primary school

    4) __ Some secondary school

    5) __ Completed secondary school

    6) __ Some professional school

    7) __ Completed professional school

    8) __ Some university

    9) __ Completed university

    __ Other: Describe: _____

8. What is the principal occupation—or the occupation in which most time is spent—of your father or of the head of the family? (The head of the family is the person who maintains the household. If your father or the head of family is retired or is deceased, enter the name of the last occupation he held).

8a. In the above occupation, what does (did) your father or head of the family actually do? (Explain what his work consists of; that is, what does he do? What does he produce? Sell? What services does he provide? Indicate here the name of the firm or institution in which he works.)

** 9. What is your marital status?

    __ Single

    __ Married

    __ Divorced or annulled

    __ Widowed

**10. How many children do you have?

    __ None

    __ One

    __ Two

    __ Three

    __ Four or more

    __ Am single

*11. What grade are you now in? _____

*12. Of the subjects you are now studying, or have studied in the past, which one do you like *most* of all?

_____

Why? _____

_____

_____

*13. Of the subjects you are now studying, or have studied in the past, which one do you like *least* of all?

_____

Why? _____

_____

*14. From which one have you learned the *most*? _____
Why? _____

_____

*15. From which one have you learned the *least*? _____
Why? _____

_____

*16. When you complete your schooling, which is the occupation you would most like to have? (Select only *one* from the following list):

      1) ___ Worker
      2) ___ Skilled worker
      3) ___ Farmworker
      4) ___ Whitecollar worker
      5) ___ Professional
      6) ___ Businessman or industrialist
      7) ___ Technical expert
      8) ___ Other: (Explain) _____

_____

*17. What do you suppose your chances are of getting the occupation that you most want to have?

      1) ___ Very good
      2) ___ Good
      3) ___ About 50-50
      4) ___ Poor

*18. How far do you think you will go with your schooling? (Indicate the highest level you think you will reach):

      1) ___ Complete primary school
      2) ___ Begin, but not finish secondary school
      3) ___ Complete secondary school
      4) ___ Begin, but not finish professional school

5) __ Complete professional school
6) __ Begin, but not finish university
7) __ Complete university
8) __ Other: (Explain) _____

_____

*19. What do you suppose your chances are of getting this education?

1) __ Very good
2) __ Good
3) __ About 50-50
4) __ Poor

*20. Whom would you most like to marry, a person who is: (Choose one)

1) __ Worker
2) __ Skilled worker
3) __ Farm worker
4) __ White-collar worker
5) __ Professional
6) __ Businessman or industrialist
7) __ Technical expert
8) __ Other: (Explain): _____

_____

**21. Indicate the number of organizations to which you belong: _____

**22. During the past six months:

a. Have you attended a political meeting?   __ Yes   __ No
Have you attended a union meeting?   __ Yes   __ No
Have you discussed politics with
an acquaintance?   __ Yes   __ No
Have you discussed politics with friends? __ Yes   __ No
Have you participated in a public
demonstration?   __ Yes   __ No
Have you worked actively in politics?   __ Yes   __ No

**23. Should some groups of persons be prohibited from entering into the teaching profession?

__ Yes   __ No

If "Yes" which ones? Why? _____

**24. Indicate the *highest* level of schooling you have had:

1) __ Some primary school
2) __ Completed primary school
3) __ Some secondary school
4) __ Completed secondary school
5) __ Some professional school

6) __ Completed professional school
7) __ Some university
8) __ Completed university
9) __ Did not attend school

25. [Question number omitted]

*26. Have you had to repeat a course at any time?

__ Yes
__ No (If "No," check "Never" in the list below.)

26a. How many times have you had to repeat a course?

1) __ Never
2) __ Once
3) __ Twice
4) __ Three times
5) __ More than three times

27. [Secondary students only] What activity do you engage in most in school?

1) __ Student center
2) __ Sports
3) __ School publications
4) __ Music groups
5) __ Theater
6) __ Academic & literary groups
7) __ Religious groups
8) __ Boy Scouts and Girl Guides
9) __ Other: Which? _____

28. [Secondary students only] How long do you think your family will be able to support your schooling? (Check most applicable):

1) __ My studies now involve a great economic sacrifice
2) __ Until I complete secondary school
3) __ Until I complete professional school
4) __ For some years at the university, but not to graduation
5) __ Until I complete university
6) __ As long as I wish to continue studying
7) __ As long as I wish and pay for my schooling (my family does not need my economic help)
8) __ Other: Indicate: _____
_____

29. [Secondary students only] Would you consider studying a technical subject?

__ Yes
__ No

29a. (If your answer is "No," give the reason why not): _____

_____

_____

PART II

30. In your opinion, what is the position of your family in the community?

   1) ___ Very high
   2) ___ High
   3) ___ Intermediate
   4) ___ Low
   5) ___ Very low

31. To which group do you or your family belong?

   1) ___ Rich
   2) ___ Comfortable
   3) ___ Modest
   4) ___ Humble
   5) ___ None of the above. Which? _____

32. Of the following groups, to which do you or your family belong?

   1) ___ Ruling class
   2) ___ Traditional class
   3) ___ Middle class
   4) ___ Popular class
   5) ___ None of the above. Which? _____

33. In relation to you or your family, what is the position of your closest friends?

   1) ___ The same social position
   2) ___ In a lower social position
   3) ___ In a higher social position
   4) ___ In different positions

34.[a] Should you seek to realize your aspirations in life, principally for

   ___ the benefit of the family?
   ___ your own benefit?

35. In your opinion, is the basic social unit

   ___ families?
   ___ individuals?

36. Do you think that a child's education should be determined according to the advice of parents?

   ___ Yes
   ___ No

---

[a]Although varied in the interviewing, answers to questions 34–63 are presented so that the first is the "traditional" and the second the "modern" response.

37. The family:

       ___ is basically the same in all societies

       ___ varies according to the society

38. As time passes, do you expect that your relations with your family:

       ___ will remain more or less the same

       ___ will change greatly

39. What do you think is the principal duty of a good parent?

       ___ to maintain the continuity and stability of the family

       ___ to stimulate his children to realize themselves

40. (In this question, first select the situation that applies in your case, then within that alternative select one of the two answers given.)

You comply with religious practices principally because of:

       ___ family custom

       ___ personal religious

       __ sentiments

You do not comply with religious practices because:

       __ your family seldom engages in them either

       __ of a lack of religious conviction

41. Do you believe that most people hold their religious beliefs:

       ___ out of custom

       ___ because of personal convictions

42. Do you believe that religious beliefs:

       ___ aid a person in carrying out his work

       ___ hinder a person in carrying out his work

       ___ have no influence on how a person carries out his work

43. Do you think that a person can be moral in his economic and political life without being a religious believer?

       ___ No

       ___ Yes

44. Regarding your religious beliefs in the future, do you think:
If you are a believer that

       ___ they will become stronger?

       ___ they will become weaker?

If you are a non-believer, that you will feel

       ___ indifference?

       ___ rejection?

       ___ curiosity and interest?

45. Do you think that the religion of our elders can help us in the development of our country?

       ___ Yes

       ___ Not necessarily

46. What is the principal reason for your going to school:
    ___ because it is expected of a person of my age
    ___ because it can provide knowledge necessary for life

47. What would you say is more important, that education should:
    ___ give the individual general knowledge
    ___ prepare the individual to be a productive member of society

48. You attend school principally:
    ___ to take your proper place in society
    ___ to find a place for yourself in society

49. Education ought to teach people, principally:
    ___ moral principles
    ___ to think for themselves

50. Is the education you are now receiving in school more helpful:
    ___ to adapt to the present situation, or
    ___ to adapt to changes that might occur

51. Primary education ought to be principally:
    ___ different according to the social origins of the student
    ___ equal for all

52. Whom would you prefer to work with or to employ:
    ___ a member of the family
    ___ any qualified person

53. One ought to seek an occupation that principally:
    ___ will be well regarded by those of one's own social station
    ___ permits one to express one's personal capacity

54. One performs one's work well because, principally:
    ___ it is what is expected of a proper person
    ___ it helps one to achieve what one may wish

55. The economy ought, principally:
    ___ to be at the service of social justice
    ___ to promote production

56. When you begin to work, you will take a position that:
    ___ accords with the situation of your family and friends
    ___ permits you to develop your personal ability

57. Do you think that people ought to be:
    ___ content with an income with which they can live well
    ___ trying always to raise their economic level

199

58. As a citizen or future citizen what is your principal function?

    ____ to defend the national honor and sovereignty of the country

    ____ to be concerned with the progress of the country

59. Do you think that the principal function of the state is:

    ____ to preserve the national culture

    ____ to be responsive to the decisions of its citizens

60. Do you comply with the laws primarily because:

    ____ it is your obligation

    ____ it allows one to live together better with others

61. Do you think that a good law:

    ____ is inspired by human nature

    ____ responds to the changing needs of the population

62. Do you (will you) vote because:

    ____ it is your obligation as a citizen

    ____ you may be able to influence social events

63. Political activity ought to have as its goal, preferentially:

    ____ the maintenance of public order

    ____ the orientation of the country's development

**64. Do you believe that the state should make divorce possible for all those who may desire it?

    ____ No

    ____ Yes

65. Should the principal function of the state be a concern for the well-being of the family?

    ____ Yes

    ____ No

66. Should teaching in school be free from all political influence?

    ____ No

    ____ Yes

67. Should the price of essential goods be fixed by the government?

    ____ Yes

    ____ No

68. Should teaching in school be free from all religious influence?

    ____ No

    ____ Yes

69. Should the principal function of education be the strengthening of the unity of the family?

      ____ Yes

      ____ No

70. Should the principal function of the school be the preparation of individuals to earn a living?

      ____ No

      ____ Yes

71. In case of some conflict between the public welfare and the legitimate interests of each of the following, which one would you support?

a.   ____ family unity
        ____ the public welfare

b.   ____ religious beliefs
        ____ the public welfare

c.   ____ private education
        ____ the public welfare

d.   ____ private enterprise
        ____ the public welfare

72. Now, in the event of conflict between the educational system, and each of the following, which one would you choose?

a.   ____ religious beliefs
        ____ the educational system

b.   ____ family unity
        ____ the educational system

c.   ____ economic needs
        ____ the educational system

73. Which is the better criterion by which to judge a man?

    ____ his contribution to society

    ____ his talents and capacities

74. Now, considering the following aspect, which is the better criterion by which to judge a man?

    ____ his family situation   ____ his personal accomplishments

75. And again, which is the better criterion by which to judge a man?

    ____ his personal religious convictions

    ____ his moral principles as regards society

76. In your opinion, how important is (will be) your vote?

    ____ very important   ____ somewhat important   ____ without
    ____ important   ____ of small importance   importance

77. In your opinion, social changes occur principally as a result of:

        —— the action of natural forces

        —— the action of social groups

78. Social changes occur principally as a result of:

        —— inevitable historical conditions

        —— the wishes of groups who hold power

79. Social changes occur principally as a result of:

        —— the actions of great men

        —— the perspectives and power of a whole people

80. What presents the greater obstacles to the development of a society?

        —— the physical characteristics of a country

        —— the way of thinking of its population

SAMPLE CHARACTERISTICS

Table A-3 SELECTED CHARACTERISTICS OF SAMPLES: CHILE

Characteristics	SAMPLES				
	Primary Students	Secondary Students	University	Teachers	Parents
Number of cases	1526	1202	514	637	622
Mean age (in years)	11.9	17.7	20.5	34.6	45.4
Marital status (per cent)					
Single				37.6	4.8
Married				57.0	84.4
Widowed-Divorced				5.4	10.8
Per cent male	50.1	51.5	68.7	30.1	78.0

Table A-4 SELECTED CHARACTERISTICS OF SAMPLES: VENEZUELA

Characteristics	SAMPLES			
	Primary Students	Secondary Students	Teachers	Parents
Number of cases	1904	1452	578	888
Mean age (in years)	12.9	17.6	31.1	43.0
Marital status (per cent)				
Single			41.6	18.4
Married			52.2	71.8
Widowed-Divorced			6.2	9.8
Per cent male	48.1	52.3	31.9	45.5

202

Table A-5 EDUCATIONAL LEVELS OF TEACHERS: CHILE (In Per Cent)

Highest Grade Reached	BY SCHOOL SYSTEM			BY LOCALE			
	Public	Private	Catholic	Santiago	Chillan	Antofagasta	Molina
Some primary	.2	0	0	0	.5	0	0
Primary completed	0	0	1.6	.6	.5	0	0
Some secondary	.8	7.7	12.4	2.3	5.9	2.4	1.1
Secondary completed	8.7	3.8	24.0	9.1	16.4	4.3	18.0
Some professional	2.6	7.7	9.3	2.3	5.0	4.3	5.6
Professional completed	49.6	34.6	10.9	45.7	32.0	36.0	65.2
Some university	6.1	19.2	11.6	9.7	5.5	11.6	2.2
University completed	28.9	26.9	27.1	25.7	32.9	38.4	4.5
None and no answer	3.0	0	3.1	4.6	1.4	3.0	3.3
NUMBER OF CASES	487	26	124	173	213	162	89

Table A-6   EDUCATIONAL LEVELS OF PARENTS: CHILE (In Per Cent)

Highest Grade Reached	BY SCHOOL SYSTEM			BY LOCALE			
	Public	Private	Catholic	Santiago	Chillan	Antofagasta	Molina
Some primary	27.2	35.7	13.5	18.3	7.6	11.8	44.9
Primary completed	22.8	21.4	11.9	18.3	10.2	17.2	26.3
Some secondary	26.4	21.4	32.0	32.1	41.4	27.2	16.7
Secondary completed	5.6	3.6	13.5	11.9	12.7	9.5	3.0
Some professional	4.2	7.1	7.4	2.8	5.1	10.7	3.0
Professional completed	6.9	7.1	10.2	8.3	9.6	11.2	4.5
Some university	1.9	0	4.9	3.7	4.5	4.1	.5
University completed	2.5	3.6	6.1	3.7	5.7	7.1	0
None and no answer	2.5	0	.4	.9	3.1	1.2	1.0
NUMBER OF CASES	356	28	238	105	154	166	197

Table A-7 EDUCATIONAL LEVELS OF TEACHERS: VENEZUELA (In Per Cent)

Highest Grade Reached	BY SCHOOL SYSTEM			BY LOCALE			
	Public	Private	Catholic	Caracas	Barquisimeto	Maracaibo	Ocumare
Some primary	0	0	0	0	0	0	0
Primary completed	0	1.4	0	0	0	.7	0
Some secondary	1.1	1.4	2.1	.5	0	3.6	2.0
Secondary completed	2.2	2.9	4.2	1.4	2.4	6.5	1.0
Some professional	2.2	2.9	1.4	1.4	1.6	1.4	5.0
Professional completed	14.7	13.0	17.5	6.0	7.1	42.0	7.9
Some university	69.0	58.0	51.7	76.4	80.2	15.9	79.2
University completed	7.1	7.2	18.9	7.9	2.4	26.8	2.0
None and no answer	3.8	13.0	4.2	6.5	6.3	2.9	3.0
NUMBER OF CASES	366	69	143	215	126	138	99

Table A-8 EDUCATIONAL LEVELS OF PARENTS: VENEZUELA (In Per Cent)

Highest Grade Reached	BY SCHOOL SYSTEM			BY LOCALE			
	Public	Private	Catholic	Caracas	Barquisimeto	Maracaibo	Ocumare
Some primary	32.7	13.8	17.6	21.9	24.8	18.1	42.4
Primary completed	24.2	24.6	26.1	23.6	25.4	24.1	25.2
Some secondary	10.1	16.9	10.5	15.6	8.0	10.3	9.5
Secondary completed	1.7	6.2	8.0	5.5	2.1	9.5	1.0
Some professional	2.4	4.6	5.5	5.1	2.4	6.0	1.4
Professional completed	4.8	7.7	8.4	6.8	6.1	9.5	2.9
Some university	.9	3.1	.8	1.3	1.2	1.7	0
University completed	1.2	15.4	9.7	10.5	2.1	6.9	0
None and no answer	22.1	7.7	13.4	9.7	27.8	13.8	17.6
NUMBER OF CASES	587	65	236	237	327	114	210

Table A-9   OCCUPATIONAL PRESTIGE OF PARENTS: CHILE (In Per Cent)

Occupational Prestige	BY SCHOOL SYSTEM			BY LOCALE			
	Public	Private	Catholic	Santiago	Chillan	Antofagasta	Molina
Upper	4.2	0	13.1	9.2	14.0	8.4	.5
Middle	40.6	17.9	46.7	38.5	55.4	53.9	23.7
Lower	46.1	67.9	30.7	50.5	18.5	33.5	60.6
No answer	9.2	14.3	9.4	1.8	12.1	4.2	15.2
NUMBER OF CASES	356	28	238	105	154	166	197

Table A-10   OCCUPATIONAL PRESTIGE OF PARENTS: VENEZUELA (In Per Cent)

Occupational Prestige	BY SCHOOL SYSTEM			BY LOCALE			
	Public	Private	Catholic	Caracas	Barquisimeto	Maracaibo	Ocumare
Upper	1.7	18.5	16.0	12.2	2.8	15.5	1.9
Middle	33.9	41.5	36.1	40.5	26.3	29.3	45.7
Lower	24.4	13.8	10.5	13.9	7.3	19.0	46.7
No answer	40.0	26.2	37.4	33.3	63.6	36.2	5.7
NUMBER OF CASES	587	65	236	237	327	114	210

Table A-11   OCCUPATION WANTED BY PRIMARY SCHOOL STUDENTS: CHILE (In Per Cent)

| Occupation Wanted | BY SCHOOL SYSTEM | | | BY LOCALE | | | |
	Public	Private	Catholic	Santiago	Chillan	Antofagasta	Molina
Worker	2.0	6.4	1.6	1.4	1.9	2.9	2.5
Skilled worker	3.4	1.3	2.7	3.0	2.6	1.8	5.0
Farmworker	.7	0	.9	1.2	.6	0	.8
White collar	7.0	5.1	6.9	3.8	4.2	9.9	13.9
Professional	66.4	60.3	66.4	68.6	68.8	63.6	59.2
Businessman	3.4	2.6	2.9	2.6	5.2	2.9	2.1
Technician	14.3	19.2	6.5	7.6	8.8	16.8	12.6
Other	2.2	3.8	11.1	10.4	7.5	1.6	2.9
No answer	.7	1.3	1.0	1.4	.3	.5	.8
NUMBER OF CASES	713	76	737	624	297	372	233

Table A-12   OCCUPATION WANTED BY SECONDARY SCHOOL STUDENTS: CHILE (In Per Cent)

Occupation Wanted	BY SCHOOL SYSTEM			BY LOCALE				
	Public	Private	Catholic	Santiago	Chillan	Antofagasta	Molina
Worker	0	0	0	0	0	0	0
Skilled worker	0	0	0	0	0	0	0
Farmworker	.1	0	.4	0	.7	0	3.3
White collar	3.5	0	3.6	4.0	3.0	1.9	23.3
Professional	83.5	100.0	87.8	84.8	87.1	86.9	60.0
Businessman	1.6	0	1.9	2.8	1.3	.8	0
Technician	8.1	0	4.0	6.4	5.0	7.8	0
Other	2.5	0	1.9	1.6	2.3	2.4	10.0
No answer	.6	0	.4	.4	.7	.3	3.3
NUMBER OF CASES	677	1	524	499	300	373	30

Table A-13   OCCUPATION WANTED BY PRIMARY SCHOOL STUDENTS: VENEZUELA (In Per Cent)

| | BY SCHOOL SYSTEM | | | BY LOCALE | | | |
Occupation Wanted	Public	Private	Catholic	Caracas	Barquisimeto	Maracaibo	Ocumare
Worker	1.4	1.4	.7	.8	.5	1.0	2.6
Skilled worker	3.0	2.8	1.2	1.7	3.3	1.8	2.8
Farmworker	.8	2.8	.9	.3	1.2	1.8	.8
White collar	13.5	0	7.7	11.2	11.4	10.2	10.6
Professional	34.7	64.8	50.1	41.7	31.0	59.8	34.0
Businessman	5.4	9.9	3.5	4.1	4.4	3.4	8.2
Technician	31.9	14.1	22.0	25.5	38.0	11.3	36.3
Other	8.2	2.8	13.6	13.3	9.6	10.5	3.6
No answer	1.2	1.4	.3	1.4	.7	0	1.0
NUMBER OF CASES	1147	71	686	707	429	381	387

Table A-14   OCCUPATION WANTED BY SECONDARY SCHOOL STUDENTS: VENEZUELA (In Per Cent)

Occupation Wanted	BY SCHOOL SYSTEM			BY LOCALE			
	Public	Private	Catholic	Caracas	Barquisimeto	Maracaibo	Ocumare
Worker	0	0	0	0	0	0	0
Skilled worker	.1	0	.2	0	.3	.3	0
Farmworker	0	.4	.2	.3	0	0	0
White collar	4.5	1.3	1.6	3.7	2.1	1.4	8.8
Professional	83.8	88.5	87.6	83.8	85.0	92.3	75.4
Businessman	.7	2.7	1.0	.9	.6	2.2	0
Technician	6.3	5.3	5.3	6.2	9.6	1.1	8.8
Other	4.3	1.3	4.1	4.7	2.4	2.7	7.0
No answer	.3	.4	0	.4	0	0	0
NUMBER OF CASES	716	226	510	697	334	364	57

Table A-15   INTERCORRELATIONS OF CLASS-RELATED MEASURES: CHILE

Variables	TEACHERS					
	1	2	3	4	5	6
1-Parents' education	-	.36	.12	.12	.21	.11
2-Father's occupation		-	.15	.17	.29	.18
3-Respondent's education			-	.09	.09	.01
4-Class I measure (Q. 30)				-	.31	.24
5-Class II measure (Q. 31)					-	.17
6-Class III measure (Q. 32)						-

Variables	PARENTS						
	1	2	3	4	5	6	7
1-Parents' education	-	.51	.49	.36	.28	.38	.27
2-Father's occupation		-	.38	.47	.28	.41	.26
3-Respondent's education			-	.50	.37	.49	.32
4-Respondent's occupation				-	.39	.43	.30
5-Class I measure (Q. 30)					-	.57	.42
6-Class II measure (Q. 31)						-	.51
7-Class III measure (Q. 32)							-

Table A-16   INTERCORRELATIONS OF CLASS-RELATED MEASURES: VENEZUELA

Variables	TEACHERS					
	1	2	3	4	5	6
1-Parents' Education	-	.38	.02	.08	.26	.15
2-Father's occupation		-	.07	.16	.16	.15
3-Respondent's education			-	0	.02	.03
4-Class I measure (Q. 30)				-	.46	.52
5-Class II measure (Q. 31)					-	.44
6-Class III measure (Q. 32)						-

Variables	PARENTS						
	1	2	3	4	5	6	7
1-Parents' education	-	.48	.14	.34	.37	.42	.41
2-Father's occupation		-	.10	.43	.37	.36	.34
3-Respondent's education			-	.15	.08	.04	.05
4-Respondent's occupation				-	.31	.33	.27
5-Class I measure (Q. 30)					-	.55	.49
6-Class II measure (Q. 31)						-	.14
7-Class II measure (Q. 32)							-

CHECKS ON INTERNAL CONSISTENCY

We had written the questionnaire so as to include groups of questions that we believed would cluster together as separate units, as for example, the sets of six questions for each of the institutional areas. Our intention from the start was to add up the individual's answers to each cluster and to analyze that total score.

Given this objective, it is necessary to determine whether or not the individual questions in any cluster are, indeed, correlated with the total score that is obtained by adding up the individual answers. Thereby, a high correlation means that the answers given to any single question are related to the answers given to all the questions in the particular cluster. Tables A-17 and A-18 present these intercorrelations for each of the five institutions and for each of other groups of questions dealing with the subjects indicated.

A glance at the correlations reveals that they generally are quite high, with the possible exception of Question 44 under *Religion* in Table A-17. We decided to retain all of the questions we had used for our analysis in view of the strong support these correlations gave for internal consistency.

Table A-17   INTERCORRELATIONS OF INDIVIDUAL QUESTIONS TO TOTAL SCORES BY INSTITUTION

FAMILY		Chile	Venezuela	RELIGION		Chile	Venezuela
Q. 34	Aspirations	.45	.41	Q. 40	Practices	.53	.51
Q. 35	Society	.55	.41	Q. 41	Beliefs	.31	.33
Q. 36	Child's educ.	.63	.57	Q. 42	Work	.56	.57
Q. 37	Family	.57	.56	Q. 43	Morality	.59	.57
Q. 38	Relations	.30	.41	Q. 44	Future	.28	.27
Q. 39	Good parent	.56	.61	Q. 45	Development	.66	.60

EDUCATION		Chile	Venezuela	ECONOMY		Chile	Venezuela
Q. 46	School	.47	.40	Q. 52	Work with	.59	.62
Q. 47	Education	.50	.50	Q. 53	Occupation	.63	.66
Q. 48	Attend school	.47	.51	Q. 54	Performs	.51	.50
Q. 49	Ought to teach	.54	.62	Q. 55	Economy	.51	.50
Q. 50	Helps one	.53	.54	Q. 56	Position	.56	.61
Q. 51	Ought to be	.41	.41	Q. 57	Ought	.56	.55

POLITICS		Chile	Venezuela
Q. 58	Citizen	.58	.55
Q. 59	State	.50	.50
Q. 60	Laws	.55	.63
Q. 61	Good law	.56	.57
Q. 62	Vote	.67	.59
Q. 63	Activity	.64	.63

213

INTERCORRELATIONS OF INDIVIDUAL QUESTIONS
TO TOTAL SCORES BY SPECIFIED SUBJECTS

INSTITUTIONAL DIFFERENTIATION	Chile	Venezuela
Q. 65 State/Family	.51	.42
Q. 66 Education/Politics	.52	.40
Q. 67 Economy/Politics	.38	.45
Q. 68 Education/Religion	.56	.51
Q. 69 Education/Family	.50	.43
Q. 70 Education/Economy	.30	.30

PUBLIC GOOD		
Q. 71a Public Good/Family	.62	.72
Q. 71b Public Good/Religion	.73	.78
Q. 71c Public Good/Education	.78	.81
Q. 71d Public Good/Economy	.74	.76

IMPORTANCE OF EDUCATIONAL SYSTEM		
Q. 72a Education/Religion	.62	.63
Q. 72b Education/Family	.73	.74
Q. 72c Education/Economy	.69	.66

JUDGE A MAN		
Q. 73 Society/Talent	.62	.60
Q. 74 Family/Accomplishments	.68	.67
Q. 75 Religion/Morality	.62	.68

SOCIAL CHANGE		
Q. 77 Natural forces/Social groups	.70	.72
Q. 78 History/Social groups	.66	.68
Q. 79 Great men/All people	.46	.47
Q. 80 Physical characteristics/Thinking	.63	.59

Table A-19   INTERCORRELATIONS OF THREE SUBJECTIVE CLASS
MEASURES

	CHILE		
	Class I	Class II	Class III
Q. 30 Class I	1.00	.41	.43
Q. 31 Class II	.41	1.00	.40
Q. 32 Class III	.43	.40	1.00

		VENEZUELA		
		Class I	Class II	Class III
Q. 30	Class I	1.00	.51	.52
Q. 31	Class II	.51	1.00	.44
Q. 32	Class III	.52	.44	1.00

Another facet of "consistency" arose in connection with the comparisons between students and their parents and their answers to factual and plainly evaluative questions. We became interested, thereby, in how the two groups compared when they were asked about the family's class position and about the parent's education. Obviously, the relationships in this instance are not methodological in the sense that the preceding correlations were, but instead, are more revealing of individual perceptions and evaluations; in short, they are attitudinal in character.

In order to reconstruct from our data the most closely matching groups of students and parents, we classified by locale, school level, and school system. In this manner, for instance, we were able to compare the primary, public-school students in Caracas with those parents who had a child attending a primary public-school in Caracas. We then determined the means for each of these groups for parent's education (students—"father's education"; parents—"respondent's education"), and for each of the three estimates of the family's class position. The results are presented in Table A-20 for the Chileans and in Table A-21 for the Venezuelans.

The coding of educational levels was such that a higher number meant a higher level of education attained. However, in the case of the class measures, the coding was reversed, so that a *lower* number indicated a *higher* class. For example, Question 30, which we have designated as a Class I measure, was scored so that 1 meant "very high," 2, "high," 3, "intermediate," and so on. Therefore, in reading the results of Tables A-20 and A-21, these different coding categories must be kept in mind.

The incontestable and overwhelming results of Tables A-20 and A-21 are that the students assign their parents higher educational levels than the parents themselves say they have, and additionally, the students judge their family's class position to be consistently higher than their parents judge it to be. There are only scattered instances of a reverse order; for example, the first three groups in Barquisimeto for parents' education. There are but scattered instances of ties between the means for students and for parents.

215

Table A-20 COMPARISONS OF MEANS OF STUDENTS AND PARENTS ON CLASS-RELATED MEASURES: CHILE

Sample	PARENT'S EDUCATION		CLASS I		CLASS II		CLASS III	
	Students	Parents	Students	Parents	Students	Parents	Students	Parents
SANTIAGO								
Primary public	4.9	2.4	2.6	3.4	2.6	3.1	2.8	3.2
Primary private	3.7	3.7	2.7	3.0	2.9	2.8	2.8	3.0
Primary Catholic	6.2	3.9	2.5	3.0	2.4	2.6	2.5	3.2
Secondary public	5.1	3.0	2.9	3.1	2.6	3.0	2.7	3.3
Secondary Catholic	6.3	4.0	2.6	3.0	2.3	3.0	2.2	2.5
CHILLAN								
Primary public	3.8	3.7	2.7	3.2	2.7	3.0	2.6	3.2
Primary Catholic	4.9	3.9	2.4	3.0	2.6	2.8	2.6	3.1
Secondary public	5.0	3.7	2.9	3.0	2.6	3.3	2.9	3.0
Secondary Catholic	5.5	4.2	2.6	2.9	2.2	2.6	2.4	2.8
ANTOFAGASTA								
Primary public	3.9	3.5	2.7	3.0	2.9	3.0	2.9	3.2
Primary Catholic	4.8	3.6	2.7	3.0	2.7	2.8	2.3	3.0
Secondary public	4.7	3.7	3.0	3.1	2.7	2.9	2.9	3.2
Secondary Catholic	5.2	4.1	2.9	3.0	2.6	2.6	2.7	2.8
MOLINA								
Primary public	2.7	1.7	3.0	3.3	3.1	3.2	3.0	3.4
Primary private	-	-	3.3	-	-	-	3.2	-
Primary Catholic	3.1	2.3	3.0	3.3	3.0	3.2	2.7	3.2
Secondary public	3.1	1.7	3.2	3.0	2.6	2.6	2.9	2.7

Table A-21 COMPARISONS OF MEANS OF STUDENTS AND PARENTS ON CLASS-RELATED MEASURES: VENEZUELA

Sample	PARENT'S EDUCATION		CLASS I		CLASS II		CLASS III	
	Students	Parents	Students	Parents	Students	Parents	Students	Parents
CARACAS								
Primary public	3.5	3.2	3.1	3.3	3.0	3.3	3.4	3.4
Primary Catholic	5.0	3.4	2.8	3.0	2.4	3.0	3.0	3.5
Secondary public	3.6	3.4	3.0	2.7	3.0	3.1	3.3	3.3
Secondary private	5.6	4.8	2.8	2.9	2.7	2.7	2.9	3.2
Secondary Catholic	5.5	4.5	2.7	2.8	2.5	2.7	2.8	2.9
BARQUISIMETO								
Primary public	2.9	3.7	3.0	3.2	3.0	3.0	3.1	3.4
Primary Catholic	3.5	4.3	3.0	3.0	2.7	3.1	2.8	3.0
Secondary public	2.7	2.9	3.1	3.2	3.1	3.4	3.3	3.2
Secondary private	4.1	3.3	2.7	2.8	2.6	2.8	2.7	3.1
Secondary Catholic	4.1	2.7	2.9	3.0	2.8	3.1	2.9	3.1
MARACAIBO								
Primary public	3.2	3.4	2.9	3.1	2.7	3.4	3.1	3.5
Primary private	5.9	-	2.2	-	1.9	-	2.4	-
Primary Catholic	4.5	3.0	2.8	3.4	2.5	3.5	3.0	3.5
Secondary public	3.7	3.5	3.0	3.0	3.0	3.2	3.2	3.0
Secondary private	4.1	-	2.6	-	2.5	-	2.7	-
Secondary Catholic	4.9	5.1	2.7	2.8	2.6	2.7	2.8	2.9
OCUMARE								
Primary public	2.2	3.1	3.1	3.4	3.3	3.3	3.4	3.6
Primary private	2.3	2.9	2.9	3.1	3.3	3.1	3.2	3.3
Primary Catholic	3.2	1.8	2.9	3.3	2.5	3.5	3.1	3.3
Secondary public	2.7	2.7	2.9	3.0	3.0	3.1	3.3	3.6

CONSTRUCTION OF THE TYPOLOGY

As explained in the text (Chapter III), the typology of belief-sets was constructed from three batteries of questions. The first set included the questions about institutional differentiation as follows:

		TRADITIONAL RESPONSE	MODERN RESPONSE
		(SCORE = 1)	(SCORE = 2)
Q. 65	The principal functions of the state ought to be concerned with the well-being of the family	Yes	No
Q. 66	The student's education should be free from any political influence	No	Yes
Q. 67	The price of essential goods ought to be fixed by the government	Yes	No
Q. 68	The student's education should be free from any religious influence	No	Yes
Q. 69	The principal function of education is to reinforce the unity of the family	Yes	No
Q. 70	The principal function of the school is to prepare individuals to earn a living	No	Yes

The range of scores for this set of questions could vary from 6 to a high of 12. We dichotomized these scores so that those from 6 through 8 were classified as "low," and those from 9 through 12 as "high."

The second set of questions upon which the typology was based was as follows:

		TRADITIONAL RESPONSE	MODERN RESPONSE
		(SCORE = 1)	(SCORE = 2)
Q. 73	Which is the better criterion to judge a man?	by his contribution to society	by his talents and capacities

		TRADITIONAL RESPONSE (SCORE = 1)	MODERN RESPONSE (SCORE = 2)
Q. 74	Considered from the following aspect, which is the better criterion by which to judge a man?	by his family situation	by his personal accomplishments
Q. 75	And again, which is the better criterion by which to judge a man?	by his personal religious conviction	by his morality as regards society

The range of scores in this set could vary from 3 to a high of 6. We dichotomized total scores, classifying scores of 3 and 4 as "low," and scores of 5 and 6 as "high."

The third and final dimension used to create the typology was based upon answers to the first two questions in each series about institutions, for a total of ten questions as follows:

		RITUALISTIC RESPONSE (SCORE = 1)	RATIONALIST RESPONSE (SCORE = 2)
Q. 34	Should you realize your aspirations in life principally for	the benefit of the family	the benefit of oneself
Q. 35	In your opinion, is society formed basically for the unit of	families	individuals
Q 40	You comply with religious practices principally because of	family custom	personal religious sentiments
	or		
	You do not comply with religious practices because	the family seldom engages	of a lack of religious conviction
Q. 41	Do you believe that most people hold their religious beliefs	because of custom	because of personal conviction

		RITUALISTIC RESPONSE	RATIONALIST RESPONSE
		(score = 1)	(score = 2)
Q. 46	What is the principal reason for going to school?	it is expected of a person of my age	it can provide knowledge necessary for life
Q. 47	Education is primarily important because	it gives the individual general knowledge	it prepares the individual to be a productive member of society
Q. 52	Whom would you prefer to work with or prefer to employ	a member of the family	any qualified person
Q. 53	One ought to seek an occupation that principally	reflects one's social situation	permits one to express one's personal abilities
Q. 58	As a citizen (future citizen) what is your principal function?	to defend the national honor and sovereignty of the country	to be concerned with the progress of the country
Q. 59	Do you think that the principal function of the state is	to preserve the national culture	to be responsive to the decisions of its citizens

The range of scores for the above set of questions could vary from 10 to a high of 20. These scores were dichotomized so that those from 10 through 16 were classified as "low," and those from 17 through 20 as "high."

On the basis of his answers to these sets of questions each individual was simultaneously classified into one of the 8 possible combinations that can be developed by considering the combinations of "high" and "low" on the three sets of questions.

Two additional typologies were considered but not further explored. The typology just described relied upon the first two questions in each set of questions about the five institutional areas. The *next* two questions in each of those sets asked about the standards the individual used in explaining his behavior, as for example Question 36: "Do you think a child's education should be decided according to the advice of parents?" By substituting these 10 questions for the ritualist/rationalist set we used, we would have the basis for a second typology. Similarly, the *last* two questions asked in each set about the five institutional areas referred to the individual's judgments about future changes in his beliefs or actions, as for example Question 38: "As time passes, will your relations with the family remain more or less the same" or "change greatly." Again, a third typology could be constructed based upon substituting these 10 questions for the ones that we used.

Relatively little new information about our respondents was revealed by employing these two additional typologies. For one thing, the high correlations among the several questions within each institutional set meant that there was no noticeable shifting of types from one kind of typology to the second or the third. For another thing, the fact that all three typologies still were based upon the same set of questions in part (institutional differentiation and the criteria for judging a man) meant that individuals would not very likely shift from one type to another as the different typologies were employed. We did compare the distributions of the samples between the types in all three typologies, and as expected, we found the differences to be on the order of 2–3 percent, and never more than 5 percent. We made the judgment, therefore, to use only the typology of ritualism/rationalism that we have described.

DISCRIMINANT FUNCTION ANALYSIS

The particular problem of analysis that we confronted in describing the typology was a meaningful statistic that would allow efficient summarization of our data, which were in the form of a discrete dependent variable and a number of, essentially, continuous independent variables. A χ^2 analysis was cumbersome when interpreted as a measure of "goodness of fit," since it required close inspection of 80–90 separate tables, each with as many as 40 cells in the cross-classification. Multiple regression statistics, based as they are upon a continuous dependent variable, we judged to be incorrect for our purposes. With our requirements in mind, we chose discriminant function analysis, and particularly, the stepwise, multiple discriminant analysis—a relatively new computer program in the *Statistical Package for the Social Sciences*.[1]

Briefly, the SPSS program can handle from 2 to 40 groups in the dependent variable, and up to 40 variables as independent. As in a stepwise regression program, one variable from the independent set is considered at each step and it is selected according to the following equivalent criteria:[2]

1. The variable with the largest F value.

2. The variable which when partialled on the previously entered variables has the highest multiple correlation with the groups.
3. The variable which gives the greatest decrease in the ratio of within to total generalized variance.

The multiple discriminant function program quite obviously fulfilled the requirements we had in mind for our analysis. For one thing, it provided a statistical summary that was both efficient and clear. For another thing, the form and type of our data matched the requirements for this analysis. Our dependent variable was the eight types of belief-sets; types that were classified so that they were not continuous and were mutually exclusive. Our independent variables varied from 7 to 11, depending upon the particular sample we were analyzing. Not all of these were continuous (sex, urban or rural residence, and the like), but they were defined as dummy variables in line with the practice for such an analysis.

The information produced by the SPSS program, and upon which our description in Chapter IV is based, is reproduced in the following tables. The diagrams in Chapter IV, as far as we know, are the first use made of the F matrix comparing the several types in this manner. The idea for handling the data in this manner came from a set of diagrams drawn by C.R. Rao[3] using Mahalanobis D^2 as his basis.

Table A-22   DISCRIMINANT ANALYSIS: MULTIVARIATE F RATIOS
PRIMARY STUDENTS: CHILE

Muitivariate F		Degrees of Freedom = 7, 1419	
School type	2.67**	Parents' education	2.09*
Class III	1.30	Father's occupation	1.07
Sex	2.05*	Class I	3.00**
Urban	1.97	Class II	1.51

Total F = 1.98**   Degrees of Freedom = 56, 8191.09

F Matrix			Degrees of Freedom = 8, 1419			
Type	1	2	3	4	5	6	7
2	1.82						
3	1.30	1.00					
4	2.23	1.21	.94				
5	1.57	2.95	1.29	2.42			
6	1.69	3.46	1.74	1.71	3.39		
7	2.19	1.93	2.43	2.10	2.25	2.25	
8	1.99	2.16	.96	1.23	2.92	1.89	2.15

Table A-23 DISCRIMINANT ANALYSIS: MULTIVARIATE F RATIOS
SECONDARY STUDENTS: CHILE

Multivariate F		Degrees of Freedom = 7, 1114	
School type	6.12**	Parents' education	1.15
Class III	2.66**	Class I	3.59**
Sex	1.08	Father's occupation	.50
Urban	58	Class II	.64

Total F = 2.04** · Degrees of Freedom = 56, 6431.89

F Matrix			Degrees of Freedom = 8, 1114			
Type	1	2	3	4	5	6	7
2	1.05						
3	.65	2.29					
4	1.22	.96	1.58				
5	1.05	.46	2.33	1.38			
6	1.21	.56	3.29	3.78	.37		
7	.55	.51	1.45	.81	.91	1.10	
8	1.72	.80	3.78	4.77	.54	1.80	1.63

Table A-24 DISCRIMINANT FUNCTION: MULTIVARIATE F RATIOS
PRIMARY STUDENTS: VENEZUELA

Multivariate F		Degrees of Freedom = 7, 1805	
School type	2.55**	Parents' education	2.57*
Class III	.34	Father's occupation	3.32**
Sex	1.66	Class I	1.15
Urban	4.80**	Class II	1.47

Total F = 2.94** Degrees of Freedom = 56, 10417.49

F Matrix			Degrees of Freedom = 8, 1805			
Type	1	2	3	4	5	6	7
2	3.82						
3	1.31	.81					
4	9.26	4.29	1.06				
5	1.62	2.45	1.07	5.29			
6	3.83	.73	.98	4.08	3.33		
7	1.64	1.55	.47	1.17	1.54	1.57	
8	7.69	4.23	1.42	1.86	6.71	3.01	1.51

Table A-25   DISCRIMINANT ANALYSIS: MULTIVARIATE F RATIOS
SECONDARY STUDENTS: VENEZUELA

Multivariate F		Degrees of Freedom = 7, 1397	
School type	5.69**	Parent's education	1.04
Class III	.48	Father's occupation	.41
Sex	4.65**	Class I	.42
Urban	1.83	Class II	1.54

Total F = 2.36   Degrees of Freedom = 56, 7528.38

F Matrix   Degrees of Freedom = 8, 1397

Type	1	2	3	4	5	6	7
2	1.10						
3	.85	.79					
4	2.39	3.40	1.47				
5	1.48	.54	.84	.87			
6	2.20	2.48	2.13	5.36	.38		
7	2.00	1.06	1.39	.83	.49	1.03	
8	2.70	4.79	2.45	4.57	.62	2.36	.54

Table A-26   DISCRIMINANT ANALYSIS: MULTIVARIATE F RATIOS
UNIVERSITY STUDENTS: CHILE

Multivariate F		Degrees of Freedom = 7, 446	
Sex	.31	Class I	2.16*
Political activity	.50	Class II	.73
Parents' education	2.52*	Class III	1.59
Father's occupation	.58		

Total F = 1.47*   Degrees of Freedom = 49, 2268.69

F Matrix		Degrees of Freedom = 7, 446				
Type	1	2	3	4	5	6	7
---	---	---	---	---	---	---	---
2	4.26						
3	1.72	.71					
4	3.23	1.25	.40				
5	4.89	1.31	1.59	1.78			
6	4.63	1.38	.90	1.19	1.01		
7	1.87	1.15	.42	.41	1.71	.97	
8	3.55	1.94	.66	.42	1.80	1.39	.53

Table A-27 DISCRIMINANT ANALYSIS: MULTIVARIATE F RATIOS
TEACHERS: CHILE

Multivariate F		Degrees of Freedom = 7, 550	
School types	2.16*	Respondent's education	1.77
Class III	.69	Father's occupation	.71
Sex	1.81		
Urban	1.93	Class I	1.72
Parent education	.70	Political activity	1.32
		Class II	1.32

Total F = 1.29* Degrees of Freedom = 70, 3616.05

F Matrix	Degrees of Freedom = 10, 550						
Type	1	2	3	4	5	6	7
2	1.21						
3	1.76	1.76					
4	1.24	.62	1.34				
5	1.27	.82	1.94	1.41			
6	1.36	1.15	1.68	2.32	.68		
7	1.35	.76	1.32	.92	1.34	1.28	
8	1.39	1.04	1.77	1.93	.82	1.06	1.56

Table A-28 DISCRIMINANT ANALYSIS: MULTIVARIATE F RATIOS
PARENTS: CHILE

Multivariate F		Degrees of Freedom = 7, 582	
School types	.88	Respondent's education	3.40**
Class III	1.50	Father's occupation	.42
Sex	1.02	Respondent's occupation	.42
Urban	1.49	Class I	1.78
Parent's education	.64	Political activity	.89
		Class II	.29

Total F = 1.41** Degrees of Freedom = 77, 3825.89

F Matrix	Degrees of Freedom = 11, 582						
Type	1	2	3	4	5	6	7
2	1.33						
3	1.07	1.00					
4	.54	.89	1.26				
5	1.24	.98	.87	.78			
6	2.16	1.51	1.15	1.15	1.06		
7	1.20	.64	1.26	.56	.46	.34	
8	2.04	3.56	1.18	1.12	1.68	2.49	.75

225

Table A-29 DISCRIMINANT ANALYSIS: MULTIVARIATE F RATIOS
TEACHERS: VENEZUELA

Multivariate F		Degrees of Freedom = 7, 543	
School type	2.68**	Respondent's education	1.17
Class III	.31	Father's occupation	.20
Sex	1.97	Political activity	.93
Urban	.94	Class I	.56
Parent's education	.59	Class II	1.05

Total F = 1.22** Degrees of Freedom = 70, 3452.51

F Matrix			Degrees of Freedom = 10, 543				
Type	1	2	3	4	5	6	7
2	.51						
3	.62	.65					
4	.65	2.25	.68				
5	.74	1.31	1.02	1.83			
6	.85	.65	.79	2.58	1.73		
7	.45	.41	.45	.75	.35	.55	
8	1.06	1.35	1.09	3.20	1.93	.56	.71

Table A-30 DISCRIMINANT ANALYSIS: MULTIVARIATE F RATIOS
PARENTS: VENEZUELA

Multivariate F		Degrees of Freedom = 7, 813	
School type	2.31*	Respondent's education	1.21
Class III	.88	Father's occupation	.46
Sex	3.80**	Respondent's occupation	.59
Urban	1.33	Class I	.84
Parents' education	1.03	Political activity	.81
		Class II	2.04*

Total F = 2.03** Degrees of Freedom = 77, 5340.66

F Matrix			Degrees of Freedom = 11, 813				
Type	1	2	3	4	5	6	7
2	2.17						
3	1.47	1.40					
4	3.95	1.62	1.10				
5	1.00	2.04	1.11	3.45			
6	2.88	2.93	2.31	3.70	3.24		
7	.81	.87	.75	1.21	.74	1.22	
8	3.45	1.47	1.87	1.20	3.69	2.43	1.08

226

Footnote 9 of Chapter III describes the results of breaking the typology down by autonomist responses contained within each type, and then drawing comparisons among the groups and across the countries. The following are the percentages coming out of this rearrangement of the data, and their graphic presentation.

Accept autonomy for:	Oneself	Others	Society
CHILE			
Primary	11.4	64.7	38.8
Secondary	70.8	92.1	74.2
University	73.4	89.6	74.5
Teachers	58.5	87.6	72.0
Parents	28.0	83.6	73.4
VENEZUELA			
Primary	19.6	66.2	41.1
Secondary	62.8	92.9	58.6
Teachers	52.1	91.9	51.3
Parents	30.1	80.4	48.0

We would note in concluding this discussion that we have found relatively little use made of discriminant function analysis in social-science research. It has been used in biomedical research to solve the problem of classification. Apparently, it has not had wide use in education and psychology, according to Tatsuoka and Tiedeman,[4] who concluded, "About as many applications of discriminant analysis have been made for the purpose of *illustrating* the method as for *using* the method as a research tool with little explanation of it." An interesting application of the analysis to evaluating economic development was published by Adelman and Morris,[5] who were concerned with "criteria for identifying a set of promising countries as potential foreign-aid recipients."

From its usefulness for our analysis we have become convinced that social scientists could make wider use of discriminant function analysis, especially as they—like we were—are confronted with similar kinds of statistical problems of classification and summarization of data.

Notes

notes to chapter one

1. For the best description and analysis of this incident see Irving Louis Horowitz (editor), *The Rise and Fall of Project Camelot: Studies in the Relationship Between Social Science and Practical Politics*, (Cambridge: MIT Press, 1967). It is worth stating, perhaps, that our project was in no way connected with U.S. Government financing or sponsorship.

notes to chapter two

1. Luis A. Costa Pinto, "Studies on Students," October, 1972, ms., p. 15.
2. Among many works that could be cited are I.L. Horowitz, *Three Worlds of Development*, (New York: Oxford University Press, 1966); André Gunder Frank, *Latin America: Underdevelopment or Revolution*, (New York: Monthly Review Press, 1969; Fernando Henrique Cardoso and Enzo Faletto, *Dependencia e desenvolvimento na América Latina, Ensaio de Interpretação Sociológica* (Rio de Janeiro: Zahar Editores, 1970).
3. Alain Touraine, *The Post-Industrial Society* (New York: Random House, 1968); Zbigniew Brzezinski, *The Technetronic Society* (New York: Viking Press, 1970).
4. Gino Germani, "Urbanization, Social Change, and the Great Transformation," in Gino Germani (ed.), *Modernization, Urbanization, and the Urban Crisis* (Boston: Little, Brown & Co., 1973), p. 45.
5. S. N. Eisenstadt, "Social Change, Differentiation, and Evolution," *American Sociological Review*, XXIX, (June, 1964), p. 376.
6. Alex Inkeles, "Making Men Modern: On the Causes and Consequences of Individual Change in Six Developing Countries," *American Journal of Sociology*, September, 1969, p. 210. The complete report of this research study is contained in Alex Inkeles and David H. Smith, *Becoming Modern* (Cambridge, Mass.: Harvard University Press, 1974.)
7. Joseph A. Kahl, *The Measurement of Modernism: A Study of Values in Brazil and Mexico* (Austin: University of Texas Press, 1968), p. 132.
8. Allan Schnaiberg, "Measuring Modernism: Theoretical and Empirical Explorations," *American Journal of Sociology*, November, 1970, p. 420.
9. W. G. Runciman, *A Critique of Max Weber's Philosophy of Social Science* (Cambridge: Cambridge University Press, 1972), p. 14. The basis for the distinction here is that in the value-rational context, the individual is motivated to pursue some value or set of values, whereas in the end-rational context there are multiple ends. "[R]ationality involves on the one hand the weighing of the relative importance of their realization, on the other hand, consideration of whether undesirable consequences would outweight

the benefits to be derived from the projected course of action. . . . [A]s Weber's analysis proceeds, there is a tendency of the meaning of these terms to shift, so that *Wertrationalität* comes to refer to a system of ultimate ends, regardless of the degree of their absoluteness, while *Zweckrationalität* refers primarily to considerations respecting the choice of means and ends which are in turn means to further ends. . . ." Max Weber, *The Theory of Social and Economic Organization,* transl. A. N. Henderson and T. Parsons (New York: Oxford University Press, 1947), p. 115*n*.

notes to chapter three

1. S. N. Eisenstadt, "Social Change, Differentiation and Evolution," in *System, Change, and Conflict,* ed. N. J. Demerath III and R. A. Peterson (New York: The Free Press, 1967), pp. 217–18, 228–29.
2. Alex Inkeles, "Making Men Modern: On the Causes and Consequences of Individual Change in Six Developing Countries," *American Journal of Sociology,* LXXV (September, 1969), pp. 210 and 224.
3. *Ibid.,* p. 225.
4. Arun Sahay, "The Importance of Weber's Methodology in Sociological Explanation," in Arun Sahay (ed.), *Max Weber and Modern Sociology* (London: Routledge & Kegan Paul, 1971), p. 73, says the following on this point: "The ideal-type concept, in fact, is the realization of the principle of sociological rationality, which is Weber's basic and original contribution to scientific analysis. Its contents are only relatively objective, and the purpose of sociological analysis is to decide which particular one—or a combination—of these relatively objective but *possible* descriptions of facts is the completely valid one, i.e., which gives the correct cause of an event or action."
5. Robert Redfield, *The Folk Culture of Yucatan* (Chicago: University of Chicago Press, 1941), pp. 355–56.

notes to chapter four

1. Martin Nicolaus, in the "Foreword" to Karl Marx: *Grundrisse: Introduction to the Critique of Political Economy* (Harmondsworth: Penguin Books, 1973), p. 36.
2. Robert Derathé, "Jean Jacques Rousseau," *International Encyclopedia of the Social Sciences,* IV, 566. These ideas have been further elaborated in the theories of George Herbert Mead, *Mind, Self and Society,* (Chicago: University of Chicago Press, 1934), and in the imaginative research of Jean Piaget, *The Moral Judgment of the Child,* (New York: Harcourt, Brace, 1932). Both Mead and Piaget describe the stages of experiential, moral, and social development of children, from an early stage of unyielding adherence to absolutistic norms to the more adult, more relativistic stage of reciprocity and social interaction. Maturation abetted by education broadens perception permitting the individual to recognize differences and ambiguities, as well as to learn to live with them.
3. Preface, "A Dissertation on the Origin and Foundation of the Inequality of Mankind, "*The Miscellaneous Works of Mr. J. J. Rousseau* (New York: Burt Franklin), 160. (Reprinted from the original edition, London: T. Becket & P. A. DeHondt, 1767.)
4. Karl Marx, *Early Writings,* transl. and ed. T. B. Bottomore (New York: McGraw-Hill Paperbacks, 1963), p. 127.

notes to chapter five

1. Shlomo Avineri, *The Social and Political Thought of Karl Marx,* (Cambridge: Cambridge University Press, 1968), pp. 44–45. The quotation from Max Stirner is from his

Der Einzige und sein Eigentum (1845), quoted by Avineri from K. Löwith (ed.), *Die Hegelsche Linke* (Stuttgart, 1962), p. 69.

2. The Coleman report was published under the title of *Equality of Educational Opportunity* (Washington, D.C.: Government Printing Office, 1966). The other citation refers to Christopher Jencks *et al., Inequality: A Reassessment of the Family and Schooling in America,* (New York: Harper Colophon Books, 1973). The quotation in the text is from pp. 7–8.

3. Amanda Labarca, *La historia de la enseñanza en Chile* (Santiago: Imprenta Universitaria, 1939), p. 28.

4. See José M. Muñoz, *Historia elemental de la pedagogía chilena* (Santiago: Imprenta Universo, 1918). In speaking of these elementary schools, Muñoz adds, "In some schools they enlarged those rudiments with an explication of Christian doctrine and notions of grammar" (p. 17).

5. Aníbal Bascuñán Valdés, *Pedagogía juridical* (Santiago: Editorial Jurídica de Chile, 1954), pp. 29–30.

6. Máximo Pacheco Gómez, *La Universidad de Chile* (Santiago: Editorial Jurídica de Chile, 1953, p. 31).

7. From *Escritos de don Manuel de Salas*, I, 571, as quoted in Octavio Azócar Gauthier, "La enseñanza industrial en relación con la economía nacional," thesis for the *licenciatura* degree in economics, Faculty of Juridical and Social Sciences, University of Chile (Santiago: Editorial Jurídica de Chile, 1951), p. 41.

8. According to a census completed in 1778, the city of Santiago then had a population of 24,318 persons. (See Corporación de Fomento de la Producción, *Geografía Económica de Chile* [Santiago: 1965], pp. 346–47.) The population of the city is given as about 50,000 in Fernando Campos Harriet, *Desarrollo Educacional, 1810–1960* (Santiago: Ed. Andrés Bello, 1960), p. 12.

9. For the text of the regulation, see Ricardo Anguita, *Leyes promulgadas en Chile hasta el 1° de junio de 1912* (Santiago: Imprenta Barcelona, 1912), I, 36.

10. Gauthier, *op. cit.,* p. 46.

11. Campos Harriet, *op. cit.,* p. 56.

12. For "Lancastrianism" in Chile, see Labarca, *op. cit.,* p. 86, and Campos Harriet, *op. cit.,* pp. 15–16.

13. For an easily available and excellent source in English on Chilean national history, see Frederick B. Pike, *Chile and the United States, 1880–1962* (South Bend, Ind.: University of Notre Dame Press, 1963). Also particularly useful for understanding the Conservative-Liberal split at this time is J. Lloyd Mecham, *Church and State in Latin America* (rev. ed.; Chapel Hill, N.C.: University of North Carolina Press, 1966), chap. IX.

14. As given in Anguita, *op. cit.,* I, 225.

15. Muñoz, *op. cit.,* p. 100, cites the decree, in part, as follows: "In each convent . . . the prelates must establish, within a period of four months, a primary school in the place and with the capacity that the local governors may designate. The education will be adjusted to the general school plan which the executive shall issue. If after four months those establishments have not been set up, it shall be done by the municipalities at the expense of the convents."

16. O. Poblete Muñoz, "Un servidor de la enseñanza," *Anales de la Universidad de Chile,* CXII, Nos. 90–92 (1953), 286.

17. *Ibid,* p. 287.

18. Labarca *op. cit.,* p. 88. The total national population is estimated at 1,010,322 in 1835, and 1,083,801 in 1843. See Corporación de Fomento de la Producción, *op. cit.,* p. 350.

19. M. L. Amunátegui, *Estudios sobre instrucción pública* (Santiago: Imprenta Nacional, 1898), II, 103–5. This publication is Amunátegui's report as Minister of Public Instruction for the year 1877.

231

20. *Loc. cit.*
21. Eugenio González Rojas, "Andrés Bello y la Universidad de Chile," in Fac. de Filosofía y Educación, *Andrés Bello,* (Santiago: Univ. de Chile, 1966), pp. 13–14.
22. As quoted in W. Rex Crawford, *A Century of Latin-American Thought* (rev. ed.; New York: Frederick A. Praeger, 1961), p. 56.
23. Anguita, *op. cit.,* I, 396. Articles 8–13 of the statute, establishing the faculties and their special attributes, are given on pp. 396–97 of this source.
24. Labarca, *op. cit.,* p. 113.
25. Muñoz, *op. cit.,* p. 111.
26. Roberto Munizaga Aguirre, *En torno a Sarmiento* (Santiago: Ediciones de la Universidad de Chile, 1958), p. 26.
27. An easily available life of Sarmiento in English is A. W. Bunkley, *The Life of Sarmiento* (Princeton, N.J.: Princeton University Press, 1952). By the same author and publisher, see also *A Sarmiento Anthology* (1948).
28. Campos Harriet, *op. cit.,* p. 23.
29. Ignacio Domeyko, "Reseña de los trabajos de la Universidad desde 1855 hasta el presente," *Anales de la Universidad de Chile,* CXII, Nos. 90–92 (1953), 209.
30. Abdón Cifuentes, *Memorias* (Santiago; Editorial Nascimento, 1936), I, 397–98. Cifuentes gave another example of the effect of the chain of command, this time concerning a teacher's request for maternity leave. By the time the permission "reached the hands of the teacher, the child already had teeth" (*ibid.*). Cifuentes took a leading role in the Church-state conflicts concerning education which broke out in the 1870s.
31. Anguita, *op. cit.,* II, 96.
32. These data are based on a compilation of information in Labarca, *op. cit.,* p. 147; Campos Harriet, *op. cit.,* p. 26; and Dirección General de Educación Primaria, *op. cit.,* whose numbers differ somewhat from the other two sources, but support the importance of the growth.
33. Poblete M., *op. cit.,* p. 291.
34. For the development of study plans and more details on this subject, see Domingo Amunátegui, *El progreso intelectual y político de Chile* (Santiago: Editorial Nascimento, 1936).
35. From Domeyko's memoirs, as quoted in Guillermo Feliú Cruz, "Domeyko en la evolución cultural de Chile," *Anales de la Universidad de Chile,* CXII, Nos. 90–92 (1953), 20–21.
36. Cifuentes, *op. cit.,* I, 26.
37. The first figure is from Domeyki, *op. cit.,* p. 205. The second is from Amunátegui, *op. cit.,* II, 104
38. Azócar G., *op. cit.,* p. 51.
39. As quoted in Anguita, *op. cit.,* II, 200.
40. As quoted in Tatiana Román Belyramin and Juan Antonio Loyola Opazo, *El culto religioso en Chile y su aspecto constitucional,* Memoria de Prueba, Escuela de Derecho, Universidad Católica, Santiago: Editorial Universitaria, 1963, p. 31.
41. See Cifuentes, *Colección de discursos de don Abdón Cifuentes* (Santiago: Imprenta de "El Independiente," 1882), pp. 236–38 for pertinent portions of the decree.
42. *Ibid.,* pp. 239–42.
43. For Barros' version of events, see Diego Barros Arana, *Mi destitución, Apuntes para la historia del Instituto Nacional* (Santiago: Imprenta de "El Ferrocarril," 1873).
44. For the text of the decree, see *Anales de la Universidad de Chile,* XLVI, 1874, 18–20.
45. From his speech in the Chamber of Deputies of June 17, 1873, as quoted in Roberto Munizaga A., *El estado y la educación,* (Santiago: Imprenta Universitaria, 1953), pp. 50–51.
46. Miguel Luis Amunátegui, *Discursos parlamentarios,* I, 494–95. (The statement was made on June 19, 1873.)

47. *Ibid.*, I, 496 (speech given on June 19, 1873).
48. *Ibid.*, I, 497 (speech as in preceding note).
49. *Ibid.*, I, 510–12, 507 (speech delivered on June 24, 1873).
50. Anguita, *op. cit.*, II, 464.
51. As quoted in Leonardo Fuentealba Hernández, "Valentín Letelier y el Pensamiento educativo en la ópoca de la fundación del Instituto Pedagógico," in *Instituto Pedagógico* (Santiago: Universidad de Chile, 1964), p. 64.
52. For details of the steps leading to the founding of the Institute, see Guillermo Feliú Cruz, "El Instituto Pedagógico bajo la dirección de Domingo Amunátegui Solar, in *Instituto Pedagógico, LXXV aniversario de su fundación* (Santiago: Universidad de Chile, Fac. de Filosofía y Educación, 1964).
53. Valentín Letelier's best know book is *La lucha por la cultura* (Santiago: Imprenta Barcelona, 1895). The essay therein entitled "El Instituto Pedagógico," pp. 366–97, describes Letelier's self-ascribed role in the Institute's founding as well as some of his views concerning teacher-training.
54. Letelier, *op. cit.*, p. 366.
55. From a speech at the *Gran Convención Liberal* given in Valparaíso on January 17, 1886, as quoted in Hernán Rampirez N., "Panorama de la vida chilena en la época de la fundación del Instituto Pedagógico," *Instituto Pedagógico, op. cit.*, p. 53.
56. As translated and quoted in W. Rex Crawford, *op. cit.*, pp. 75–76.
57. Letelier, *op. cit.*, pp. 44, 47.
58. Letelier, *Teoría de la instrucción publica* (Santiago: Ediciones de los Anales de la Universidad de Chile, 1957), pp. 29–30. (This edition was edited by Roberto Munizaga Aguirre.)
59. *Ibid.*, p. 112.
60. Letelier, *La lucha . . .* , p. 259.
61. For an analysis of Herbartian ideas, see Labarca, *Nuevas orientaciones de la enseñanza* (Santiago: Imprenta Santiago), 1927.
62. *Ibid.*, p. 32.
63. Eduardo Hamuy, *Educación elemental, analfabetismo y desarrollo económico* (Santiago: Editorial Universitaria, 1960), p. 17. See chap. 1 for a highly synthetic quantitative summary of changes in Chilean education up to the late 1950s.
64. *Ibid.*, Eduardo Hamuy, *op. cit.*, pp. 29–30.
65. Ricardo Donoso, *Recopilación de leyes, reglamentos y decretos relativos a los servicios de la enseñanza pública*, (Santiago: Imprenta de la Dirección General de Prisiones, 1937), p. xxxiii.
66. For an excellent account of the politics of higher education, and especially of student movements in contemporary Chile, see Frank Bonilla and Myron Glazer, *Student Politics in Chile* (New York: Basic Books, 1970).
67. Comisión de planeamiento integral de la educación, *Algunos antecedentes para el planeamiento integral de la educación chilena*, (Santiago: Ministerio de Educación Pública, 1964), p. 258.

notes to chapter six

1. Gallegos' most famous novel, *Doña Bárbara*, is considered a classic. Betancourt's best known book is *Venezuela, Política y petróleo* (Mexico: Fondo de Cultura Económica, 1956). His presidential papers, published in four volumes, make interesting and instructive reading. The title is *La revolución democrática en Venezuela* (Caracas: Imprenta Nacional, 1969).
2. Virgilio Tosta, *Ideas educativas de venezolanos eminentes* (2d ed.; Caracas: Ediciones Villegas, 1958).

3. Jose A. Silva Michelena, *The Illusion of Democracy in Dependent Nations* (Cambridge, Mass.: The MIT Press, 1971), pp. 42–43.
4. Frank Bonilla, *The Failure of Elites,* (Cambridge Mass.: The MIT Press, 1970), pp. 34–35.
5. Idefonso Leal, *Historia de la Universidad de Caracas (1721-1827)* (Caracas: Universidad Central de Caracas, 1963), a work which provides a good general view of ethnic and other biases associated with colonial education in Venezuela.
6. *Ibid.,* p. 18.
7. José Gil Fourtoul, *Historia constitucional de Venezuela* (5th ed.; Caracas: Ediciones Sales, 1964) I, 147–48.
8. Leal, *op. cit.* , p. 379, quoting from Title XVIII of the University statute.
9. Federico Brito Figueroa, *Historia económica y social de Venezuela* (Caracas: Universidad Central de Caracas, 1966) I, 160.
10. As translated and cited in Bonilla, *op.cit.*, p. 43; in turn cited in Fortoul, *op.cit.*, p. 478.
11. Bonilla, *op. cit.,* p. 46.
12. The minister's name was Antonio Leocadio Guzmán; he was the father of Antonio Guzmán Blanco, the country's leader between 1870 and 1887. As quoted in Fortoul, *op. cit.,* III, 28.
13. Jose María Vargas, *Exposición de la Dirección General de Instrucción Pública,* as as reprinted in Laureano Villanueva, *Biografía del Doctor José Vargas* (Caracas; Imprenta Nacional, 1954), p. 295. This book was written to celebrate the centenary of Vargas' death as a means of promoting Venezuelan patriotism.
14. *Ibid.,* p. 296.
15. Mariano Picón Salas, *Formación y proceso de la literatura venezolana,* pp. 140–41, as quoted in Angelino Lemmo, *La educación en Venezuela en 1870* (Caracas: Univ. Central de Caracas, 1961), p. 19.
16. Bonilla, *op. cit.,* pp. 52–53.
17. All references to the law from Lemmo, *op. cit.,* pp. 118–19.
18. *Ibid.,* pp. 62–65.
19. Brito Figueroa, *op. cit.* I, 310.
20. Alexis Márquez Rodríguez, *Doctrina y proceso de la educación en Venezuela* (Caracas: private ed. 1964, p. 71).
21. Miguel Angel Mudarra, *Historia de la legislación contemporánea en Venezuela* (Caracas: Ediciones del Ministerio de Educación, 1962). p. 64 and p. 82.
22. Silva Michelena, *op. cit.,* p. 49.
23. Daniel H. Levine, *Conflict and Political Change in Venezuela* (Princeton, N.J.: Princeton University Press, 1973), pp. 14–15.
24. *Ibid.,* p. 14.
25. Bonilla, *op. cit.,* p. 54. This book is a study of Venezuela's elites as they confront the problems of the 1960s and, by implication, the 1970s. Thus, it is directly to the point of the question posed in the text above, and of great suggestive import to our study.
26. *Ibid.,* p. 315.
27. For a detailed statement of these laws and regulations, see R. González Baquero, *Análisis del proceso histórico de la educación urbana (1870–1932) y de la educatión rural en Venezuela (1932–1957)* (Caracas: Universidad Central de Venezuela, 1962), pp. 23–71, as well as Mudurra, *op. cit.,* pp. 73–139, and Márquez Rodríguez, *op. cit.,* pp. 79–99. The González Baquero work is a translation of a doctoral dissertation prepared for the University of Michigan in 1960. The English title of the dissertation is *A Historical Analysis of Venezuelan Education with Particular Reference to Programs of Rural Education.*
28. Márquez Rodríguez, *op cit.,* p. 87.
29. González Baquero, *op. cit.,* pp. 40–41.

30. See Márquez Rodríguez, *op. cit.*, p. 91, for the matter of coeducation; and for the reasoning behind the introduction of graded school, see *Memoria que presenta el Ministro de Instrucción Pública* (Caracas: Imprenta Nacional, 1912), I, xxiii-xxxi.

31. Márquez Rodríguez, *op. cit.*, pp. 88–89.

32. *Memorias . . . 1912, op. cit.*, pp. 81–95.

33. Ministerio de Instrucción Pública, *Decreto orgánico de la instrucción nacional y documentación*, (Caracas: Imprenta Nacional, 1914), p. 3.

34. *Memoria del Ministerio de Educación Nacional, Años 1945 y 1946* (Caracas: Tipografía Americana, 1947), p. 216.

35. *Memoria del Ministro de Instrucción Pública, 1929* (Caracas: Tipografía del Comercio, 1929), p. 458. The reason that the number is uncertain is that some students may have enrolled in more than one school of the University.

36. *Memoria . . . 1929, op. cit.*, pp. 628–29.

37. From the census of 1926, as analyzed in Brito Figueroa, *op. cit.*, II, 531.

38. K. H. Silvert, "The University Student," in John J. Johnson (ed.), *Continuity and Change in Latin America* (Stanford, Calif.: Stanford University Press, 1964), pp. 206–66.

39. Silva Michelena, *op. cit.*, 56–57. See also Levine, *op. cit.*, pp. 18–23.

40. D. H. Levine, *op. cit.*, pp. 28–29 for the citation, and Chapt. III for a descriptive analysis of this entire process. Levine's book is a study of contemporary Venezuela as a success story in party pluralization, demonstrated by the ability of the political mechanism as a whole to handle discord. One of the two essential cases studied by Levine is conflict concerning education. As such, the book is of great use to us in these discussions; we have drawn upon it freely. Some other easily available and useful books on contemporary Venezuelan politics are Robert J. Alexander, *The Venezuelan Democratic Revolution* (New Brunswick, N.J.: Rutgers University Press, 1964); John D. Martz, *Acción Democrática*) Princeton, N.J.: Princeton University Press, 1966); Edwin J. Lieuwen, *Petroleum in Venezuela* (Berkeley, Calif.: University of California Press, 1954); and by the same author, *Venezuela* (London: Oxford University Press, 1969).

41. Silva Michelena, *op. cit.*, p. 62.

42. Population figures are from the censuses of 1936 and 1941. The age groups for primary-school students range from 5 to 14 years, and for secondary-school students from 15 to 19. Comparative census figures for Venezuela can be found in Julio Páez Celis, *Situación demográfica de Venezuela 1950* (Santiago: Centro Latinoamericano de Demografía), 1963.

43. Enrollment figures are from Márquez Rodríguez, *op. cit.*, p. 108, and from *Memoria del Ministerio de Educación Nacional, 1946–47* (Caracas: Tipografía Americana, 1947), pp. 88–90, 203–4, 209, 216, and 117.

44. *Memoria . . . 1946–47, op cit.*, p. 204.

45. Joel M. Jutkowitz, *Venezuelan Classrooms and Venezuelan Values: Education's Role in Value Formation* (unpublished ms., 1971), p. 36.

46. *Memoria . . . 1946–47, op. cit.*, p. 204.

47. The complete decree is contained in *Ibid.*, pp. 362–76.

48. The full text of the law can be found in Luís Beltrán Prieto Figueroa, *De una educación de castas a una educación de masas*, (La Habana: Editorial Lex, 1951), pp. 221–43. The quote given in the text is from p. 222. Beltrán Prieto was Minister of Education in the short-lived Gallegos government, and one of the principal intellectual authors of the educational changes of the *trienio*.

49. *Ibid.*, p. 88.

50. From a refined table in Jutkowitz, *op. cit.*, p. 37. Original statistics can be found in the several issues of the Venezuelan Official Gazette (*Gaceta Oficial de la República de Venezuela*).

235

51. *Memoria y cuenta del Ministerio de Educación Nacional, 1966* (Caracas: Imprenta de la Dirección Tecnica, 1967), II, 7 and 199.
52. *Ibid.,* II, 489.
53. For a discussion of the meaning of university autonomy in the Venezuelan context, and of the events leading to government intervention of the Central University, see Foción Febres Cordero, *Autonomía universitaria,* (Caracas: Universidad Central de Venezuela, 1959); and, by the same author, *Reforma universitaria* (Caracas: Universidad Central de Caracas, 1959).
54. Betancourt, *op. cit.,* pp. 606–97.
55. See Silva Michelena, *op. cit.,* pp. 64–68 for a useful description, with excellent citations, of this aspect of the Pérez Jiménez period, and for the political dynamics behind the events leading to his overthrow.
56. *Ibid.,* pp. 68–69.
57. Levine, *op. cit.,* pp. 53–54. Levine's italics.
58. Cordiplan, *Plan Cuatrienal, Plan VI—Educación,* May 25, 1960, p. 1.
59. All the figures in this discussion are from *Memoria . . . 1966,* II, 7, 199, 305, 405, 473, 489, and from UNESCO, *Statistical Yearbook 1968* (Paris: UNESCO, 1969), p. 81.
60. Figures from *Memoria . . . 1966,* I, 2, and II, ix, xv-xvi, xxix, xxxii–xxxiii, 58–59.
61. In addition to *Memoria . . . 1966,* see also República de Venezuela, *Noveno censo general de la República, Resumen general de la República, Parte A* (Caracas: Oficina Central de Censo, 1964), p. 123.
62. Gordon C. Ruscoe, "The Efficacy of Venezuelan Education," paper read at a conference on "Venezuela: Panorama 1969," at the Johns Hopkins University School of Advanced International Studies, Washington, D.C., November 10–11, 1969, mimeo., pp. 21–22.
63. Bonilla, *op. cit.,* p. 302.
64. All data in this paragraph from AVEC, *Planteles y estadísticas, Curso 1965–66* (Caracas: Fundación Editorial Escolar, 1966), Tables I and I-3a, no pagination.
65. Bonilla, *op. cit.,* pp. 321 and 322.
66. Levine, *op. cit.,* p. 259.

notes to chapter seven

1. "The Human Prospect," *The New York Review of Books,* XX, Nos. 21 & 22 (January 24, 1974), 21.
2. W. Lloyd Warner, Robert J. Havighurst, and Martin B. Loeb, *Who Shall be Educated? The Challenge of Unequal Opportunites* (London: Kegan Paul, 1946), p. 56.
3. Christopher Jencks, "Schooling Has Limits," *New York Times, Annual Education Review,* January 15, 1974, p. 57 and 86. We have already cited relevant portions of Jencks *et al., Inequality: A Reassessment of the Effect of Family and Schooling in America, op. cit.,* in Chapter VI.
4. Frederick Mosteller and Daniel P. Moynihan, "A Pathbreaking Report," in Mosteller and Moynihan (eds.), *On Equality of Educational Opportunity* (New York: Vintage Books, 1972), p. 27.

notes to appendix

1. *SPSS Update Manual,* July 1973 Revisions (National Opinion Research Center) A-020-244-01 ff. A related program, but with different outputs, is described in W. J. Dixon (ed.), *Biomedical Computer Programs,* (Berkeley, Calif.: University of Califor-

nia Press, 1970), "BMD05M, Discriminant Analysis for Several Groups" and "BMD07M, Stepwise Discriminant Analysis."

2. *SPSS Update Manual*, p. 9.

3. C. R. Rao, *Advanced Statistical Methods in Biometric Research* (New York: Wiley, 1962). Mahalanobis D^2 is a "measure of distance rather than a criterion for testing the hypothesis of zero-distance;" i.e., a measure of the distance between each pair of groups. *Cf.* Maurice M. Tatsuoka and David V. Tiedeman, "Discriminant Analysis," *Review of Educational Research*. XXIV (December, 1954), 402–20; also *Biomedical Computer Programs, op. cit.*

4. *op. cit.*, p. 415, and accompanying bibliography.

5. Irma Adelman and Cynthia Taft Morris, "Performance Criteria for Evaluating Economic Development Potential: An Operational Approach," *Quarterly Journal of Eeonomics*, LXXXII, 1968, 260.

Index

Kerr, Clark, 103n
Keynes, John Maynard, 139
Khrushchev, Nikita, 163

Letelier, Valentín, 129–132
Leoni, Raúl, 166
Levine, Daniel, 148, 155, 171–172
Liberalism, 109, 117, 130
Liberals, 54–57, 111–113, 116–117,
    119–120, 122–128, 133, 135–136,
    139, 163
Libertarianism, 113
Liceo de Chile, 120
Lira, Máximo, 125
Locke, John, 64
López Contreras, Eleazar, 154

Marshall, Alfred, 139
Marx, Karl, 66–67, 69–74, 83, 101
Marxism, 9, 35, 55, 72–73, 102, 163
Marxist coalition, 136
Medina Angarita, Isaías, 154–156
Mexican Revolution, 138
Mexico, 25, 55
    in 1930s, 155
Mill, James, 113, 139
Mill, John Stuart, 139
Ministry of Public Education, 157, 170
    creation of in Venezuela, 147
Missile Crisis, 163
Miranda, Francisco de, 140
Montt, Manuel, 113–117
Movement of the Revolutionary
    Left (MIR), 165
"Multiversity," 103
Mussolini, Benito, 56, 133

National Constitution (Venezuela)
    and freedom of instruction, 152
National Institute, 110, 113, 115, 117,
    120–121, 123–124
Nazi movement (in Latin America), 56
Neo-Kantianism, 9
Neopositivism, 54
Normal School of Paris, 129
Normal School of Preceptors, 116–117

Onganía, General Juan
    regime in Argentina, 56–57
Opus Dei, 46, 170
Organic Law of Education (1948),
    159
Ortega Díaz, Pedro, 165–166

Páez, José Antonio, 144
Paraguay, 164
Parsons, Talcott, 39n
Pedagogical Institute, 129, 132, 157,
    168
Pérez Jiménez, Marcos, 158–162,
    164–166
Perón, General Juan, 163
Peronismo, 56
Peru, 156, 164
Pluralism, 9–10
Popular Front, 135–136, 155–156
Popular Unity, 135
Portales, Diego, 148
Positivism, 9, 70, 102–103, 126, 128,
    132, 139, 157
Prebisch, Raúl, 139
Primary schools (Chile)
    class bias in, 120, 135
    development of, 117–119, 127
Primary schools (Venezuela)
    enrollment in, 152–153, 157–160,
        167
    establishment of, 145–146,
        150–151
Primo de Rivera, Miguel, 56, 133
Project Camelot, 3, 12, 163

Quiroga, Facundo, 116

Radical Party, 55–57, 136
Radicals, 56–57, 123–124, 128, 133,
    135–136, 140
Real Universidad de San Felipe, 108
Redfield, Robert, 43
Reed, John H., 89n
Revolution of 1891 (Chile), 133